# MACINTOSH
# 3-D
# WORKSHOP

Hayden
Books

# MACINTOSH

# 3-D

# WORKSHOP

Sean Wagstaff

## Hayden Books

Macintosh 3-D Workshop

**©1993 Hayden Books, a division of Prentice Hall Computer Publishing**

Library of Congress Catalog No.: 93-79998

ISBN: 1-56830-061-1

95  94                4  3  2

Interpretation of the printing code: the rightmost double-digit number is the year of the book's printing; the rightmost single-digit number is the number of the book's printing. For example, a printing code of 93-1 shows that the first printing of the book occurred in 1993.

# Dedication

To Mom and Dad,

for their sense of perspective.

# Credits

**Publisher**
David Rogelberg

**Acquisition Editor**
Karen Whitehouse

**Developmental Editor**
Rosie Blankenship

**Production Editors**
Dave Ciskowski
Judy Everly

**Publishing Coordinator**
Mat Wahlstrom

**Cover Designer**
Tim Amrhein

**Interior Designer**
Kevin Spear

**Production Team**
Gary Adair
Diana Bigham
Jeanne Clark
Tim Cox
Meshell Dinn
Mark Enochs
Howard Jones
Beth Rago
Greg Simsic

# About the Author

## Sean T. Wagstaff

Sean Wagstaff recently left a three year post as *MacWEEK's* Associate Editor of Reviews. He now divides his time between writing, rendering, playing with pictures, and giving shape to ideas. Some of his ideas have nothing to do with computers.

In addition to *MacWEEK*, Wagstaff's recent writing, photography, and editing credits include *Insight's Guides to California, Northern California,* and *Southern California*; *Wind Surf Magazine, California Angler Magazine, Mexico Magazine,* and *Skiing Magazine*.

Chronicles of his adventures in graphics, multimedia, and four dimensions—both synthetic and natural—will continue to appear in *MacWEEK* and other prominent locations.

# Trademark Acknowledgments

This book mentions too many companies and products to list every trademark on this page. Because we are environmentalists, and because paper is a valuable (and costly) commodity, we limit our trademark acknowledgments to the following statements:

# Acknowledgments

Many people helped make this book possible, or at least tolerated the author's countless transgressions, absences, and absentminded blunders during its creation. To family, friends, and others who stubbed toes on my floatsam without a wimper, I extend an open invitation to dinner—I'm cooking. At *MacWEEK*, Rick LePage exhibited extraordinary patience, and frequently turned a blind eye to my "rendering" as one deadline after another soared by. To my other colleagues at *MacWEEK*, I also extend thanks for the years of education and discussion that led to this project. To the many people in the Mac industry who lent their time and ideas and patiently re-sent floppy disks and documentation as originals disappeared into the maelstrom of my desk, I extend the hope that Mac 3-D will one day be as common as Times Roman. Among the two dozen industry people who contributed, Gina Rubattino of Pixel Relations was particularly helpful in getting and keeping the ball rolling. Thanks to David Rogelberg at Hayden Books for believing in this project, even when others closer to home did not. Rosie Blankenship, at Hayden Books, was a kindred spirit when somebody outside the sphere of my fawning finally sat down to read. Ben Long has often bandied the possibility of stringing cables through yards and over fences, hedges and telephone poles to network our Macs. He willingly matched me in a daily game of "What Did We Learn Today?" which—more than anything—was the source of ideas for this book. Neil McManus, long-time lunch mate and co-conspirator, used phrases like "Zowie!" and other subtle piques, to indicate where things had run completely amuck. As an editor, he bravely did more to keep my rogue metaphors and stampeding puns in check than a great-white hunter with an elephant gun. Finally, Dorit Fehrensen constantly and kindly reminded me that in reality, not all things are virtual. For her, I hope the wait was worth it.

—stW

# We Want To Hear from You

What our readers think of Hayden is crucial to our sense of well-being. If you have any comments, no matter how great or how small, we'd appreciate your taking the time to send us a note.

We can be reached at the following address:

David Rogelberg
Hayden Books
201 West 103rd Street
Indianapolis, IN 46290

(800) 428-5331 voice
(800) 448-3804 fax

E-mail addresses:

| | |
|---|---|
| Internet | hayden@hayden.com |
| America Online | Hayden Bks |
| AppleLink | hayden.books |
| CompuServe | 76350,3014 |

If this book has changed your life, please write and describe the euphoria you've experienced. Do you have a cool book idea? Please send your proposal to us at the above address.

# Contents

# chapter 1

# Introduction

W hat sculpture is to painting, three-dimensional graphics is to illustration. Three-D graphics is the modeling and rendering of three-dimensional objects, including all of the visual information found in the real world: perspective and depth, light and shadow, form and texture, and sometimes motion. Using these techniques, a designer can produce images of imaginary worlds that are so realistic that they resemble photographs.

Three-dimensional graphics can be a powerful medium. For example, a package designer can show beforehand exactly what a perfume bottle will look like in a display case; an illustrator can create a company logo out of chrome, complete with reflections of the surrounding landscape; a video animator can wrap a decorative map of the world around a spinning globe then send type into orbit around his planet; a corporate trainer can create a realistic simulation of an airplane cockpit.

In contrast, an artist using traditional materials must photograph intricate scale models or turn to friskets and airbrushes. Realistic animations can take the problem to the extreme; they can require thousands of individual hand-painted cells. Even Macintosh 2-D techniques are taken to their limits when simulating traditional perspective design (see figure 1.1). Adobe's Illustrator and Aldus FreeHand users must draw in perspective and create many blends to simulate shadows and highlights. Users of Adobe's Photoshop and Fractal Design's Painter must create masks and airbrush each element of a scene to affect realism.

Using 3-D software, you need not skip details such as shadows and reflections simply because they are too difficult to paint. More importantly, using 3-D software you can move around and change your perspective. However, once you create an image in 2-D, there is little you can do with it. If, for example, you need to see more of the front of the motorcycle you've drawn, you must start over from scratch. With 3-D, you simply move the camera that controls your point of view, or rotate the bike just as you would a real model, and render the image again. Because your models are objects in space, you can easily view the object from the top or side, front or back, inside or outside. Three-D is a vehicle users can ride into any space.

**Figure 1.1.** Illustration modeled and rendered in Alias Sketch!

The Apple Macintosh is the ideal graphics platform for artists and designers because it is easy to use and capable of producing a variety of professional artwork. It also has the advantage that it easily can move files between programs and other users. Yet, 3-D is one of the most demanding applications for the computer. The millions of calculations required to render light and shadow in a 3-D world taxes even the most powerful Macintoshes (see figure 1.2).

**Figure 1.2.** Rendering 3-D illustrations can require powerful Macintoshes.

3

Fortunately, Apple is constantly building more powerful, less expensive workstations. This has brought the computing performance required for 3-D into the range of desktop designers and illustrators as well as multimedia developers, video producers, architects, engineers, and product designers. Add-on accelerators and distributed processing also help to speed things up. Macintoshes based on the PowerPC chip—due to hit the streets not long after this book—should have a substantial increase in performance over current desktop computers.

Not all 3-D programs devour Macintosh system resources. There are now a number of powerful 3-D illustration packages that can run well on low- to mid-range Macintoshes.

This book breaks the sometimes complex world of 3-D graphics into its basic components. It explains how to create 3-D and how to optimize 3-D techniques.

# What is 3-D?

Three-D graphics, as created on the Macintosh, is divided into several parts: modeling, scene building, rendering, and animation. All of them are closely-related activities, but each takes highly-specialized forms so they are treated separately. Often, the different tasks require different software applications.

- **Modeling** is the creation of 3-D objects. Models are the building blocks that are used to create 3-D scenes.

- **Scene Building** is where you put the models together. It also is where you give them textures and physical properties, and add lighting and atmospheric effects.

- **Animation** is scene building with the added element of time. It enables you to move objects and cameras to create movies depicting events in a 3-D world.

- **Rendering** is the final production of finished images. It is used for both still images and animations. As a director, you say, "This is how I want the picture to look." The renderer is the software that takes these directions and paints a picture.

# Why Macintosh 3-D Workshop ?

The evolution of the Macintosh into a graphics workstation has occurred with startling speed. Even as I write, new Macintoshes (such as the PowerPC) are being developed that will leave the fastest Quadras behind. Realistic 16- and 24-bit color is a standard feature of many new Macintoshes rather than an expensive option. Color graphics boards are inexpensive compared to a year or two ago; and large monitors—needed to view a 3-D object from many angles at once—are also cheaper than ever. Even users with low-cost Macintoshes, such as LCs and Color Classics, can use basic 3-D illustration tools.

Computers communicate with the user via flat screens, flat print, and flat video. Most computer users are comfortable thinking in only two dimensions, so 3-D requires considerable explanation. The lexicon of new terms is long and many techniques are unique to the format. However, once the hurdles are behind you, 3-D opens up a whole new world of imagery (see figure 1.3).

**Figure 1.3.** A close encounter of the 3-D kind, modeled in Alias' Sketch! and rendered in the Electric Image Animation System.

For those who use 3-D software already, such as architects using CAD applications, *Macintosh 3-D Workshop* will help explore the techniques needed to take their 3-D designs to a high level of realism. Beginners will find an eye-popping number of new 3-D tools designed specifically to make 3-D easy for illustrators and first-time animators.

# The softwares

Even more impressive than the rapid introduction of new Macintoshes and peripheral hardware is the unprecedented development of 3-D software. At last count, there were over fifty 3-D products for Macintosh users. These include modelers, scene builders, animators, and renderers, as well as a host of supporting products: texture libraries (made up of materials such as marble and granite that you can apply to your models); texture generators that enable you to create your own materials; 3-D illustration packages that create realistic-looking PostScript artwork; 3-D type programs that create realistic 3-D logos; hardware accelerators and distributed rendering software that speed up the computationally-intensive task of 3-D rendering; CAD programs for highly-accurate architectural and engineering design; and many hybrid products.

Each of these software categories can be further divided. Some modelers can construct solids, while others deal only in surfaces; some use polygonal surfaces, while others are based on smooth splines; renderers offer many different options that render textures, reflections, refractions, and shadows; some modelers include renderers; and some scene builders offer animation.

There are high-end software products (such as Electric Image Animation System) that target the professional video and film market and sell for the price of an economy car. Other products, such as RayDream's Designer, are aimed at the illustrator and cost less than most word processing programs.

*Macintosh 3-D Workshop* attempts to explain the tools offered by these diverse programs. Appendix A, "Product directory," will guide you to where specific products fall within the wide spectrum of 3-D applications.

# What's your task?

Like anything else in life, you need to know where you want to go before you can figure out the best way to get there. Knowing more about these various 3-D professions can help you to do both.

- Illustration and graphic arts

- Product and package design

- Animation and video

- Multimedia

- Architectural and industrial design

# Illustration and graphic arts

Just as you got used to creating artwork on a computer in two dimensions and mastered the difficult world of blends and gradient fills, you're suddenly faced with programs such as Adobe's Dimensions, RayDream's addDepth and Designer, Alias' Sketch!, Pixar's Typestry, Specular's LogoMotion, and StrataType 3d—all of which are designed to provide easy entry into the world of 3-D. If Adobe's Illustrator, Aldus FreeHand, and Deneba's Canvas are your tools of trade, you will find help on importing and adding light and depth to PostScript art in chapter 4, "Basic shapes and fonts," which discusses 3-D PostScript.

Three-D type, also discussed in chapter 4, should appeal to almost every designer. Graphic designers, like illustrators, are under intense deadline pressure and the demands of their craft are severe. Now a designer can create 3-D beveled type quickly without friskets and airbrushes; it is a simple matter to chisel type out of marble, to wrap text around a sphere, or to turn a logo into shining gold (see figure 1.4).

**Figure 1.4.** Three-D makes creating gold letters easy—and inexpensive.

**Color Images**

The color image editing programs have enjoyed a boom, making them too numerous to mention here.

Artists used to the bitmapped painting and image editing world of Adobe Photoshop and Fractal Designs' Painter and ColorStudio can skip willy-nilly through this book.

Examples of using 3-D images in 2-D applications can be found in chapter 11, "Working with images." With only a few exceptions, still images from 3-D programs are generated as high-resolution bitmap, PICT, TIFF, or other standard image files. You can, for example, import 3-D images and combine them with scanned photos. Or, you can use images from your image editing and paint programs as backgrounds and textures within 3-D applications.

Many illustrators have come into computing reluctantly as work increasingly depends on instant color separations and their capability to combine earlier creations into new projects. Fortunately, some 3-D applications are simplified for illustration. For example, with Adobe's Dimensions and RayDream's addDepth, you can take existing Illustrator or FreeHand artwork and can turn it into 3-D models. You can then place colored lights, position labels, and render images that would take hours using Illustrator's blends and fills alone. The resulting image retains the benefits of illustrations created in a

PostScript drawing package, including resolution independence when printing and relatively compact file size. You can even open a 3-D image created in addDepth or Dimensions and edit it using FreeHand or Illustrator. Examples are provided in chapter 4, "Basic shapes and fonts."

Alias' Sketch!, meanwhile, is a full-featured 3-D program designed for ease of use and targeted at print illustrators and designers. Unlike Dimensions, it is capable of creating very complex models which can be matched to the perspective of scanned photographs. Sketch! offers photorealistic ray tracing and exports to other 3-D applications. RayDream's Designer is a low-cost 3-D program that, like Sketch!, is designed for easy production of 3-D illustrations. It also features the tools required to create fairly complex scenes and models, although it is somewhat less complex than Sketch!.

Three-D offers a unique opportunity to the illustrator. Artwork in the form of 3-D models can be used over and over in many new ways. A model of an airplane can be duplicated and combined with models of buildings and viewed from a distant point to illustrate an airport, or you can zoom in to view the passenger compartment or cockpit. Once rendered, images even can be returned to 2-D applications for touch-up and enhancement.

# Product and package design

Product and package designers were among the first to embrace the power of 3-D computing. Few things will sell a concept better than a photorealistic picture or animation of a finished industrial design. With 3-D software, a designer can build a box or a bottle, make it green plastic or red cardboard, and wrap a label created in a 2-D illustration program around the package. The result is then placed in a flattering setting, lights are positioned, and the image is rendered as though you were taking a photo of the package. Beyond packaging, you can bring industrial designs to life, proving to the venture capitalists that your newest invention is a bright idea (see figure 1.5).

**Figure 1.5.** The coffeepot of the future, modeled in VIDI Presenter Professional. Rendered with MacRenderMan.

If you are an experienced designer—but new to the Macintosh—then chapter 11, "Working with images," will prove enlightening. If you have experience with 3-D on high-end dedicated graphics worksta-tions, you may also want to investigate the discussion of acceleration that explains how you can squeeze Silicon Graphics' Indigo-level rendering performance out of your Macintosh system.

Production-oriented designers intent on exporting designs to computer-aided design (CAD) and computer-aided manufacturing (CAM) systems, can turn to the discussions of CAD presented in chapter 11. A well-made 3-D rendering is virtually indistinguishable from a photograph of the actual object—and is even better if it avoids costly prototyping and production mistakes.

A popular toy-making firm, for instance, models and renders a new design in VIDI's Presenter Professional, imports the result into Macromedia Director, and adds sounds and active buttons. The company then shows the new "toy" to children, who can push the buttons and get real responses. Based on kids' reactions, the com-pany decides whether or not to move to the next stage of production.

# Animation and video

Animation, whether for QuickTime movies, broadcast video, or film, is the ultimate expression of the 3-D art. Just about anything you can do in 3-D, you can set to motion. This book explains key frames, morphing, animated shaders, machine control, and alpha channels for compositing graphics with video. Also described are esoterica such as using QuickTime animations as surface textures, and important basics such as beveling to catch highlights and animating reflections.

For humans, animation is a labor-intensive task requiring 24 to 30 images for every second of film or video. Unlike a human illustrator, a computer is tireless. Build a model, specify starting and ending points (*key frames*) and paths for the motion of objects, lights, and cameras, and the Macintosh will render the frames between the points.

The most recognizable purveyors of animation and special effects have used these techniques extensively in Hollywood. Television producers use Macintosh-generated fly-by titles, spinning logos, animated illustrations, three-dimensional maps, and a host of other slick graphics. In fact, viewers will be hard-pressed to find a television station that doesn't broadcast flying 3-D logos at every commercial break.

Three-D is such a staple of Sunday sports broadcasts and beer commercials that one company has released a collection of sports balls (clip models and textures of golf balls, footballs, basketballs, and so on) that producers can send flying into America's living rooms.

Even the showplace of television graphics, MTV, has taken a serious interest in Macintosh-generated 3-D animations. Work created using Electric Image Animation System and Macromedia Three-D appears regularly from this frenetic broadcaster.

While many professional animators currently use expensive workstations (such as those from Sun, Silicon Graphics, and Hewlett-Packard) to churn out thousands of renderings, the distinction between these computers and the Macintosh is beginning to blur. Accelerators based on RISC chips, and optimized applications such as Electric Image's Animation System and NetRenderMan, effectively provide RISC-speed rendering on the Macintosh. The first PowerPC Macintosh—comparable to the fastest workstations—should bring the Macintosh fully up to workstation performance.

# Multimedia

Chapter 11, "Working with images," describes the use of 3-D in interactive and otherwise dazzling multimedia productions. Animated buttons, interactive rooms, animations synchronized with sound, and optimized color palettes are also covered. The ethereal world of virtual reality (that is, real-time interactive 3-D) also gets a look.

Multimedia productions incorporate sound, graphics, animation, video, and interactivity. This field is seen by many as the future of modern communications.

As the most modern and sophisticated tool for creating still images and animation, 3-D fits in everywhere. Interactive presentations need realistic backgrounds and buttons. Many interactive presentations feature rooms where you can pick up realistic 3-D objects or walk through corridors to discover new scenery.

A developer of training presentations can create a simulated switchboard where a train operator learns to reach for the appropriate stop and go buttons without ever stepping inside a train. This kind of simulation demands realistic 3-D renderings of the switchboard, complete with separate versions with warning lights turned on and off. Woe to the designer who has to paint all those switchboards by hand!

A developer of presentations can create a "pie" chart of profits on a spinning globe that flies apart when the presenter clicks on "miscellaneous expenses."

It's possible to create a travel kiosk where the viewer selects a destination and a 3-D airplane suddenly takes off, banks, and flies across a map of the world!

With a 3-D program, (such as Specular's Infini-D, that can import QuickTime video as a "texture"), a television can be rendered in 3-D and by clicking on the channel changer new video clips will appear on the screen. An architect can show the interior of a new theater, complete with the latest movie.

A kiosk developed by a well-known shoe company enables users to click on shoes in a 3-D store to order products and automatically fill out invoices.

Macromedia, Virtus, and Strata all offer "virtual-reality" software that enables even novices to take self-guided walk-through tours of models you've created.

# Architectural and mechanical design

Architects have a whole world of 3-D CAD applications at their disposal. Three-D CAD is so powerful that 2-D-only applications are falling by the wayside. It is now common to design a structure in 3-D and create realistic renderings to show clients. Mechanical designers, similarly, can render their designs for documentation or provide early marketing materials to the business department.

While CAD applications are highly specialized, architects often use general 3-D applications to design parts of their structures, such as decorative moldings and furniture. Chapters 5, 8, and 10, "Modeling," "Lighting," and "Rendering," should all prove useful. CAD topics include time-of-day and -year rendering, importing and rendering CAD models with ray tracing, mathematical accuracy, and perspective matching for fitting 3-D models to photos of an existing site.

Because architects and engineers must work extensively with negative spaces, volumes, quantity and weight of materials, their world demands a picture that is more than pretty on the surface. Solid modeling enables users to interface objects with each other using simple but powerful techniques known as Boolean operations. Solid modelers can even keep track of how much material is involved in a design. Engineers can use solid modeling and rendering to check for interfering or overlapping parts.

Using 3-D, architects can give clients realistic renderings of building designs. Animated renderings and real-time walk-through software can take clients on a walk down hallways to enter rooms and look around, peek out windows at other parts of a compound, or view a new design in the context of surrounding landscape. Some programs enable you to set the time of year and watch where shadows will fall in a courtyard at different times on different days.

An architect can greatly enhance the prospects of selling a design when a client can see a photorealistic rendering of the building's sparkling interior, tastefully decorated, with sunlight streaming through windows.

Engineers use 3-D to visualize relationships and conflicts in a model, or to show the foundry what's expected in the finished product. A complex machine made of many parts can be exploded and rendered for documentation. At the far end of the spectrum, 3-D designs can be exported to computer aided manufacturing (CAM) systems to control manufacturing machinery.

# How to use this book

The author's hope is that a newcomer to 3-D can use this book to gain a solid understanding of 3-D graphics on the Macintosh. It is not a user's manual for any one software package, but—where possible— there are step-by-step examples of useful techniques which you can adapt to the 3-D software package of your choice. Where techniques are unique to a particular software package, you should find that program identified.

Many techniques are general, but each 3-D application has its own approach to doing similar things. Techniques are divided into the four somewhat arbitrary classifications of user: Beginner, Intermediate, Advanced, and Very Advanced.

Again, in appendix A, "Product directory," you will find a listing of the many 3-D software applications available, along with a list of what categories the program falls into for each of the disciplines of 3-D (modeling, scene building, rendering, and animation). While it would be nice to include a complete listing of features for each product, to do so would be a disservice both to readers and the software vendors, as features are added and modified daily. Like all software markets, 3-D is highly competitive and it is hoped that the vendors of the different programs will play catch-up in features, so that a generalization that doesn't hold today will do so tomorrow.

Where particular programs offer unusual features, credit is given where it's due. On the other hand, we also strive to avoid boring the reader with endless attribution. If a feature is the rule, rather than the exception (which is often the case), it is illustrated and described in general terms.

While 3-D tools are not necessarily hard to use once the concepts are clear, the creators of software are in such a mad dash to keep up with one another that all-too-important documentation is often an afterthought. It is all the manual writers can do to keep up with new and improved features. Unfortunately for the user, the theory and clear visual examples behind the tools are often left for a later revision. This book aims to fill some of these cracks in the sidewalks.

Furthermore, this book offers many techniques and tricks of the trade used to speed work along, to bring new levels of detail and realism to renderings, and to boost the impact of animations. This is by no means an exhaustive collection. Each program offers its own pitfalls and opportunities. But the hope is that you will glean a strong enough understanding of how things are done that you will know when it's time to move on to more powerful tools.

# What level of 3-D user are you?

Just as there's a difference between replacing a sink's faucet washer and replacing a sink, there's a difference of skill level in producing 3-D imagery. Necessarily, you can only benefit from some honest self-examination in determining the kinds of tasks you can execute. But don't worry—this book will be here for you every step of the way!

- Beginner

- Intermediate

- Advanced

- Very advanced

# Beginner

You sat drop-jawed through the latest Hollywood spectacular featuring molten-metal cyborgs sparring on Jupiter. You need a 3-D logo for your Jumping Frog newsletter. You're determined to become the first 3-D whiz on the block. The catch: you've never touched a computer. While this book doesn't teach Macintosh basics, it will guide you through building a basic geometric shape like a sphere (a crude approximation of Jupiter), creating knockout logos and completed still images, and even generating otherworldly video and film animations. If you don't know where to start, then chapter 2, "Getting started," is a good place to find out what hardware and software you'll need to make 3-D happen.

The new user, totally unfamiliar with 3-D tools or geometry, can read from cover to cover with the expectation of finding a useful overview of what's involved in creating 3-D.

# Intermediate

Those readers who have considerable computer or graphics experience, but are just entering the world of computer 3-D (as well as those who need a little brushing up on geometry lessons long forgotten) will find the basic principles of 3-D described in chapter 5, "Modeling," chapter 6, "Scene building," and chapter 10, "Rendering." If your understanding of illumination extends only as far as the wall switch or the flash in your Instamatic camera, then chapter 8, "Lighting," will guide you safely out of the dark.

In addition to describing what 3-D is, this book describes limitless ways you can put it to use, such as importing a rendered image into Photoshop using alpha channel transparencies.

The intermediate user of 3-D can turn to relevant chapters in time of need. The different parts of 3-D are broken into their basic components and grouped accordingly. If you cannot make heads or tails of environment maps, for example, you can find an explanation under the heading "Environment maps," in chapter 7, "Materials." Where topics become unruly and cross boundaries—a cylinder can be extruded or lathed, for example—the heading "Cylinder" discusses the duality, while the headings "Lathing" and "Extrusion," in chapter 5, "Modeling," explain how each can be accomplished.

# Advanced

If you're already using one or more 3-D applications, the pages within will serve as a supplement to sketchy software tutorials, an introduction to new techniques, and a source of ideas. Are you building intricate models, but your renderings come up flat? Perhaps it's time to take on reflection, bump, and environment mapping. You'd like to add motion blur to a speeding bullet, but you don't know how. Maybe you're wondering how to animate RenderMan shaders or make convincing neon tubes. This book aims to shed light on these problems and many more.

If multimedia is the message, the postman delivers twice: chapter 9, "Animation," and chapter 11, "Working with images," cover 3-D in the new media age.

The person who is already a regular user of Macintosh 3-D tools, or who has used 3-D on other platforms, but is investigating Macintosh, will find the basic descriptions of techniques helpful as a refresher. Many of the tips throughout the book have been contributed by expert users and some of them may be valuable additions to the reader's tool chest. For those who hope to further advance their capabilities, some of the advanced topics may lend new insight and ideas.

# Very advanced

Just because you know it all, it doesn't mean you won't forget. Think of this as a cookbook for the ultimate meal. Find your favorite recipes and fold the corners for future reference. The following is a taste of the subtle and the spicy within:

- Reverse kinematics and physical modeling: drag-and-drop animation.

- Solids: more than meets the eye.

- Sipping splines smoothes your NuRBs: cures for the common DXF.

- Visible lights: a glowing account.

- Putting it in perspective: matching a model to a site and a texture to a model.

- Radiosity, field rendering, RISC, and PowerPC; distributed rendering; animated textures; frame-by-frame output, and more.

The author acknowledges that there are many expert users of 3-D who, given the time and the patience for book writing, could and probably will eventually provide a more experienced, minutely-detailed guide to the individual products involved in 3-D. So what's in it for you? In addition to being a suitable doorstop, and occasional primer for new employees, this book has benefited from the author's several years of weekly contact with the vendors of 3-D and their products. Appendix A provides an account, from a single source, of the capabilities of every 3-D tool currently available to the Macintosh user, as well as where to find them.

# The CD-ROM

The CD-ROM included with this book realizes a great opportunity. Color is the natural media of 3-D, but color printing all of the hundreds of illustrations included in the examples here would have driven the cost the book into the fourth dimension. Many of the best examples have been reproduced on the disc, so you can see the images in their natural form.

Animation, a caged tiger on the printed page, is set free through the innovative medium of QuickTime. Software interfaces are also given a shakedown, so you can see some of the basic techniques in a live-action format.

Several interactive tutorials guide users through key 3-D concepts, such as lathing, extrusion, lighting, texture mapping, and navigating. A visual reference to different lighting and rendering techniques also is presented in interactive format.

Finally, included are some unique 3-D models in DXF and RIB formats (usable in most 3-D programs) and a collection of matching backgrounds, seamless textures, and bump maps.

There was a time when floppy disks came with books and authors had to labor over what to put on the disk and what to leave off because there was only so much space. Now that there's so much space, it's only a matter of time. It is the author's hope that the content of the disc offers many things of value to every reader interested in 3-D. For those lacking CD-ROM drives, the author suggests trading time on a friend's drive for a peek at the cool animations.

Directions for using the disc are located in appendix B, "How to use the CD-ROM." Look for the CD-ROM icon; it highlights material that is on the disk.

# Summary

- Three-D on the Macintosh enables users to create highly realistic still images and animations.

- Three-D involves several stages: modeling, scene building, animation and rendering.

- The *Macintosh 3-D Workshop* was inspired by the emergence of fast Macintoshes and a wealth of powerful 3-D software.

- Macintosh 3-D software is useful to illustrators, industrial designers, animators, multimedia producers, and architects.

- This book is supplemented by interactive tutorials, illustrations, and examples on the included CD-ROM.

# chapter

# 2

# Getting started

M acintosh 3-D graphics—and this book—owe their existence to the rapid development of Macintosh computers. The seemingly endless pace at which Macintosh computers have accelerated year after year has delivered the power—missing only one year ago—to meet the demands of 3-D.

The president of a 3-D graphics software company summarized the importance of speed: "Imagine word processing and waiting 15 minutes for the cursor to return after you type a paragraph. That doesn't just affect the way you work, it affects the way you think."

When creating an image, the need for instant feedback is critical. If you are forced to wait for several seconds or minutes to see what you're making, the creative muse will soon become a frustrated, irritable ogre. Three-D graphics place such high demands on your computer system that every action can result in a several second redraw of the screen. This delay between what you do and what you see can be frustrating. If you draw a shape, you need to see it *now*. When you apply a texture, you want to see the result right away.

To some extent, software developers have responded to this need by writing faster and faster software and creating interface tricks (such as prebuilt previews of textures), to enhance visualization. Often, you can see real-time updates of objects and scenes as you draw. But this is far from real-time rendering, where you see a completely fin-ished image appear as fast as you draw. Most programs force you to accept boundary boxes and wireframe views as a compromise between no feedback and real-time realism.

Even the ElectricImage Animation System (currently the fastest high-quality renderer available to Mac users) will take a minute or two to render an average model on a fast Mac.

Meanwhile, programs such as Virtus WalkThrough Pro, that enable you to move through a shaded, texture-mapped model in real time, are changing the landscape. While it will not be mistaken for reality any time soon, real-time visualization of complete scenes is coming soon to a screen near you.

Inevitably, high-quality rendering will take time—sometimes hours—so anything you can do to speed the process will help. The best way to overcome the problem is to have the fastest hardware and software possible. Otherwise, there are several tricks and techniques to help speed things up.

# Working for speed

Although the fastest Macintosh available will help any 3-D user, even owners of slower Macs can benefit from the following tips. They apply to all phases of 3-D:

- **Use groups, names, and layers**. One way to speed up 3-D is to work on individual parts of the puzzle separately wherever possible. For example, if you are modeling a complex engine, "hide" all of the parts except the gear on which you are currently working. This way the computer only has to redraw the gear—not the whole engine. Likewise, when it comes time to preview part of a model, hide all the parts but the ones you need to see in the preview. Your Macintosh will calculate only the appearance of the visible objects, and the rendering will proceed much faster. Some programs accomplish this with a hierarchical grouping structure. While CAD programs, in particular, depend on "layers."

- **Hide the previews**. When working in a program that offers a real-time shaded preview, try hiding the preview window when you do not need it. This will significantly speed things up.

- **Name views and switch between them**. Because open views of a scene will need to be redrawn each time you make a change, it is much faster to hide or close superfluous views until you need them. Saving views also makes it quicker to move between views.

- **Use coarse wireframes**. Work in a coarse wireframe view until it comes time to make critical alignments and render. Then switch to a detailed wireframe to ensure the best rendering possible.

# Hardware

The Macintosh model you will need to work in 3-D depends on the complexity of the images you plan to create and how fast you need to do it. If you only plan to create the occasional 3-D PostScript rendering for use in an illustration program, any standard business-level Macintosh (such as the IIvx or Centris 610), is probably adequate. On the other hand, if you plan to do serious 3-D work (especially photorealistic rendering or animation), the fastest Mac money can buy will be worth the money spent.

# Accelerators

It is also possible to accelerate your work with a variety of additional hardware and software. Accelerators that speed up your Macintosh (such as those from Daystar, Fusion, and Applied Engineering) can turn a tired Macintosh into a 3-D workhorse. Currently, the fastest accelerators (such as the 68040-based boards from Daystar and Fusion) make Macintosh computers like the IIvx almost as speedy as the fastest Mac you can buy.

The Rocket, from Radius Inc., can be used as a straightforward accelerator—but it also has its own unique capability. You can plug in one or more of the boards—combined with RocketShare software—and each of the boards will operate as a separate Macintosh on a network inside your computer. You can switch between "Macs," leaving one board rendering while you model on another. This also has possibilities for "distributed rendering," described in chapter 13, "Advanced Topics."

# Monitor

A large color monitor, 16 to 21 inches, is practically a requirement for working in 3-D. If you plan to use a software product that displays four working windows simultaneously, one solution is to use two monitors: one that displays menus, toolbars, and positioning windows; and another that displays the preview window. Figure 2.1 clearly illustrates the need for plenty of screen space.

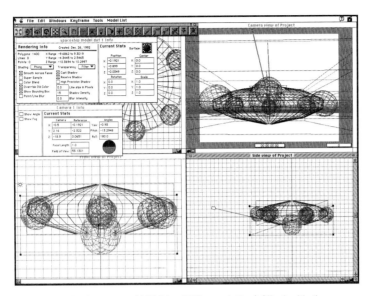

**Figure 2.1.** A 20-inch screen (1152 by 870 resolution) filled with the many windows used simultaneously in the Electric Image Animation System.

Color is extremely helpful—almost mandatory—even when creating grayscale artwork. When modeling, it is sometimes difficult to distinguish the different layers of wireframe models, as well as which model parts are active and which are not. A color display enables you to display inactive parts in black, for example; while active objects can be displayed in red or some other equally visible color.

Dimensions and addDepth (3-D illustration programs) have simple interfaces that are not as dependent on a large color monitor. You even can get away with working on a PowerBook with these programs.

# Display cards

In programs where you are working with many different layers or groups, you often can assign different colors to different layers to further distinguish objects of interest. If you decide to use multiple monitors, you'll need at least one display card to supplement your Macintosh's internal video.

While many newer Macintosh computers drive most monitors (some even in millions or thousands of colors), the older Macintosh will require a separate display card if you want to drive a large monitor or display photorealistic 16-bit or 24-bit color. This book was illustrated with the help of a SuperMac Thunder/24 board, which provides accelerated video and therefore makes modeling much snappier. Accelerated video cards are also available from RasterOps, Radius, Sigma, Mirror, and Envisio. Acceleration is particularly important when working on large, complex models—redrawing wireframe models on the screen can be painfully slow.

# Hard disks

Three-D applications themselves do not require huge amounts of storage. The serious 3-D artist, however, may use many textures, geometry libraries, reflection maps, and so forth. Animators will require massive amounts of hard disk space to accommodate digital video and other animation formats. Three-D images, for the most part, are 32-bit bitmapped graphics: a single 640-by-480 (NTSC resolution) image occupies about 1.2M of disk space. Multiply this by the number of frames required for 30 seconds of video, and you will find you need about 1G (gigabyte) of disk space.

Although compression techniques help, a fast, high-capacity drive will make it much easier to complete your work. Drives featuring SCSI-2 and other fast technologies will significantly increase performance, when combined with one of Apple's Quadras which have special support for these drives.

In addition, FWB Inc. and other vendors offer accelerated SCSI throughput in the form of a special NuBus board.

# Long-term storage

Serious 3-D users will develop massive libraries of textures, reflection maps, bump maps, models, animations, and images. In order to maintain these as libraries, you may want to invest in a large-capacity data storage system, such as a magneto-optical (MO) drive. These drives currently hold anywhere from 650M to 1.3G of data on a cartridge that costs about $200. This makes per-M cost of media about a fifth of that of hard disks. Large format MO drives are also the ideal media for transferring animations to service bureaus (if the service bureau also has a compatible drive).

Another option for long-term storage is Digital Audio Tape (DAT). While DAT tape backup works for protecting data from loss, it doesn't provide very convenient access to images and objects when you need them. DAT drives typically store the contents of a hard disk as a backup archive. In order to regain access to files, you usually need to "restore" the entire hard disk—which typically means deleting the current contents of the hard disk. A remarkable program called DeskTape, from Optima Technology Inc., enables you to use a DAT or Exabyte tape drive as a mountable volume on the Macintosh desktop, giving you 2, 5, or even 10G of data storage on a tape that costs between $10 and $20. Combined with image cataloging software, such as Aldus Fetch or Canto Software's Cumulus, this makes for a tremendously effective and cheap storage solution.

Floppy disks continue to be a viable media for storing single 3-D model files that are fairly compact. However, you will usually store the associated texture and environment maps with your model, which will often put floppies out of the running. Floptical drives, which store about 20M of data, are a relatively low-cost compromise, although 128M MO drives are rapidly coming down in price and threatening the long-term future of flopticals.

Animators must choose their removable media more carefully. Given that every finished frame of a video animation can require as much as a megabyte of storage space and that animations involving many layers of effects will require much more, this application definitely calls for a higher-capacity transfer mechanism. There are some creative solutions available for 3-D animators. For example, ElectricImage Animation System enables you to store animations as Abekas-format backup files on an Exabyte 8mm DAT drive. These can be "restored" directly onto an Abekas video disk system that keeps images in absolutely pristine condition all the way to video.

Video people also have a new option that does the same thing for every animation program. You can copy any animation directly from your Macintosh to an Exabyte drive in Abekas format with new software from ASDG and Knoll Software's Missing Link.

# Removable hard disks

Assuming you plan to transport your images to service bureaus or elsewhere, a removable storage media (such as the Iomega Bernoulli or Syquest 88c), can greatly facilitate moving files. In general, your choice of removable media will depend on the type of images you plan to produce, as well as what drives your favorite service bureau has to offer. The 44M- and 88M-Syquest cartridges have been the standard mode of transport of large files for the past few years, but these drives are now on the low end of the capacity scale and they seem certain to eventually give way to faster, more durable magneto-optical technology. However, if you only plan to take the occasional high-resolution still image to a service bureau for output to a film recorder, these drives are up to the task and they can be found everywhere, making them likely to be in the print world for a long time.

# Scanner

One of the most useful tools you can have for 3-D work is a scanner that brings photographic images into the computer. Anyone serious about doing 3-D will eventually want to tap the real world for some of its infinite textures. Architects will find the capability to photograph a site, produce a model, and render the proposed structure against a backdrop of its intended surroundings invaluable.

Slide and film scanners (such as the Nikon CoolScan, Microtek ScanMaker 35, and Santos Mira•35), enable you to scan negatives or slides directly into the computer. Aside from digital photography—which currently is grossly expensive and of fairly low quality—this is the fastest way to capture high-quality images and get them into your Macintosh. You can shoot a roll of film (photos of textures for example), take them to the local 1-hour photo finisher, and scan them for almost instant turnaround.

Other types of scanners will work for this purpose. Inexpensive flatbed scanners are readily available for scanning the prints that you get back from a photo finisher. Flatbed scanners are too numerous to mention by name, but for best results with 3-D software seek a scanner that offers 24-bit color. If you do not own a scanner already, look for a scanner that comes bundled with the complete package of Adobe Photoshop. This software is a "must-have" for any serious 3-D user.

Hand-held scanners are an inexpensive solution and can be useful when scanning textures you plan to use as texture "tiles." But in general, they do not serve well as a professional graphics solution. A hand-held scanner combined with a full-featured 3-D program (such as RayDream's Designer) could form a complete system for the novice—but not for a serious 3-D user.

# CD-ROM Drive

There are dozens of CD-ROM titles available that ease the creation of interesting 3-D art—including the disc that comes with this book. Items that can be found on CD for the 3-D user include: print-quality photographic textures, seamless textures, video and animation loops for rotoscoping, and 3-D clip models, to name a few. While a CD-ROM drive is by no means a requirement to work in 3-D, it opens up a wealth of creative opportunities (see figure 2.2).

Several companies offer CD-ROM libraries of seamless photographic textures for use in 3-D.

For an explanation of "seamless textures," see "Texture mapping" in chapter 7, "Textures."

**Figure 2.2.** The backdrop in this image is from the Sky Volume One collection from CD Folios. The marble texture on the vase is from ArtBeats' Marble and Granite, Volume One.

The latest CD-ROM drives have "double-speed" or even "4-speed" capability and they are exponentially faster than older drives. This is important because CD-ROM drives have been notoriously slow in the past.

# Photo CD

One of the most compelling CD-ROM formats for 3-D users is Eastman-Kodak's Photo CD. You can store your photos of textures and backgrounds permanently in electronic form on CD-ROM, without benefit of a scanner. This is an excellent way to develop a library of textures and other images. You can put hundreds of images on CD-ROM for the price of the cheapest flatbed scanner, and the images are usually of very high quality—depending on your originals. Many newer CD-ROM drives that read standard CD-ROMs also will read Photo CD format. The other advantage of Photo CD is that it frees you from the burden of scanning textures. You can simply shoot photos and drop the film off at a photo finisher and pick up the disc and negatives a few days later.

> **Tip**
> The CD-ROM ToolKit from FWB Software Inc., accelerates existing CD-ROM drives through sophisticated caching and makes most CD-ROM drives—even old ones—Photo CD- and multi-session-compatible.

A sample of matched background and material textures from the Alpha Channel Expert Collection can be found on the included CD-ROM. Clip models, tutorials, an image gallery, and many sample animations are also on the disc.

# Drawing tablet

Drawing or digitizing tablets are standard in the architectural and engineering CAD worlds, where handmade drawings are converted to highly-accurate vector-based artwork. These combine a tablet (anywhere from 6 inches by 9 inches to 3-feet square) with a "pen" or a "puck" (a mouse with crosshairs), which mimic a mouse in functionality. The difference is that a drawing tablet can use absolute coordinates, unlike a mouse's relative position. This means that if your pen is one inch over and down from the upper left-hand corner of the tablet, your drawing cursor will be one inch over and down in your drawing. You can tape an existing drawing over the tablet and trace it with your pen to input a highly accurate copy into your 3-D application.

A relatively new type of tablet and pen, introduced by Wacom Inc., has completely changed the way computer artists interact with the Macintosh. The Wacom tablets feature a pressure-sensitive pen that when combined with compatible software, responds to human input very much like traditional brushes and paints. As you press harder, the brush stroke widens; press more lightly and it narrows. The result is that you can create an infinite variety of painted, drawn, inked, and smeared textures that can bring a new level of artistic detail to 3-D images (see figure 2.3).

**Figure 2.3.** The texture used to create this image was painted with a Wacom pen and tablet and Fractal Design's Sketcher software. The texture was used as a bump map when rendered on the sphere in Alias' Sketch!

When combined with a program like Painter, the Wacom tablet enables you to trace over a 3-D rendering using colors from the

**Figure 2.4.** This image shows a lamp modeled and rendered in Alias Sketch!

original to create an image that is accurate in terms of shadow and perspective—yet looks for all the world like it is hand-drawn or painted (see figures 2.4 and 2.5).

**Figure 2.5.** This image shows figure 2.4 cloned using Fractal Designs' Painter software along with a Wacom tablet.

CalComp Inc. and Kurta Inc. also make pressure-sensitive tablets that mimic the functionality of Wacom's tablets.

# 3-D digitizer

A 3-D digitizer is very much like a 2-D drawing tablet, except that a stylus is moved over the surface of the object being digitized and the tablet reports the stylus' position in three dimensions.

Many professional 3-D animators use clay models of objects; digitize them using one of these devices; and then use the resulting models in their animations. Since it is sometimes easier to create a life-like organic model (such as an animal), out of clay than with 3-D software, this is an effective technique.

Mira Imaging makes a unit called "HyperSpace" with a variety of resolutions and prices. When you digitize a model up to 15 inches high, the location of the stylus as you move it over the surface is saved in a standard three-coordinate format such as DXF. You can then import the file into a 3-D program and use it like a regular 3-D model. Because this is still a relatively obscure technology, 3-D digitizers remain expensive (in the neighborhood of $12,000 for one that captures a high degree of detail).

# Animation hardware

Most 3-D users opt to take their animations to a service bureau for output to video tape. But those who are determined to record their animations in-house will need to invest in a substantial amount of additional hardware.

## Animation deck

Animators will need a frame-accurate video animation deck. These range in price from $6,000 to $40,000. This requirement alone is the reason most animators turn to service bureaus for final output.

An animation deck is capable of stepping, one frame at a time, through an animation; and recording each frame as it goes. This seems like a simple process on the surface. But in reality, to record video, the tape must move at full speed. Since the computer cannot display the images of an animation at full speed without a high degree of compression, the animation deck must do what is known as *pre-roll*, or back up and move forward for each successive frame. Generally, the computer controls the animation decks, so it is not necessary for the user to manually operate the deck to record each frame.

While broadcast-quality video decks, such as three-quarter-inch component devices, are prohibitively expensive, there is at least one reasonably priced solution for creating near-broadcast quality video animations. Sony offers a low-end professional hi-8 deck, the EVO-9650, which produces excellent results. For users who need to create quick drafts of animations before going to a service bureau, this represents a very good solution.

# Animation controller

Animation controllers (such as the DQ-Animaq NuBus board or DQ-MAC232 software from Diaquest Inc.), enable your Macintosh to control a compatible animation video deck and automatically output completed animations to video tape. Essentially, the Diaquest system works as a traffic controller, sequentially stepping through and displaying the many frames of an animation, all the while telling the video deck when to move on and record the next frame.

Diaquest's DQ-MAC232 software-only animation product performs these functions, but without some of the other benefits of the NuBus boards, such as the capability to do "Fast Pass" video capture from professional animation decks. For users of low-end animation hardware, however, this product is well suited to the task.

# Video encoder

In order to output to video tape, the RBG images on your Macintosh must be encoded to NTSC or other appropriate video format. (The standards in Europe are PAL and SECAM.) A *video encoder* is circuitry—often on a NuBus board—that converts your computer's RBG video signals into a format that can be displayed and recorded by video equipment. Examples include the TruVision's Nuvista+, and Radius' VideoVision (see figure 2.6). There are also a wide variety of external encoders that will convert the output from your standard Macintosh internal video or display board to NTSC format.

When working on 3-D images for video—even if you plan to take your work to a service bureau—using an encoder and an external video monitor will ensure your images will display properly and that the colors you are using translate accurately to video.

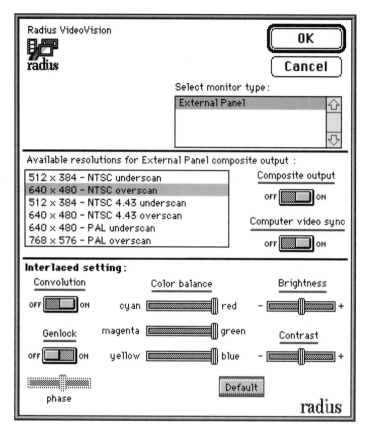

**Figure 2.6.** The control panel for Radius Inc.'s Video Vision—a combination display card, video digitizer, sound board, and video encoder.

# Video digitizer

A video digitizer (such as the RasterOps MediaTime board or the Radius VideoVision), enables you to "grab" frames of video. If used with a frame-accurate video deck and an animation controller, it can grab frames one at a time for high image fidelity. The frames of video can then be used as backdrops or textures for 3-D animations, producing startling movie effects. Some programs (such as Specular International Inc.'s Infini-D and ElectricImage Animation System), will enable you to use video or animations as moving textures. For example, you can project a "movie" of a fish swimming inside a 3-D fish bowl.

# Hardware tips

Here are some tips for getting the most performance from hardware used for Macintosh 3-D. For more ideas, see chapter 13, "Advanced topics."

- **Turn off unused and superfluous system extensions**. You can do this with a program such as Now Software Inc.'s Startup Manager. It enables you to create sets of startup extensions that you can use when you are performing different tasks. In particular, turn off AppleTalk and File Sharing unless they are in use.

- **Set your monitor to 256 colors using the Monitors control panel**. If you have a video board or a Mac that supports 24-bit (millions) of colors, be aware that performance will be much slower when you work in "millions-of-colors" mode. This is particularly true while modeling and scene building when the Mac is constantly redrawing the screen. Most 3-D programs will continue to work with a full 32 bits of color information, even when you're only displaying eight bits.

- **Use more than one computer**. This book was written and illustrated with the help of a 33-MHz Radius Rocket with RocketShare, which works essentially like a second Macintosh plugged into the NuBus. While the Mac is busy rendering, for example, you can switch over to the Rocket and continue modeling. This effectively eliminates sitting idly while you wait for things to happen. Similarly, distributed rendering systems that take advantage of networked Macintosh computers are also an effective way to speed things up. The author also made use of a NuSprint board from YARC Systems Corp. This is essentially a RISC-based computer inside the Macintosh. It currently accelerates rendering with RenderMan, Infini-D, and Presenter Professional.

- **Loading your Mac with relatively inexpensive RAM** is perhaps the best hardware accelerator of all. If the Mac must constantly load code in and out of memory—or worse yet, virtual memory—the whole system will come to a virtual standstill. How much RAM is enough? This depends on the

particular 3-D application you're using and how complicated the
images you are creating. But in general, 4M of *free* RAM (above
your system requirements) is plenty for PostScript rendering; a
practical minimum for using programs like MacroModel and
Sketch! is 8M; while 16M of RAM, or more, is required for high-
resolution renderings of complex models. Like hard disk space,
more RAM will almost always give you more speed.

---

**Tip**
The author has a mess—and he means *mess*—of friends
with carpal tunnel syndrome, sore backs, necks, and
shoulders, and other repetitive stress injuries due to long
hours working on a machine that has no compassion for
the human body. Invest in a good chair, a wrist rest for
mousing, and a comfortable, adjustable platform for
working. Design an ergonomic workspace in 3-D, if you like.
You'll be glad you did.

---

# How 3-D works

Three-D graphics are created in stages: modeling, scene building,
animating, and rendering. Many 3-D applications do more than one of
the above; some do it all. Some programs combine elements. For
example, StrataVision 3d and Infini-D model and animate in the same
space used for scene building. On the other hand, some 3-D applications (such as Presenter Professional and RayDream's Designer),
divide these four tasks into separate programs or modules, passing a
model back and forth between them. A few applications are highly
specialized and fill only one or two parts of the puzzle. For example,
Pixar's ShowPlace is only a scene builder; while VIDI's Modeler
Professional specializes exclusively in model building. Because 3-D is
so memory- and processor-intensive, almost all 3-D programs have
a separate mode for rendering. For a complete listing of which
programs offer which features, see appendix A, "Product Directory."

# Modeling

Modeling is the building of 3-D objects in space. Think of it as using a computer to sculpt clay.

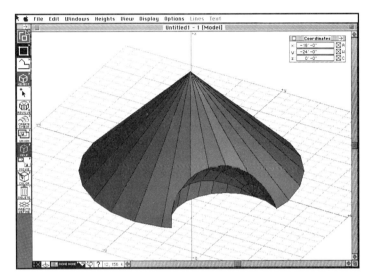

**Figure 2.7.** form•Z's single-perspective view. You can switch easily between different viewing angles.

The point of snaps in a perspective view or multiple simultaneous views is that computers have 2-D screens. In order to draw in three dimensions, you need tools to aid in visualization.

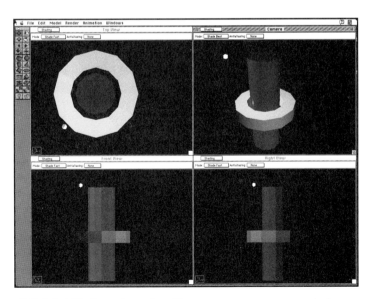

**Figure 2.8.** Infini-D's four-plane view. You can open even more windows, each with a view from a different camera angle.

39

You can accomplish this task while in a single perspective view (where drawing tools "snap" to points in space); or in a multi-window mode (where each window shows the same scene from different points of view) (see figures 2.7 and 2.8). Some programs enable you to see top, front, side, and perspective views simultaneously. An unusual program is Will Vinton's Playmation, which allows you to draw in a two-view screen.

Three-D shapes can be created in a variety of ways, many of which you can combine to form a finished model.

- *Additive modeling* involves adding pre-existing building blocks together to complete an object.

- *Constructive modeling* incorporates a number of techniques (such as extrusion, lathing, and skinning), to construct a 3-D shape out of 2-D outlines.

- *Molding* or distortion uses pre-existing shapes (primitives or constructively modeled forms like soft dough or clay) to squeeze, pinch, and distort to create unique shapes.

- *Derivative modeling* is a technique limited to solid modelers (such as form•Z or ZOOM), that enables you to use existing shapes to "carve" other shapes. This technique is sometimes called *Boolean modeling*. For example, derivative modeling enables you do things like drill a hole in a sphere with a cone, or extract a shape from the intersection of two cylinders.

# Scene building

*Scene building* is the arrangement of models, textures, lights, and cameras. While Macromedia Inc.'s MacroModel is a model-building program that offers crude rendering, users will also need a program such as Macromedia 3-D to create sophisticated animations and renderings.

Some scene builders enable you to constrain parts so that they will move in particular relationship to other parts. For example, a wheel can only turn on its axle and a piston can only move within the confines of its cylinder. Swivel 3-D, also from Macromedia, is still well known for its prowess in this regard—even though the program is otherwise out of date.

In addition to moving and placing objects, scene builders offer many of the other tools that help you create interesting renderings:

- **Texture mapping.** By attaching or mapping textures, a plain gray orb can be turned into a glowing halogen bubble, a fuzzy orange tennis ball, or a crystal oracle (see figure 2.9). Textures can be as simple as red plastic—or they can be as complex as the reflective riveted hull of an aluminum aircraft.

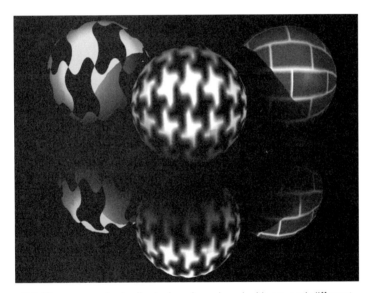

**Figure 2.9.** The same orb duplicated and rendered with several different texture maps.

- **Bump maps** are a bridge between modeling and textures. Dark and light areas in a bump map are rendered as depressions and raised surfaces (see figure 2.10).

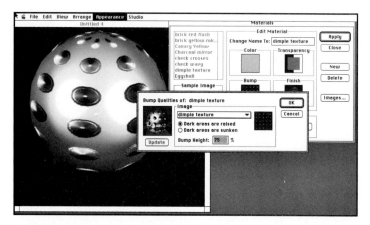

**Figure 2.10.** This model uses a simple grid of soft-edged dots as a bump map.

- **Label maps** are an extension of texture mapping and are often used in conjunction with textures. For example, you can place a wine label on a glass bottle or map a Persian rug design onto an interior floor.

- **Reflection maps and environment maps** give chrome and other reflective surfaces the appearance of reflecting the surrounding environment (see figure 2.11).

**Figure 2.11.** A landscape photograph used as a reflection map.

- **Lighting**. Just as *lighting* sets the mood of a stage play or photograph, the placement of lights profoundly affects the appearance of your final image. Types of lights include point (such as light bulbs), distant (suns), spotlights, neon tubes, and lasers to name a few. Most scene builders have multiple lights of varying intensity and color. Lights are usually invisible. Better programs (such as ElectricImage Animation System) offer lights that glow and even have an aura or halo (see figure 2.12).

**Figure 2.12.** This model was rendered using Electric Image Animation System's unique visible lights.

- **Cameras**. The *camera* is an object that represents your point of view. By moving or rotating the camera, you can change what appears in the final rendered image. Multiple cameras offer multiple points of view. Just like a real camera, you can change lenses for different angles of view and adjust apertures to change the depth of field.

- **Atmosphere and other environmental considerations.** In most scene builders, you can place simple shaded or picture backgrounds. Some enable you to employ atmospheric effects such as fog or haze that create the impression of depth by gradually obscuring distant objects.

- **Rendering interface**. Because scene building is usually the final step before rendering, scene builders often provide the interface to render an image or animation. *Rendering* is a complex series of mathematical algorithms that use your models and the composition of your scene to create a realistic image. But with the exception of Pixar's RenderMan, rendering does not lend itself to much user intervention. Scene builders enable you to set the user-configurable rendering parameters.

# Animation

Animation is really an extension of scene building. *Animation* brings 3-D designs into the fourth dimension by adding motion to objects, lights, and cameras.

While simple in concept, movie makers have used the technique called *key framing* to follow speeding spaceships through alien condominium projects. You first specify a "state of the world," including position, orientation, texture, and other attributes of objects as you normally would when building a scene. You then create a new key frame and change the scene by moving or changing objects, the camera, and so on. The software then calculates all of the frames in-between beginning and end key frames and smoothly blends any changes from one frame to the next. In some programs, objects can even be made to "morph" into one another. (Imagine glass letters magically rising out of pools of mercury, or a Fiat 500 transforming into a Cadillac El Dorado.) When you render an animation, each frame is slightly different from the last, creating a smooth, realistic animation.

# Rendering

Rendering is the final step in creating 3-D graphics. *Rendering* is where the computer calculates the appearance of the scene, including highlights and shadows, reflections and refractions, textures, labels, and bumpiness—even special effects such as motion blur. If creating an animation, the computer does this for every frame. The renderer can usually be set to save the resulting images in a variety of resolutions and file formats, ranging from high-resolution PICT files with alpha channel transparencies, to QuickTime movies for use in multimedia projects, or numbered PICT files for output to video tape.

All of these primary rendering techniques are described in detail in chapter 10, "Rendering." There are many different types of rendering, including:

- **PostScript blending**. This technique generates a smoothly shaded illustration that can be used like any image created in Adobe Illustrator or Aldus FreeHand.

- **Flat shading** gives each polygon of a 3-D object a single color, so objects appear solid, but faceted like a gem.

- **Gouraud shades** objects smoothly, but with blurred detail.

- **Phong shades** smoothly, but also accurately depicts surfaces, lighting, and can simulate reflections.

- **Ray tracing**, a complex rendering method, can accurately render mirror effects, transparency, and refraction (bending of light through clear surfaces).

- **Procedural shading**. This is the technique used for textures such as wood grain, which to some extent has to be aware of the shape receiving the texture.

Pixar's MacRenderMan relies exclusively on procedural shaders and has interesting effects all its own. In some ways, it is more realistic than ray tracing; and in other ways it is not. Radiosity, the most complex rendering system available to the Mac, renders incredibly realistic matte surfaces.

# Summary

- Speed is critical. Three-D demands a fast Macintosh and high-performance software and techniques.

- A variety of hardware will help the 3-D user get the job done. A large monitor and high-capacity hard disk are a good place to start.

- Animators require special hardware if they plan to output animations to video tape. A frame-accurate video deck, video controller hardware or software, and a video encoder are essential ingredients.

- *Modeling* is the building of 3-D objects.

- *Scene building* is the placement of objects, textures, and lights.

- *Animation* is scene building with the additional element of time and motion.

- *Rendering* calculates the final appearance of the scene, including light, shading, and surface qualities of objects.

chapter

# 3

# Navigating
# in 3-D

I magine a photographer surveying a landscape. She has the luxury of stereoscopic vision and a known point of view. This allows her to judge the length of a picket fence, the distance to a row of corn, the height of a mulberry tree, and the portliness of a grazing cow. Once she has assessed the scene, she can go about aiming her camera. By moving a few yards left, she can readjust the relationship of the cow, the fence, and the corn. If she lies on her back beneath the cow, she'll likely see a great deal of cow belly framed against blue sky—but precious little else. If she climbs the tree, she may find herself with a dizzying view of distant hills, or the wide back of the Guernsey. It all depends on her point of view.

Macintosh computers (like most others), work in two dimensions. What you see on the screen is similar to what you can print on a piece of paper. The illusion of depth in 3-D is created by perspective, highlight, shadow, and other factors (see figure 3.1). In order to achieve this illusion, you give your computer all the information relevant to true three-dimensional space.

**Figure 3.1.** Many factors create the illusion of depth.

Navigating in 3-D involves two parts: moving objects, and changing your point of view. The distinction is important—although the results can sometimes appear equivalent. Take the example of a tea pot. If you are viewing the pot from the front and you lift the lid several inches, you will clearly see the gap between the two parts. However, if you view the pot from directly above, you will not be able to determine if the lid is touching the pot or floating above it. From this point of view, both states appear to be the same.

Now, suppose you want to see the handle of the pot framed in profile in your current point of view, but the pot happens to be poised to pour tea into a cup. You can rotate the pot so that its handle is in profile in your current view, but this will change the pot's relationship to the cup. Alternatively, you can leave the pot where it is and change your point of view so that you can see the pot's handle in profile; the cup and the pot will maintain their relationship, but both will move change their position in the current view.

For most people, working in 3-D is extremely disorienting at first. After all, there's nothing normal about switching to a top view to see whether or not a table's legs are really under the table. It's sometimes helpful to think of yourself as a mosquito with super powers. You can look at your 3-D world from any point of view, and you have the power to pick things up and move them. After a while, even objects in a tri-view window will seem to take on a logical and simple sense of height, width, and depth.

# The camera

Working in three dimensions requires that you explore a virtual world much like the photographer in her landscape. While 2-D drawing limits you to a single point of view, 3-D enables you to have an infinite number of points of view (see figure 3.2). In fact, many 3-D software packages use the camera metaphor as a way to position and save different views of a scene. By aiming and placing different cameras, you can switch from view to view instantly, like a security guard monitoring a high-rise building. You can keep not only your perspective, but you can keep several, and switch among them.

The camera view shown in figure 3.2 provides the following view of the subject as shown in figure 3.3.

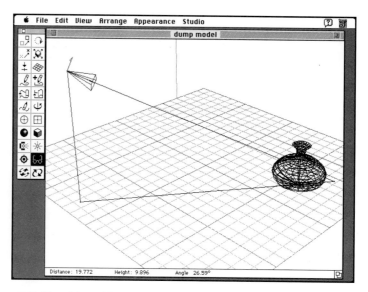

**Figure 3.2.** Sketch! enables you to easily position and aim a camera in its single-perspective view.

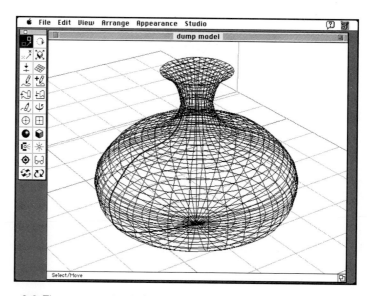

**Figure 3.3.** The camera view in figure 3.2 provides this point of view.

Some programs—particularly those that specialize in animation—enable you to move a camera while the camera remains aimed at a particular point. For example, you can circle an object with the camera to simulate a 360 degree fly by. In some animation programs, the camera can attach to and follow a moving object—a feature often called *tracking*.

The great advantage of having cameras as objects in 3-D is that you can move and reposition a camera in one view—then switch your point of view to that camera. This is critical to animators who can move a single camera to follow the action; just like a camera-man who has practically unlimited viewpoints: suspended from trucks and booms, mounted to the front of a roller coaster or a stunt man's helmet, dangled out of a helicopter, or tacked to the nose of a buzzing fly.

> The following still-image applications offer moveable cameras for setting and adjusting views of a scene:
>
> - Alias Sketch!
> - Pixar ShowPlace
> - Turbo 3-D
> - Sculpt 3-D
>
> These animation programs offer animated cameras.
>
> - Electric Image Animation System
> - Sculpt 4D
> - Presenter Professional
> - Alias UpFront
> - Macromedia Three-D
> - Infini-D
> - LogoMotion
> - StrataVision 3d
> - Strata StudioPro
> - Sculpt 4D

These 3-D programs use a single-world view:

- Swivel 3-D

- Typestry

- Strata Type 3d

- Presto 3-D

- Swivel 3-D

- addDepth

- Dimensions

# Pan, zoom, tilt

In 3-D programs that do not offer moveable cameras, there is usually a way to change points of view, and in most cases to save different viewing positions.

There are a number of ways you can change your view: by dragging the world across your view window, by rotating the world, and by zooming in or out with a magnifying glass or similar tool. Even though you may not have camera objects, per se, you can still change or move the camera you're looking through when you change your point of view. This helps you visualize the changes that you need to bring you to the desired point of view.

# Lenses

Like all good photographers, as a 3-D user you carry a goody bag full of lenses that you can interchange as necessary. Each lens has a different focal length which provides a different angle of view. The angle of view becomes narrower as the focal length increases, so a 400-millimeter lens may zero in on a single, far-off sheep—while a 15-millimeter lens will take in the pasture, mountains, and a good deal of sky.

# Moving camera versus lens length

Zooming in by moving the camera closer to the subject, and zooming in by changing lens length have two different effects (even though the term *zooming* sometimes is applied to both interchangeably). Technically, moving the camera in is called *dolly in*; moving the camera out is called *dolly out*. These two approaches have distinctly different results.

Standard human vision is approximately equal to the view provided by a 50-millimeter lens on a standard 35 mm camera. (That is why a 50 mm lens is considered normal and comes with most cameras.) When you change your lens to something other than 50 mm, you gain a sense of perspective that is not normal. With a very short (usually known as *wide*) lens of about 20 mm, things begin to take on a great deal of distortion, as if you're viewing the world through the eye of a fish in a fishbowl. At the opposite extreme, long lenses of 100 mm or more (often called *telephoto*) cause a flattening of scenes. That is, they tend to remove the sense of perspective from 3-D images. An orthogonal projection is the most extreme example of this flattening effect. (It is as if you aimed a telescope at your scene mounted on the moon.)

You can use these properties to your advantage. If you need a sense of more depth, you can use a shorter lens and move closer to the scene. This causes more wide-angle distortion, while preserving the content of the scene. On the other hand, you can use a long lens and remain farther in the back to keep foreground and background objects proportionally sized. Orthogonal views are often the best for aligning objects because you need not guess if things are really aligned or just look that way.

# Absolute position: x,y,z

Both individual objects and viewpoint cameras have a position in space as well as an orientation. For example, a camera may be above, looking down. An airplane may be at 10,000 feet, flying east. These are contextual positions—that is, the camera must be above *something* and the airplane must be east of *somewhere*. Three-D programs solve this problem by creating an "absolute world"—that is, a finite space in which all objects are located and oriented. When we refer to the position of objects, it tends to be in relationship to a known, fixed coordinate.

On maps of the real world, we use latitude and longitude to represent distance and direction from the International Dateline and the equator. In 3-D, the universal reference point is called the *origin* and everything is relative to this point. Just as we refer to an airplane's position relative to a given city, or an electron's position relative to its nucleus, 3-D requires that you have an origin for a given project and select an appropriate scale within to work.

If you're like most people who loathed high school geometry and think Cartesia is an unfriendly nation, let's start with an idea you can count on three fingers. Hold your left hand in front of you, point your index finger at the person sitting across the room, your thumb into the air, and your middle finger to your right. Each finger represents an axis, universally referred to as x, y, and z (see figure 3.4). (For the sake of conformity, we'll use the same naming scheme. But, if you prefer, you are welcome to think of the axes as "middle," "thumb," and "index," respectively.) These fingers represent positive axes. If you move your finger in a direction opposite to the direction in which they were originally pointing, you will be moving in a negative direction. (If this is particularly difficult to remember, perhaps consider tattooing +x, +y, and +z on the appropriate fingers as shown in figure 3.4.) It's important to remember that this works only with the left hand; if you make the same gesture with the right hand, the middle finger points in the negative x direction.

The x,y,z naming convention is a standard in mathematics. If you haven't learned it by now, it's about time. It is also, of course, a standard in 3-D software.

The Cartesian coordinate system is like the one you use to read a map by locating coordinates such as D-7 or A-9. The difference is that it includes in-out, left-right, as well as up-down directions. Since the map begins with x=0, y=0 and z=0 at the center of the universe; move in the direction of your pointing index finger and z increases; move up (thumb) and y increases; move right (middle finger) and x increases. Conversely, move left of center and the x value becomes negative, move down and y decreases, move in the direction opposite your pointing index finger and z decreases.

In a three-plane view, this system enables you to position and scale objects very precisely. In a top view (look down at your pointing thumb), moving an object changes its x and z values, but not its y value. Conversely, the front view can be used to change an object's x and y values, but leaves the z position untouched. For this reason, some programs label the top view window with an x-z, the front view window with an x-y, and the side view window with a y-z.

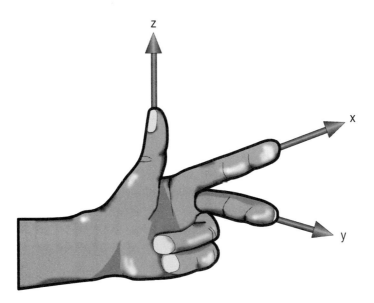

**Figure 3.4** The left hand representing 3-D.

The three-plane orthogonal view is the most common method of representing 3-D space in such a way that you can visualize what is going on at all times. Usually, this view is supplemented with a perspective view, so that you can get a realistic look at the scene while you work. The approach that's rapidly gaining favor in newer applications is the single-perspective view. This enables you to view and work on objects in a natural perspective and to switch among different perspectives to stay oriented.

> **Tip**
> Every 3-D program has some type of scene building capability. Some of the features of scene builders, however, deserve distinction. Some programs use a single view (which can make things easier to understand if well implemented) as the standard way of working. Others use multiple views, such as the tri-view or variations of it, to look at the same scene simultaneously from different angles.

Examples of single-view programs include:

- Sketch!

- form•Z

- MacroModel

- Macromedia Three-D

- Showplace

- UpFront

- addDepth

- Dimensions

- Dyna Perspective

- WalkThrough

Multiple-view programs include:

- Sculpt (all versions)

- Turbo 3-D

- Shade II

- Presenter Professional

- Presto3-D

- Playmation (2 views)

- StrataStudio Pro (one or more)

- StrataVision 3d (one or more)

# The three-plane view

The natural world generally affords us only a single perspective view—that is, we see a scene from only one point, with only one physical perspective. In Macintosh 3-D, the alternative to this single-perspective is the more traditional (although less intuitive), three-plane view. Basically, this approach provides three views of your model at all times: front, top, and side. Orthogonal views are most useful in this mode because they are free of lens distortion. You can think of an orthogonal view as one where objects have been squashed completely flat. (An orthogonal view has no perspective, like an architectural blueprint.) Usually, most 3-D applications provide a perspective preview window to show your progress.

The advantage of the three-plane view is that you can create very precise alignments. For example, in VIDI's Modeler Professional, to draw a series of circles one atop the next (as if stacking a pile of pennies), you start by drawing a circle in the top view. You then move to the front or side view (where your circle now looks like a mere straight line) and lock your drawing position an inch above the existing circle. Finally, you move back to the top view and draw another circle directly atop the first. While this system is very accurate, it is not nearly as intuitive as the single perspective view. Visualizing in three separate planes takes a good deal of practice.

To draw an object that isn't flat, such as a spiral stair's banister, you'll need to frequently lock your drawing position in one window, switch to another window, continue drawing, and then smooth the lines in the different views. This can quickly become confusing. On the other hand, the precise control afforded by this approach means you can create very accurate complex shapes sometimes impossible to build in the single-window applications.

# Single perspective

The single perspective view looks much like the place you're in right now. All objects are positioned in relation to a floor and walls (also known as *working planes*), which you can use for reference points.

The advantage of this approach is that you can easily visualize what you're doing because your view looks like the real world. The disadvantage is that you must frequently switch points of view and make extensive use of some fairly sophisticated tools, such as guides and snaps, to help you. Otherwise, what you will see in your 2-D representation of 3-D space will not necessarily coincide with your representation. For example, two blocks appear to be level with each other when viewed from the top or from an elevated perspective (see figures 3.5 and figure 3.6); but when viewed from the side (see figure 3.7) or front (see figure 3.8), it is immediately apparent that one is set far behind the other.

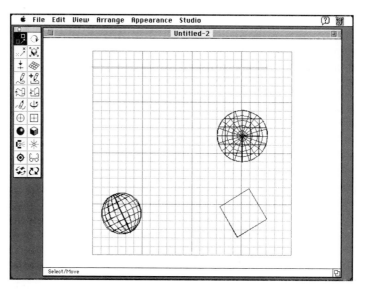

**Figure 3.5.** The top view perspective.

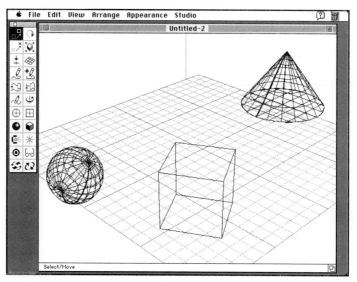

**Figure 3.6.** An elevated view perspective.

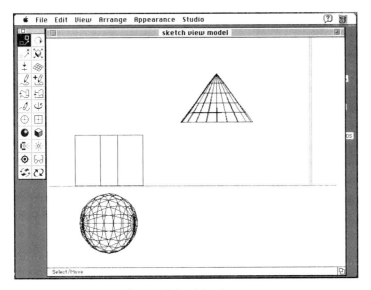

**Figure 3.7.** The perspective from a right side view.

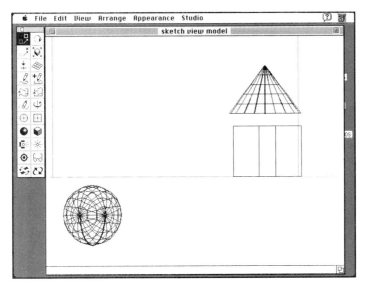

**Figure 3.8.** From a front view perspective.

# Virtual trackball

One of the most important tools for navigation in the single perspective is the *virtual trackball*. While this feature goes by a number of names, essentially it enables you to use the mouse as a handle that rotates your 3-D world in any direction. By "grabbing" the bottom of the screen and pushing it up, you roll the world away from you. By grabbing the top and pulling it down, you roll it towards you. By grabbing the left edge and pushing it right, you spin the world around the central axis of the screen. All of these movements are analogous to spinning a globe.

Some programs, such as Alias' Sketch!, enable you to select single objects, or groups of objects as the center of the universe. All rotations using the virtual trackball then revolve around this object or group of objects (see figures 3.9 through 3.12).

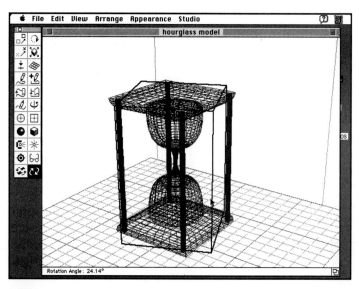

**Figure 3.9.** Turning world around y-axis.

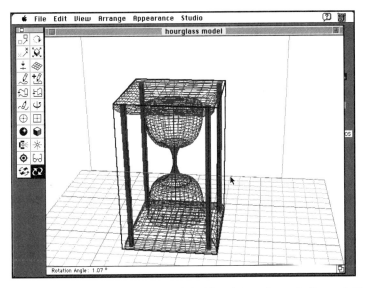

**Figure 3.10.** Turning world around y-axis in Sketch! as shown in figure 3.10, results in this view.

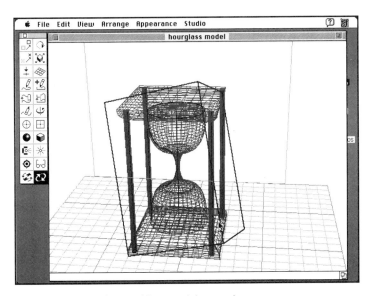

**Figure 3.11.** Revolving the world around the z-axis.

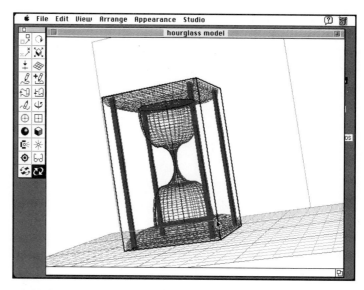

**Figure 3.12.** Revolving the world around the z-axis as shown in figure 3.11 results in this change of view.

# Moving and positioning objects

When building models and scenes, navigation takes on new importance. Now, in addition to moving a camera to change your point and field of view, you can move objects around in space. Imagine building a car: it's important that the wheels align to the car in the proper position under the fenders—where they belong, not hovering several feet above. When viewed from directly above, the wheels may appear to be aligned properly. However, when viewed from the side, the illusion may shatter. For this reason, you will almost always need to see your objects from at least two orthogonal views in order to properly align them.

The capability to represent where objects are in 3-D space, even though their position can be displayed only in two dimensions in any one window is a capability common to all 3-D software. The trick is to learn to "read" your software's representation and take advantage of its navigation tools.

# Bounding boxes

Another important tool for understanding single-perspective views is the *bounding box*. Because 3-D objects are mathematically very complex, the computer cannot redraw them nearly as fast as you can work. When moving or rotating an object in 3-D, programs usually employ a 3-D bounding box to represent your object. Because a bounding box can be redrawn very rapidly, it is an effective tool for visualizing the alignment and orientation of objects. Bounding boxes often are employed as local 3-D trackballs for modifying and rotating individual objects. The sequence shown in figures 3.13 through 3.15 shows how a bounding box can be used to represent a group of objects as the bounding box is rotated in MacroModel.

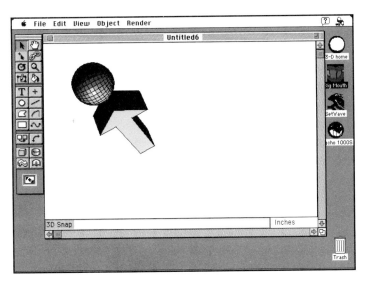

**Figure 3.13.** The object to be represented by the bounding box.

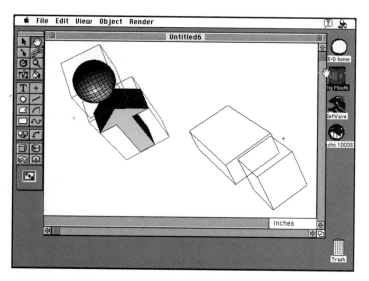

**Figure 3.14.** The object is now bounded by the box.

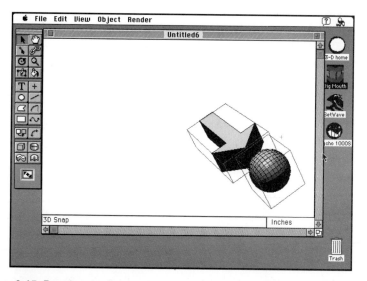

**Figure 3.15.** Rotating the figure with the use of a bounding box.

### Tip

When you need to see an object from a different perspective, you are usually better off changing your point of view than moving the object. You can generally get to your "home" point of view from other far flung perspectives. On

64

the other hand, if you move an object to see a little more of its left side, for example, it may be difficult to place it back in its original orientation to other objects. Sketch! enables you to change your point of view by using an object as a sort of handle to rotate the world. Imagine every piece of furniture in a room—the room being the 3-D world—is glued to the floor. If your omnipotent hand reaches into the room and turns the coffee table, the whole world will rotate around with it. The coffee table keeps its relationship to the world, but changes its orientation relative to you.

# Grids and snaps

*Grids* and *snaps* are navigational tools used to precisely determine your position and to help place objects. Grids are often laid out on working planes. These are flat planes positioned at a known orientation in space that are divided into a grid of squares of known size. You can use these grids to draw new objects and to place existing ones. Many programs offer a default "floor" plane which lies on the horizontal (x-z) axis. Assuming you are working in a room, anything positioned on this plane is equivalent to resting on the room's floor. If you draw a circle on the ground plane and extrude it upwards, you get a round column standing on the ground. Some programs also offer "wall planes" (which lie on the x-y and z-y axis.) More powerful programs enable you to create and position your own working planes which lie at odd angles, since not all objects are created along the three axes.

You can use *snaps* to align the cursor's position to known points in space. When drawing on a working plane, snaps can be used to confine objects to known dimensions. For example, if you want to draw a perfect square, you can snap to four equidistant corners on the grid as you draw. When positioning objects, you can snap them to a precise position on a grid. Some programs, particularly CAD programs, enable you to snap to points, lines, and even surfaces of objects. For instance, you can snap from the center of a circle to the endpoint of a distant line, or you can create a line that just touches (is tangent to) a circle.

In order to know where your object is in relation to the working planes and other objects, single-perspective view programs sometimes draw extent lines between the object being moved and existing snap points (see figure 3.16). This tells you that you are actually snapping to the desired point.

**Figure 3.16.** RayDream's Designer uses extent boxes drawn on walls to indicate the relative position of objects. You can tell that the central figure is on the ground because the extent lines on the walls touch the floor. The extent box on the floor indicates the model's relative distance to the walls.

# Reference point

When positioning an object in 3-D space, one consideration is where you place its reference point. The *reference point* is a single x,y,z point that is often the center of an object, but is easier to think of as an object's heart. Whenever you position an object in space, it is relative to this point. The reference point maintains its relationship to the rest of the object—unless you change it. When you rotate an object, the reference point is often used as the pivot point of rotation.

Some software will enable you to change an object's reference point, while other applications keep it a mystery. Your results in positioning an object in 3-D space vary greatly depending on whether you position an object's upper-left corner or its center at a given point in space. In addition, you often can use the reference point as a "pivot point" for rotation of the object. This is useful, if you want to make a hinged object rotate around one of its corners. You could also move the reference point far away from the object. You may, for instance, want to position a moon's reference point at the center of a planet so the moon orbits the planet as it rotates.

# Orientation: pitch, yaw, and roll

While it's possible to position objects absolutely in the x,y,z space, it's important to distinguish location and orientation about the coordinate axes from rotation of individual objects.

It's helpful when working in 3-D to understand the concept of pitch, yaw, and roll. Even though not all programs use these terms, they are common to aviators and they apply in general to rotation of objects in space. In simple terms, every object has its own set of x,y,z axes that it carries with it.

For example, if an airplane is flying through the air—as far as the pilot is concerned—it can *pitch* up or down; it can *roll* side to side; or it can make a flat turn so that it's sliding sideways (called *yaw*). The surprise comes when we learn that the airplane is upside down relative to the earth. Now, if the pilot pitches his plane upward—relative to himself—he is turning his plane towards the ground. If he yaws to the left—relative to himself—he yaws to the right relative to the earth, and so on.

> **Tip**
> Rotation around an object's axis is like using the axis as a
> rotisserie on which you turn a chicken. Rotation around
> the x axis means your object is skewered by, and turning
> on, the x axis. In terms of global rotation, this means you
> are literally rotating about the coordinate x axis. (The line
> where y and z are equal to zero.) In the case of local
> rotation, the object's axes are assigned when you create
> the object, and they intersect at the object's reference
> point.

Pitch, yaw and roll are relative to the current orientation of an
object—that is, if a plane is upright and heading east and you apply
90 degrees of yaw, it will head south.

Local rotation is affected by *rational order*—that is, if you apply pitch
before roll, the resulting orientation of the object is different than if
you apply the same amount of roll followed by the same amount of
pitch. This is like flinging a bucket full of water and then dumping it,
as opposed to dumping the bucket and then flinging it.

Assume that an airplane's original position has it moving forward and
flying level. Assume also that the fuselage of the plane is the z axis,
with the plane aligned flying towards positive z. In this case, pitch,
yaw. and roll can be described the following ways:

- **Pitch.** This is how much the plane points up in the air or down
  at the ground. A plane taking off from a runway is said to have a
  high degree of pitch as it leaves the ground. (Architects also will
  recognize the term pitch as referring to the steepness of a roof,
  and it is used in this context in architectural CAD.) A dive
  bomber making a pass at an enemy aircraft carrier, on the other
  hand, has a sharply negative pitch. In the x,y,z lexicon of 3-D,
  pitch is the amount of rotation around the object's x axis. In this
  case, the x axis is formed by the wings (see figure 3.17) .

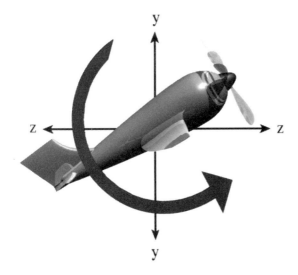

**Figure 3.17.** Pitch as represented by an airplane's takeoff.

- **Yaw**. This is the amount of "fishtailing" (y-axis) rotation of the airplane (see figure 3.18). If the plane yaws suddenly to the left, the blast of onrushing wind will hit the right side of the airplane instead of the nose cone. A car that spins out of control on an icy road also experiences yaw relative to its normal direction of travel.

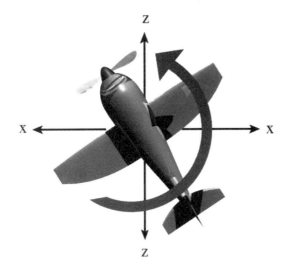

**Figure 3.18.** Yaw as represented by a plane's rotation.

- **Roll**. Roll of the "z-oriented" airplane is when it banks or tilts over on either wing (see figure 3.19). A banking turn can be accomplished with roll. From inside the cockpit, facing forward, the horizon appears to tilt to the left when the airplane rolls to the right. Roll is rotation around the z axis.

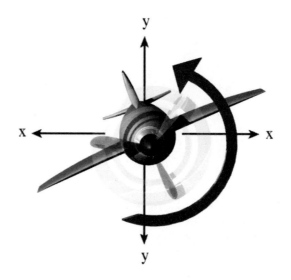

**Figure 3.19.** Roll as represented by an airplane's tilting.

Pitch, yaw, and roll are particularly useful when working with groups and in animation (discussed at length in chapter 5, "Modeling," and chapter 9, "Animation"). When two objects are grouped in a hierarchy, the orientation of a child object is relative to the parent instead of to the origin. Modeler Professional, Swivel 3D Professional, Electric Image Animation System, and Infini-D provide this type of orientation.

For example, if a ball and a stick are created with orientation settings of pitch, roll, yaw at (0,0,0), and the ball is the child of the stick, when you rotate the stick 90 degrees, the ball will still have an orientation of (0,0,0), even though it is in a new position relative to the 3-D world.

Electric Image Animation System provides precise control over these values for cameras as well (see figure 3.20).

**Figure 3.20.** Electric Image Animation System's camera rotation settings.

# Saving views

Many programs enable you save views by name. You can store these views in a menu and you can switch among them. Most 3-D applications have a view called "top" which will give an orthogonal or at least narrow-angle view of the scene from directly above. But some programs that enable you to save views also can have views such as "Top right, camera rolled left" or "Bottom view, zoomed in."

Switching between these views gives corresponding results. This capability can be very important when modeling and scene building and you need to see a particular relationship from different angles. It is also useful when you plan to render a scene from several points of view. Imagine that you have modeled a telescope that you need to see through. You can create a view that positions you to peer through the telescope. You can then return to it periodically while you align your planets.

In programs that support cameras as objects, named views correspond to different cameras. Changing the view by scrolling and zooming around changes the camera's aim; while changing the camera's aim or position changes what you see in the camera view.

# Summary

- Multiple points of view help to visualize 3-D space on a 2-D screen.

- A camera is used as a place holder for a point of view.

- Pan, tilt, and zoom are like holding a 3-D world in a box and moving the box around (without rotating it) to change your view.

- Different camera lens focal lengths change the amount of zoom and lens distortion.

- Moving the camera changes the zoom without affecting the focal length or lens distortion.

- Position in space is expressed as x,y,z values and is absolute relative to the origin.

- *Orientation* (or local rotation) can be expressed in terms of pitch, yaw, and roll, and is relative to the parent of an object.

- The three-plane view enables precise positioning of objects— while the single-perspective approach is more "natural," but often not as accurate.

- You can use a virtual trackball to rotate your world (and in some cases, single objects) as if rolling a ball in one hand.

- Grids and snaps help place objects in alignment.

- An object's reference point determines its measured location and it is usually used as the pivot point for rotation.

- Naming and saving views enables you to quickly check crucial alignments and relationships among objects.

4

# Basic shapes
# and fonts

**M**odeling is the creation of shapes. In many ways, it is like drawing on a computer in 2-D. However, drawing a simple 2-D shape is only the beginning of building a 3-D object. Once you draw or import a shape, extrusion, lathing, and loafing are just some of the operations you can perform to add the element of depth to a 2-D object.

# Simple geometry

The easiest models to create are the ones someone else builds for you. Clip models are available from the makers of 3-D software, as well as many other vendors.

Although not many high-quality 3-D model collections are currently available, the medium of CD-ROM makes it possible to distribute hundreds of objects on a single disc and it's likely to become a popular media for this purpose.

By combining two or more clip models, you can create a variety of new shapes without modeling at all. Typical examples of clip models include furniture and lamps for decorating interior models, cars, 3-D type, and dingbats. It is easy to import these models into your 3-D program and combine them into single objects and scenes.

If you're not using clip models, then you will need to create your own. The easiest place to start is with existing 2-D line art and type. You can bring these into most 3-D applications and they can be extruded or lathed into the third dimension.

Once you go beyond these simple measures, you can use basic geometries (called *primitives*). You can quickly lay them on a page like building blocks. Beyond that, there are many sophisticated tools available to the 3-D modeler that enable you to draw and manipulate objects in three dimensions.

In general, the more complex the modeler, the more difficult it is to use; the more sophisticated its features, the more expensive the product.

# A sense of scale

A common mistake made by beginning modelers is failing to properly account for the scale of objects in relation to one another. For example, a clock is not as big as the desk on which it sits and a lamp generally does not reach from the floor to the ceiling. Unless you are specifically trying to create strange-looking images, keep objects in proper proportion to each other.

Set the scale in your 3-D program to reflect the real world you are representing. This way you can size your model to natural dimensions, making it easy to keep things in proper relationship.

The most helpful tool you can use to this end is a tape measure. How big is a spaceship? Measure a car's window; compare it to the windows you would like on your starship and scale accordingly. If the ship will have 200 windows in a row along the side and the average window is 2 feet wide, make your ship at least 450 feet long in your virtual 3-D world.

Keep in mind that filling a frame completely will result in an extremely claustrophobic image—as if the borders are crushing in on the subject. One of the most important elements you can add to an image is empty space.

# 3-D PostScript

A number of programs specialize in adding depth and perspective to PostScript type and line art. Adobe Systems Dimensions and Ray-Dream's addDepth have been designed specifically for this purpose. Unlike most 3-D applications whose output is in the form of bitmapped art, these two produce editable Bézier line art that you bring back into programs such as Adobe Illustrator, Aldus FreeHand, or Deneba's Canvas. These applications quickly and painlessly create 3-D artwork. addDepth is available bundled with FreeHand, making for an all-in one purchase.

Adobe Dimensions and Aldus Free-Hand generate smooth-shaded PostScript artwork usable in Adobe Illustrator, Aldus FreeHand, and desktop publishing software that can use PostScript art. You can easily turn existing outline artwork and type into 3-D objects.

While the advantage of PostScript extruders is their extreme ease of use, they are not very powerful for creating complex 3-D scenes. The number of shapes you can build is limited; the use of textures is minimal; and animation is not well supported. Dimensions can import a model from Swivel 3-D, but it does not have the flexibility of other modelers that can exchange model files.

Many features, like texture and environment mapping, are not supported as well. Because of these limitations, these programs are sometimes referred to as "two-and-a-half-D."

On the other hand, if all you need is a good-looking 3-D logo or headline, both Dimensions and addDepth are very capable packages. For 2-D illustrators, these programs take the pain out of creating simple geometries, which you can then easily embellish with standard 2-D tools. For example, you can create a box in Dimensions, light it, and import the rendered result into Illustrator. You can add artistic embellishments to make it look like a computer, stereo, or other "boxy" object.

Some of the other modelers mentioned in this book will import EPS line art for extrusion into 3-D, and most will export Encapsulated PostScript (EPS) bitmaps. The most important distinction is that bitmapped art is capable of providing more realism; the PostScript programs, for example, don't support colored light sources or shadows. However, PostScript art is resolution independent, and it can be manipulated in a simple and efficient manner, just like other Illustrator files.

---

**Tip**
If your artwork is in EPS but not EPS AI (Adobe Illustrator) format, you can use Transverter Pro from Techpool Software to convert EPS files into EPS AI format so these 3-D programs can import them.

---

# Adobe Dimensions

Adobe's Dimensions requires that you have an illustration program (such as Illustrator, Aldus' FreeHand, or Deneba's Canvas), to create the basic 2-D artwork which you intend to extrude or lathe in Dimensions.

## Creating an Egyptian vase

In this example, a bitmapped image of an ancient Egyptian pot taken from a CD-ROM of clip art, is used as a template in Adobe Illustrator, and the contour is traced (see figure 4.1). The tracing is imported into Adobe Dimensions, lathed, textured, lighted, rendered, and finally saved in Illustrator format.

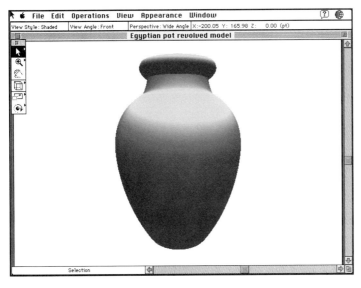

**Figure 4.1.** Bitmapped ancient Egyptian pot clip art.

1. Launch Illustrator, open the bitmap as a template and trace the left side of the vase as a single line. Save this line as an Illustrator file (see figure 4.2).

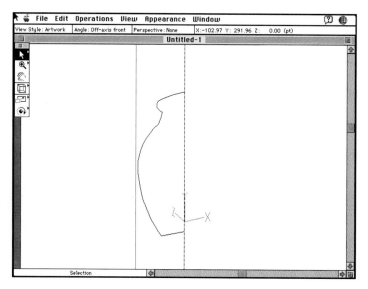

**Figure 4.2.** Single-line tracing of Egyptian pot.

2. Open Dimensions and import the Illustrator line. Revolve the line into the desired 3-D shape using Dimension's Lathe tool (see figure 4.3).

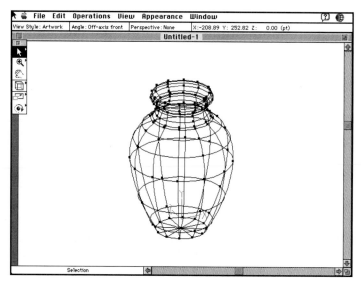

**Figure 4.3.** The Illustrator line after imported into Dimensions and lathed.

3. Apply surface color and glossiness using the Surface Properties control panel and the Lighting palette (see figure 4.4). Apply one or more lights to the scene.

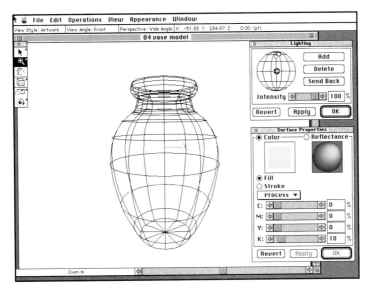

**Figure 4.4.** Adding surface color and glossiness to the Egyptian pot.

4. Render the finished pot.

> **Tip**
>
> If you have a PostScript illustration program, you can use it to export type as outline artwork for extruding in Dimensions. To do this, you must first convert the type to outlines and save it in Illustrator EPS format. Dimensions can then import it just like any other Illustrator line art.

One of the important capabilities of 3-D programs is *texture mapping*. This can be as simple as merely wrapping a label around a 3-D object—which is exactly the level of texture control allowed by Dimensions (see figure 4.5).

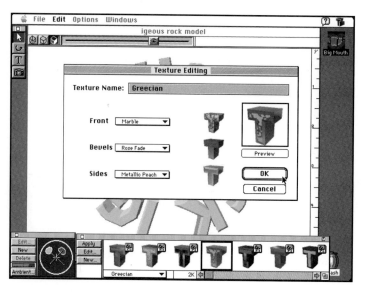

**Figure 4.5.** Applying texture to a 3-D object with Dimensions' Texture Editing dialog box.

# Creating an applesauce can

The applesauce can as seen in figure 4.6, was created in several steps using Adobe Illustrator and Dimensions.

**Figure 4.6.** This image was created using two programs: Illustrator and Dimensions.

The apple on the label actually made a couple of round trips to become finished art. The apple started as an outline in Illustrator and was saved and imported into Dimensions. In Dimensions, it was revolved to form the apple (as in the previous example of the Egyptian vase). Lights were placed, textures assigned, and the apple rendered (see figures 4.7 and 4.8). It was then exported in Illustrator format (as in the example of the Egyptian vase).

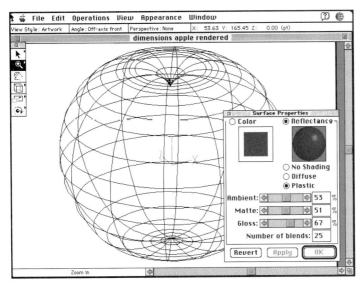

**Figure 4.7.** Applying surface properties to the revolved apple in Dimensions.

1. In Illustrator, combine the apple with type and Illustrator drawings of a stem and leaves (see figure 4.9). Save this illustration as an Illustrator file.

2. In Dimensions, create and scale a cylinder using its Primitives drawing tool (see figure 4.10).

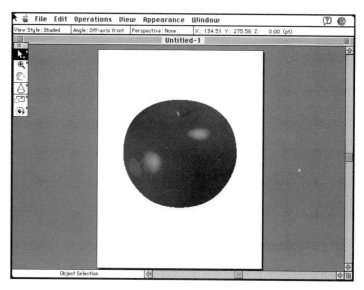

**Figure 4.8.** The rendered apple.

**Figure 4.9.** The rendered apple opened in Illustrator where leaves and type can be added.

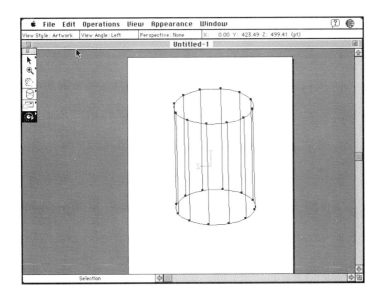

**Figure 4.10.** A scaled cylinder.

3. Import and apply the apple label illustration to the cylinder (see figure 4.11). Position the label using Dimension's mapping tool. This tool enables you to move the label up, down, and around the image in order to precisely place the label in the desired position.

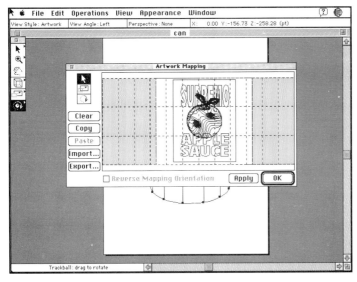

**Figure 4.11.** Applying the label to the cylinder.

4. Finally, render the image as a new Dimensions image (see figure 4.12). It is now ready for export in Illustrator format. It would be possible to import the finished can rendering into Illustrator and create a poster featuring the can and additional type.... Well, you get the idea. It's worth noting that you can create extremely complex PostScript documents by building multiple layers of 3-D; if you get too carried away—the image may never print.

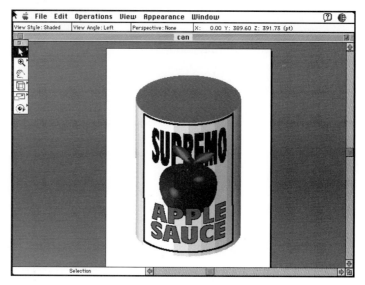

**Figure 4.12.** The finished rendered image.

# RayDream's addDepth

Like Dimensions, addDepth can extrude PostScript art into 3-D. You cannot lathe objects in addDepth, however, so you are limited to extruding curves if you want curved surfaces. For example, if you want to create a cylinder, you must start with a circle that you would extrude upwards. If you want a sphere, however, you are out of luck.

addDepth offers a set of drawing tools which theoretically means you need not use Illustrator or another drawing program as a front end—although it also supports Illustrator and FreeHand file formats. To use type (it supports both PostScript and TrueType), you simply click on the image window with the Type tool and enter the desired text. You can kern text and make other adjustments directly within the Type window.

RayDream's addDepth supports System 7's Publish and Subscribe. You can create and Publish an object in one PostScript application (a chart, for example) and Subscribe to it from addDepth. When you Publish changes to the original document, the 3-D object in addDepth is updated accordingly. You can use this feature to publish pie charts from DeltaGraph, for example; subscribe to the charts and extrude them in addDepth; and automatically update the new 3-D charts each time the DeltaGraph spreadsheet changes.

The most popular use of addDepth will undoubtedly be extruding type for use in other programs. The program offers very good control over the color and surface attributes of many of the separate elements of 3-D objects. For instance, it's easy to have a gradient fill on the face of an object, yellow on the bevels, and blue on the sides.

## Creating a "Jump!" head

To create this catchy headline of a paratrooper doing his thing required the use of Adobe Illustrator as well as addDepth (see figure 4.13).

**Figure 4.13.** Extruded type for this headline was created using addDepth.

1. Enter the text, JUMP!, in addDepth's type dialog box where you will find kerning and other standard type controls (see figure 4.14).

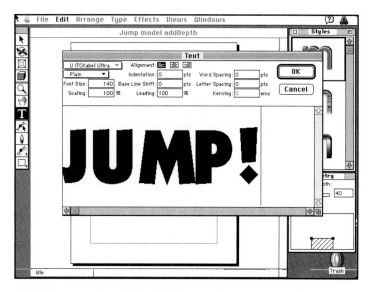

**Figure 4.14.** Enter text in addDepth's Type dialog box.

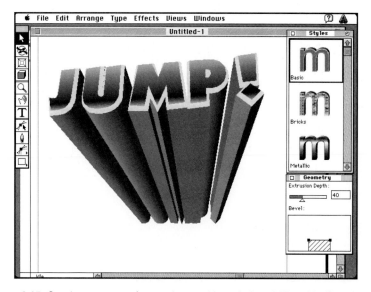

**Figure 4.15.** Set the percent of extrusion and bevels in addDepth's Geometry pop-up menu box.

2. Extrude the resulting type using the small palette found at the lower-right corner of your window (see figure 4.15). A bevel for the edges of the objects can be set in this window as well.

3. After extruding, rotate the 3-D type into the proper perspective using addDepth's virtual trackball. You can also increase the view angle using another dimensions tool to give the object more of a sense of depth.

4. Using the Color Style dialog box, add a gradient texture to one of the default surface settings and apply to the face of the 3-D type (see figure 4.16).

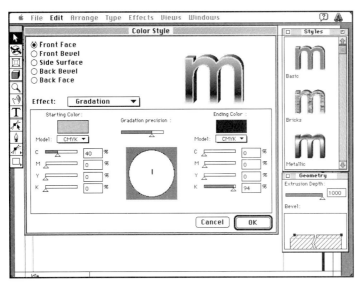

**Figure 4.16.** addDepth's Color Style dialog box.

5. addDepth automatically renders objects as you work. Once the rendering of your image is complete, the last step is to export the image in Illustrator format and combine it with the art of the paratrooper (created in Aldus FreeHand). Finally, distort the paratrooper with Illustrator's distort tool to match the perspective of the 3-D type (see figure 4.17).

**Figure 4.17.** The rendered image combined with the paratrooper.

# Working with type

Extruded, beveled, engraved, raised, and animated 3-D type treatments are the most popular uses of 3-D software. A number of vendors have responded to the demand by creating applications specifically for this purpose. Aside from the "2.5"-D PostScript programs previously described, there are a number of applications that create true, exportable 3-D geometry as well as rendering high-quality bitmapped images using all the tricks of 3-D. These include Pixar's Typestry, Strata's StrataType 3d, and Specular's LogoMotion.

Keep in mind that although you can use most TrueType and Type 1 PostScript fonts with these programs, not all fonts are ideal for 3-D use. Medium-weight sans serif fonts present the fewest problems, while serif fonts with some weight to them also work well. In general, avoid waifish, fine-lined fonts; these are often too thin to handle any beveling, as the bevels will tend to overlap one another. Thin fonts work best when extruded only slightly for embossing and "foil" type, or when extruded without bevels. On the other hand, avoid extremely heavy fonts with small openings. The holes will tend to fill in when you bevel the type.

> **Tip**
> If you have TrueType fonts and your program supports only PostScript (or vice versa), you can use a program such as FontMonger or Metamorphosis to convert one type font to another. If you have PostScript art you would like to use with 3-D type programs, but the art is not available in a font, Fontographer enables you to create new fonts from existing artwork. Once an object becomes a character in a font, you can use it with your 3-D type tool like any other font character.

# Pixar's Typestry

Pixar's Typestry is specifically devoted to creating 3-D type images and animations. Its Type tool enables you to enter a text string, specify a font, and set extrusion parameters. Its greatest strength is its reliance on MacRenderMan (which is included in the box), for rendering. This also enables you to use it with Pixar's distributed rendering system, NetRenderMan, or a RISC-accelerated version, such as YarcRenderMan; it also lets you use RenderMan's creative and unusual shaders.

One of the most powerful tools for working with 3-D images is Adobe Systems' Photoshop image editing program. The following image was created by rendering a type logo in Typestry, importing the image into Photoshop, and pasting the image over a background.

Several programs specialize in turning Type 1 PostScript, and TrueType fonts into 3-D art. They include: Pixar's Typestry, StrataType 3d, and Specular's LogoMotion. Most 3-D programs enable you to import type and extrude it directly. Among them are: Infini-D, StrataVision 3d, StrataStudio Pro, Showplace, Swivel 3-D Professional, and Presenter Professional. Other programs have special features which make them particularly useful for working with type: form•Z (solids), and Electric Image Animation System (creates bevels as separate objects).

89

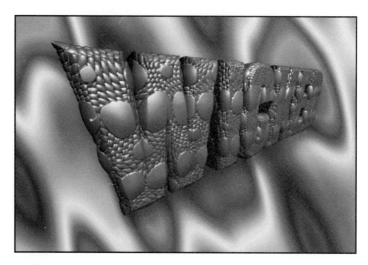

**Figure 4.18.** This logo was created using Typestry and Photoshop.

## Creating dragon type

The steps below describe how you can create the still image found in figure 4.18 above.

1.  Begin by entering text and assigning a bevel with Typestry's Type tool (see figure 4.19). Since Typestry doesn't support kerning, select individual characters in the text and move them in Typestry's 3-D space.

2.  Typestry does not enable you to save or otherwise efficiently move between views, so alignment is a bit dicey. For best results, set the Camera Lens to "Zoom—Telephoto" before moving the text into position with Typestry's Virtual Trackball tool (see figure 4.20).

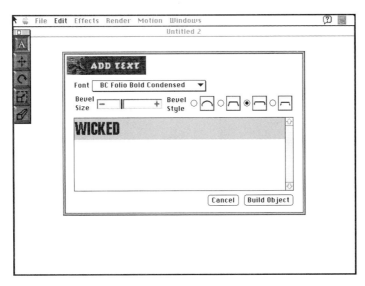

**Figure 4.19.** Assigning bevel to type in Typestry.

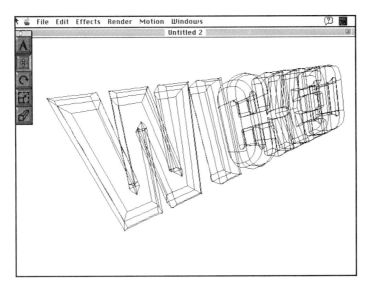

**Figure 4.20.** Moving the text into position with the virtual trackball.

3. Once you position the type, you can apply a texture (see figure 4.21). In this case, a RenderMan "Look" from the Valis Group, called "Dragon Skin" was applied.

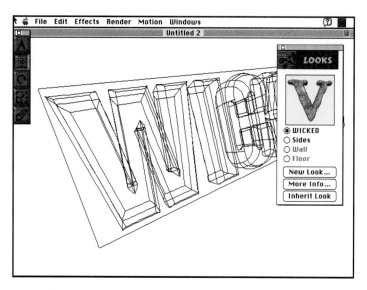

**Figure 4.21.** The texture pallete in Typestry.

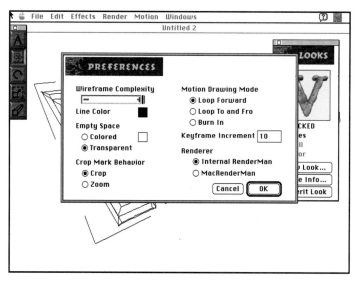

**Figure 4.22.** Setting your preferences for rendering.

4. The render settings specified that any area outside our object should be rendered as an alpha channel mask. This enables you to composite your creation seamlessly with other images in Adobe Photoshop (see chapter 11, "Working with images").

5. Apply a single overhead light to give deep texture detail. Adding more lights brightens the scene, but reduces the contrast particularly filling in the shadows in the texture. Once you have placed the lights, the type is rendered (which takes several minutes or more depending on your hardware).

6. To finish the image, a background is built in Photoshop 2.5 using Kai's Power Tools from HSC. When you open the rendered image file in Photoshop, choose the Load Selection command from the Select menu (this loads the contents of the alpha channel) and selects the "wicked" logo. Choose Copy, make the background image active, and select Paste to paste the logo over the background.

# Perforated type

RenderMan, used by Typestry, is a rendering system that offers a wealth of special effects not found in other renderers. Some of the special effects available in Typestry are in the form of "booleans" and motion blurs. The letters shown in figures 4.23 through 4.30 were created using Typestry's boolean rendering features (which Typestry refers to as "Perforations"). Booleans enable you to create a letter with holes in it, or to create a letter-shaped "hole" filled with objects. You also can specify the size, shape, and distribution of these holes or objects. Another feature of booleans is that they enable you to subtract a letter, or combination of letters, from a surface. This enables you create engraved type or type "stencils." The following are examples of rendered boolean letters shown with the perforation settings used to create the letters on the right.

**Figure 4.23.** Letter filed with holes.

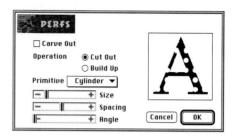

**Figure 4.24.** Dialog box setting for letter filled with holes.

**Figure 4.25.** Letter-shaped hole filled with objects.

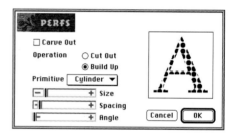

**Figure 4.26.** Dialog box settings for letter-shaped hole filled with objects.

**Figure 4.27.** Letter-shaped hole filled with square rods.

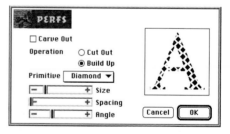

**Figure 4.28.** Dialog box settings for letter-shaped hole filled with square rods.

**Figure 4.29.** Letter shape subtracted from surface of solid.

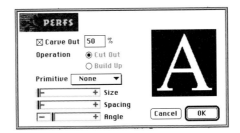

**Figure 4.30.** Dialog box settings for letter shape subtracted from surface of solid.

**Tip**
Fonts like Zapf Dingbats and LetraSet's Fontek Design Fonts contain many interesting shapes you can use in 3-D type programs. Often symbol fonts have arrows, stars, and other interesting and whimsical symbols you can extrude. The Fontek fonts are actually clip art libraries, whose images you can use in any program that supports type.

In addition to supporting all of the basic features needed to create still images, Typestry enables you to generate simple animations suitable for use in video or multimedia (see chapter 9, "Animation").

# StrataType 3d

StrataType 3d, from StrataVision Inc., works very much like Typestry. It does not support animation. However, it is a capable type creation tool, and its Phong shading is quite a bit faster than Typestry's use of RenderMan.

Booleans operations are not supported by StrataType 3d's Phong shading. On the other hand, StrataType 3d offers a variety of preconfigured text layouts, extensive kerning, and other type controls. It has very good control over automatic beveling and it enables you to make your own bevels and textures. One unusual feature is that you can apply separate textures to different surfaces of an object. You can even apply chrome to the front, brass to the bevels, and granite to the sides.

Objects can be rendered with an alpha channel or PICT background for seamless compositing with other images.

## Creating an Igneous Rock logo

The steps below describe how you can create the Igneous Rock logo shown in figure 4.31 below.

**Figure 4.31.** The Igneous Rock logo created in StrataType 3d.

1. To create this image shown in figure 4.31 above, enter text in StrataType 3d's Text Edit window. Select a circular type path from StrataType's library of prebuilt configurations, and a standard extrusion-and-bevel combination (see figure 4.32 and 4.33).

2. If necessary, kern the letters give them a pleasing distribution.

3. Adjust the camera's angle of view to wide angle using the slider at the top of the screen (see figure 4.34).

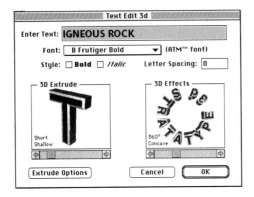

**Figure 4.32.** Selecting extrusion and bevel combinations from Strata Type's library of configurations.

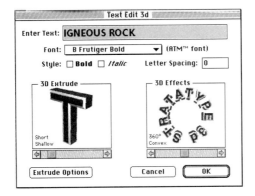

**Figure 4.33.** You can also adjust type attributes, such as spacing, style, the font, and so forth in the Text Edit dialog box.

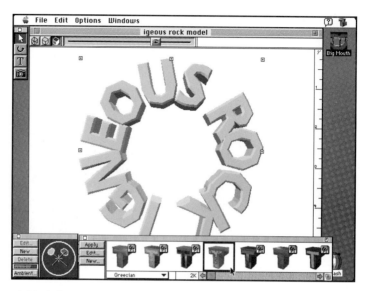

**Figure 4.34.** Adjusting the camera's angle with the slider at the top of the window.

4. Use Strata's Texture Editing dialog box, apply a "rock" texture with metallic sides to the object.

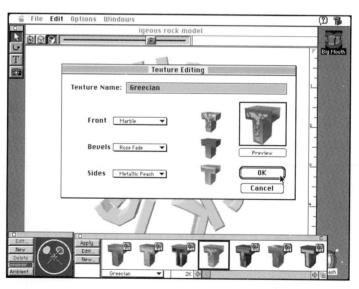

**Figure 4.35.** Applying the texture to the object.

5. Finally, render the image, and if you like, import it into an image editing program (such as Photoshop) and use the alpha channel for compositing with a background image, as shown in figure 4.36.

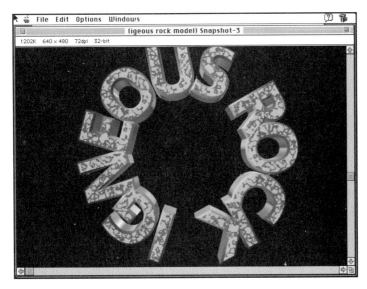

**Figure 4.36.** The finished rendered image.

# LogoMotion

LogoMotion is Specular International Inc.'s new low-cost 3-D modeling, rendering, and animation tool. (It wasn't ready in time for inclusion in this book.) Like StrataType 3d and Typestry, it is primarily designed to import and extrude fonts for use in flying logos and other type graphics. It features Gouraud shading to achieve smooth renderings, but the rendering is not as detailed as Typestry's RenderMan, StrataType's rendering, or Phong shading.

# Engraved type

One way to create realistic engraved type (as in a tombstone or statue) is to use boolean subtraction, such as that shown above in the Typestry example.

Solid modelers, meanwhile, can actually subtract one object from another, so that you can remove the intersection between an object and solid type that is embedded in the surface. form•Z, for example, has a title tool that enables you to make solid type which can be subtracted from other surfaces.

---

**Tip**
To create engraved type with a standard surface modeler without booleans, you can extrude a plane that uses type for "holes" and sandwich it on top of another plane of the same size without the holes.

---

# Bump-mapped type

*Bump mapping* is an extremely quick and easy way to simulate embossed type. You simply create a bump map image containing black type and set the renderer to use black as raised areas. Light will then catch the edges of the type when you render. The same approach can be used to affect stamped or engraved type: simply switch the bump map to treat black as depressions. (For a thorough explanation, see "Bump maps" in chapter 7, "Materials.")

# Embossed type

To achieve a really spectacular type treatment, you can import type and give it a bright surface, extrude it minutely, and place it on another surface of duller appearance. This technique can be used to create chrome lettering on a black object, for example.

A similar effect can be created in programs such as Specular's Infini-D, which support reflection mapping. By using type as a reflection map, the black of the type will reflect its surroundings, but where the reflection map is white it will not (see chapter 7, "Materials").

# Animated type

Animated 3-D type is a favorite use for 3-D graphics. Three-D software enables you to create a wealth of compelling 3-D video logos and titles quickly. While animation is covered in detail later in chapter 9, "Animation," animated type deserves special mention. Most of the applications that support 3-D animation offer some means to extrude and animate type. Multimedia producers will enjoy a chance to put animated type in their QuickTime and interactive projects.

As mentioned earlier, bevels are important in animating type, particularly since they tend to outline extruded type making it easier to read. Bevels also will catch and reflect glimmers of light, making the scene shine.

Bevels also prevent that bar-of-soap look which simple extruded surfaces tend to have.

---

**Tip**
When creating beveled type, use small, simple bevels for fonts with narrow strokes as large bevels will tend to overlap and cause problems—particularly at sharply-angled corners. Heavyweight fonts can handle larger, fancier bevels. Avoid large fancy bevels with fonts that have very small openings that can fill in when extruded (such as Antique Olive Black).

---

# Mr. Font

Mr. Font is the type extrusion program that ships with Electric Image Animation System. In early versions of EIAS, Mr. Font was a separate utility program. Mr. Font is now part of the unified Electric Image software. Unlike other type programs, Mr. Font was designed specifically to output 3-D models for use in Electric Image. However, this is a very powerful type-extrusion program and you can export models from Mr. Font to other 3-D applications via the DXF file format. One of the critical capabilities of Mr. Font is that it generates font models with the option of building the bevels as separate objects. This

101

means that you can give gold or chrome bevels to a marble object for an interesting effect. The capability to do separate bevels is critical in animation, where you want the bevels to catch and reflect light to make objects sparkle.

# Other 3-D font support

Many programs—each having many other high-end features and covered in subsequent chapters—also support direct importing and extrusion of type into 3-D (see sidebar, earlier this chapter). In these applications, 3-D type can be modified and/or rendered just like any other 3-D model (see figure 4.37).

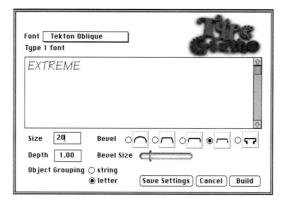

**Figure 4.37**. One of the modeling extensions that comes with the new Showplace is Type Gizmo. It looks like the type entry dialog box in Pixar's other 3-D scene builder, Typestry.

# Solid type

The following sequence of images, as shown in figures 4.38 through 4.40, illustrate how you can generate type as a solid model in form•Z, then using boolean operations such as subtraction, you can create interesting effects.

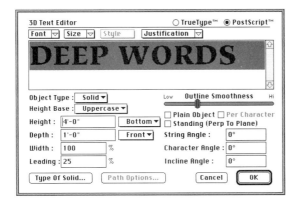

**Figure 4.38.** Type is entered in this dialog box and given a series of specifications.

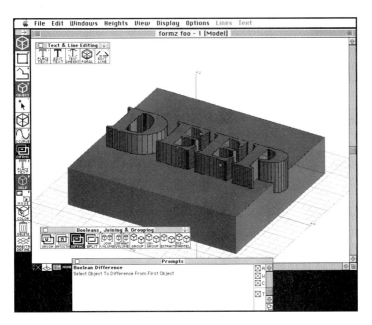

**Figure 4.39.** Extruded type is positioned to intersect with another model. In this case a simple rectangular solid. Using the Difference command, the type is subtracted from the solid.

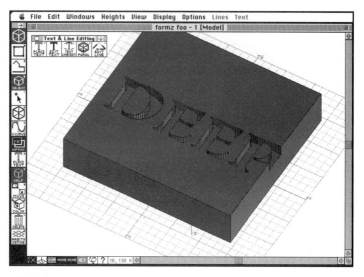

**Figure 4.40.** The result is a solid with a "stamp" where the type previously sat.

# Summary

- Use clip models for quick scene building or when you need a few props.

- Maintain a sense of scale for realism.

- Dimensions and addDepth create 3-D Illustrator-format images from simple outlines and type.

- Typestry, StrataType 3d, and LogoMotion all specialize in creating 3-D bitmapped artwork from typefaces.

- Typestry creates perforated or indented type by using RenderMan's boolean shading.

- Animated type is one of the most popular uses for 3-D software and font support is present in all but a few 3-D applications.

- Bevels add legibility and sparkle to animated type. They make things look "softer" and more natural.

# Modeling

Three-D begins with the model. Just as kids build airplanes from kits to hang from their ceilings, computer-based modeling is a process of putting together many small parts. Essentially, it's not that different from the way many manufactured goods are produced. For example, take an everyday object—a standard pencil. Every school child knows that a pencil is made of five parts: a "lead," two halves of wood, a metal ring, and an eraser. While it may be possible to form a vaguely pencil-like object in one stroke, to create the real thing, one has to take at least one step for every part. The same is true for 3-D modeling. While 3-D sometimes makes it possible to create the effect of several objects at one time, the easiest approach is *additive modeling*: putting lots of small parts together to form a whole.

**Figure 5.1.** Most 3-D objects are made of lots of small parts.

# Additive modeling

In its simplest form, additive modeling begins with *primitives*—geometric shapes with very simple mathematical descriptions. Many programs make it so easy to create primitives that all you have to do is point the mouse to where you want a cone, for example, and click. Putting the pieces together merely involves moving them into position. A few stand-alone scene builders, such as Electric Image Animation System, Macromedia Three-D, and Pixar Showplace, don't have modelers at all; they treat every object you import as a primitive, allowing you only to modify their size and position. For example, the following figures show a model built entirely from primitive objects— primarily cubes, spheres and cylinders (see figure 5.2), put together with simple additive modeling (see figure 5.3).

# Joining objects

Since much 3-D model building is designed to produce a representational model, not a manufacturing-accurate design, building models is usually a fairly simple process. 3-D programs are smart about bonding objects together. Imagine attaching one of those little knobs to thc top of a flagpole. In the real world, you would have to drill a hole in the knob that would exactly match the end of the flagpole, then join the two together with threads or a welded seam. In 3-D, you simply put the ball on the pole; the software takes care of the rest. In fact, no glue or anti-gravity devices are required, since there are no forces in the virtual world of 3-D to pull things apart. (This assumes, of course, that the hole in the ball and the threads on the pole aren't important to your design. If they are, you will have to model them.) When eyeball measurements aren't up to the task, simple modelers give way to more precise (and more difficult to use) computer-aided design (CAD) systems. The essential differences between basic modelers and full-fledged CAD are really in the details. CAD systems are often highly specific to a particular chore and can contain many specialized tools.

# Constructive modeling

While additive modeling is used to put parts together, it often fails to address a simple problem: what if you don't have the parts you need? Three-D software has its own techniques, analogous to those used in the real world, which can be applied to building your own components. These techniques are known as "constructive modeling."

Constructive modeling uses 2-D outlines to form new 3-dimensional shapes. For example, a square can be extruded to form a post, or the outline of a vase can be lathed to form the round vase itself. Lathing and extrusion are the basis of constructive modeling. There are advanced variations of each, and even hybrids, such as *sweeping,* that combine the two.

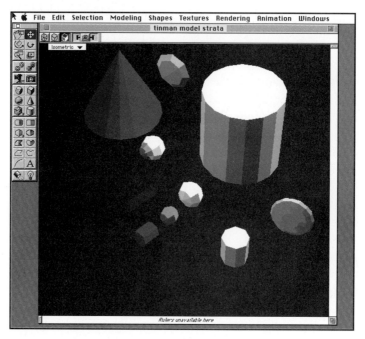

**Figure 5.2.** The primitive parts of a model.

# Extrusion

Extrusion is one of the simplest methods for creating 3-D objects. You begin with a 2-D outline, either drawn or imported, and add a third dimension. Basic extrusion is perpendicular to the plane of your 2-D object, like a cookie cutter. If the outline of the cookie cutter (a 2-D shape) is the shape being extruded, then the cookie (the 3-D object) is the resulting extrusion. When extruding an object, there is no practical limit to the depth of the cookie dough, so you could extrude a circle into a long straw or a thin ring.

**Figure 5.3.** A model made of the primitive parts from figure 5.2.

If you extrude a surface, rather than a simple outline, you will end up with a "solid" object. (An extruded circular outline creates a pipe, while an extruded solid circle creates a solid column.) The solid object typically has "caps" on the end. More sophisticated 3-D programs enable you to make changes to the end caps without affecting the extruded "walls."

Variations of extrusion include extrusion along a path, extrusion with bevels and swept extrusion along a specific curve.

**Figure 5.4.** The 2-D outline (the "cookie cutter").

**Figure 5.5.** The outline will be extuded in the direction of the arrow.

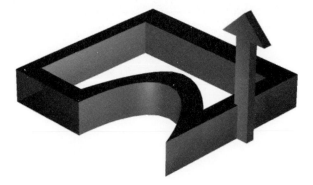

**Figure 5.6.** The extrusion begins…

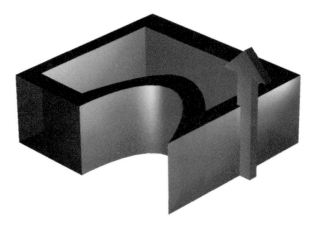

**Figure 5.7.** Continuing the extrusion…

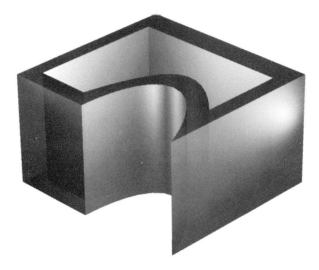

**Figure 5.8.** The finished product.

# Extrusion techniques

Extrusion is the most commonly used constructive modeling technique. Essentially, it can be used to create any object that has a consistent cross section.

As explained earlier in this chapter, extrusion is like using a cookie cutter. To create an intricately beveled molding you could draw the molding's outline, then extrude it to the desired length.

## Extruding an Illustrator outline

While many programs allow you to import a finished 2-D drawing from a vector-based illustration program as a starting point for a building a 3-D model, Specular's Infini-D uses a novel approach to creating an extrusion from an outline generated in Adobe Illustrator—System 7's Publish and subscribe. To use this method effectively, you have to be running System 7 and have enough free RAM to launch both Illustrator and Infini-D simultaneously.

1. You begin by drawing a shape in Illustrator—in this case, the profile of a football helmet logo (see figure 5.9).

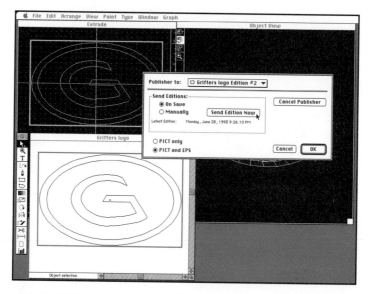

**Figure 5.9.** The 2-D shape created in Illustrator.

2. You then publish the drawing, which is roughly like saving the illustration.

3. After opening the outline in Infini-D, you subscribe to the EPS drawing within the Extrusion module. The outline is immediately extruded; you can add a bevel if you choose (see figure 5.10).

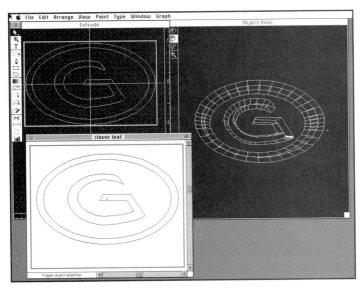

**Figure 5.10.** Importing the 2-D outline into Infini-D automatically creates an extrusion, with beveled edges if desired.

4. If you switch back to Illustrator, modify the drawing and publish the changes (see figure 5.11).

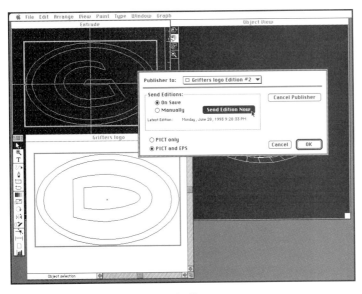

**Figure 5.11.** Modifying the 2-D outline in Illustrator.

5. The changes appear immediately in the Infini-D modeling window, even before you switch Infini-D back to the foreground (see figure 5.12).

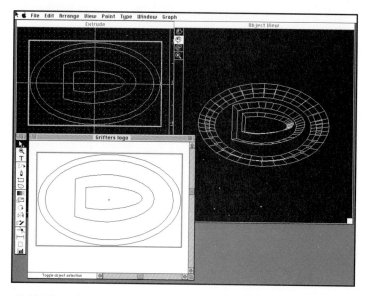

**Figure 5.12.** Your changes appear automatically.

# Slabs

A slab is geometric, like a block. It is made by extruding a rectangular shape over a short distance. If you extrude the shape at an angle other than perpendicular to the shapes surface, you can create a trapezoidal solid. Any rectangular solid shape can be made the same way (see figures 5.13 and 5.14).

# A star-shaped tube

Any irregular shaped extrusion begins with the cross sectional shape—in this case, a star burst extruded in MacroModel (see figure 5.15). The shape is extruded along the designated path. This can often be accomplished numerically, for precision, or visually (see figure 5.16). The resulting shape has a consistent star-shaped cross section (see figure 5.17).

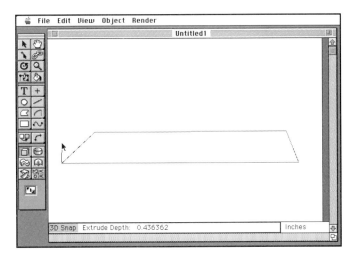

**Figure 5.13.** Preparing to extrude a slab.

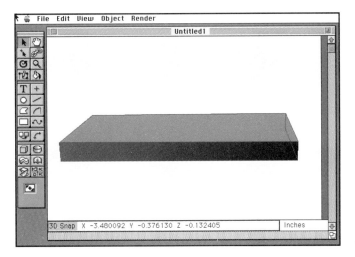

**Figure 5.14.** The extruded slab.

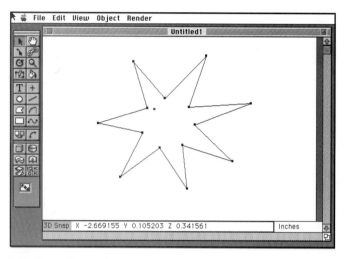

**Figure 5.15.** The 2-D star shape.

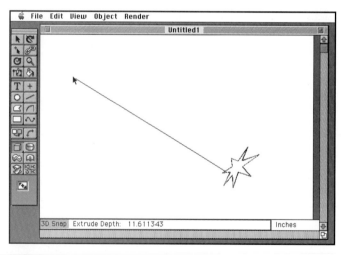

**Figure 5.16.** Visually defining the extrusion path.

# Extrusion on a path

Extrusion on a path enables you to have a shape follow a path, rather than just a straight line. If you were to extrude the molding outline used in the previous example along a square path, you will end up with a picture frame. Path extrusion is a very powerful technique for creating any object that has a consistent cross section along a crooked line (see figures 5.18 and 5.19).

The following are other common examples of path extrusions: handrails, garden hoses, telephone cords, and drain pipes.

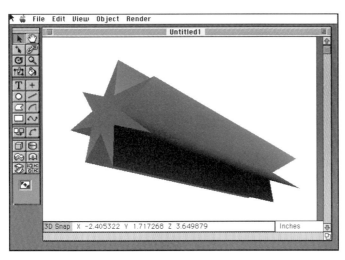

**Figure 5.17.** The extruded star.

# Lathing

Lathing is the primary modeling counterpart to extrusion. In the real world, lathing is used to cut shapes from fast-spinning lengths of wood and metal. A baseball bat or a round chair leg can be turned on a lathe. A potter's wheel is the equivalent of a lathe for working with clay. As the clay spins, it slips through the potter's fingers to become a bowl or a vase. Although they can have almost any outline, lathed objects are always round when viewed along their turning axis (imagine a flower vase viewed from above), unless they've been squashed into an oval shape or distorted by other means. Because lathing involves revolving a shape around an axis, the terms "revolve" and "lathe" are interchangeable.

Lathing in 3-D works by turning an outline or profile of the intended object around an axis. The path followed by the profile along the way becomes the final object. Figures 5.20 through 5.24 show the process of lathing a shape.

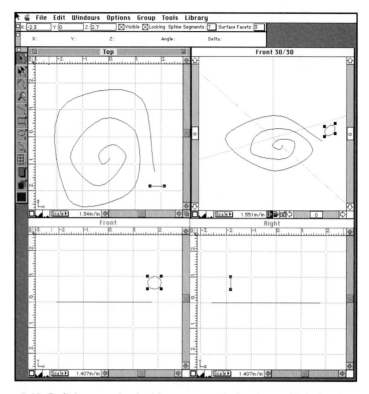

**Figure 5.18.** Defining a path—in this case, a spiral—along which the shape will be extruded.

If there is a difficult concept to grasp when it comes to lathing, it's that an object can be lathed around virtually any axis in space. Simple modelers, like the ones offered by Infini-D and RayDream Designer, have a separate lathing module. Infini-D's interface involves a two-window view, one showing the shape to be lathed aligned to an axis, the second showing the finished shape. Since this removes you temporarily from the 3-D space, it's easy to visualize the effect of your changes. Modelers that strive to give you more flexibility and control, however, allow you to lathe objects directly in space and to move the axis of rotation. Figure 5.25 shows the lathing interface in Alias Sketch! The curved shape at the left (used to create the previous example) is about to be revolved around the vertical axis. The curve at the right is a projection of the cross section that will result. By holding the Option key and moving the mouse, you can tilt the axis of rotation to a different angle. Releasing the mouse causes the curve to be lathed.

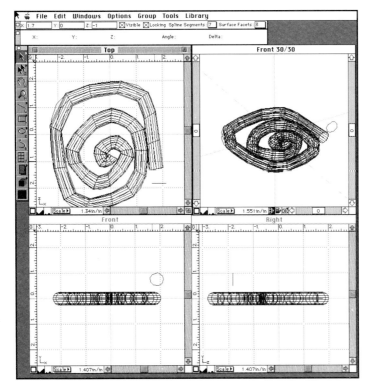

**Figure 5.19.** The end result of extruding a circle along the spiral path.

**Figure 5.20.** The 2-D shape to be lathed.

**Figure 5.21.** The shape will be rotated along the curved path.

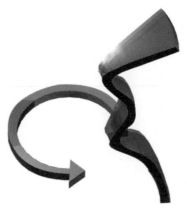

**Figure 5.22.** Beginning the lathing.

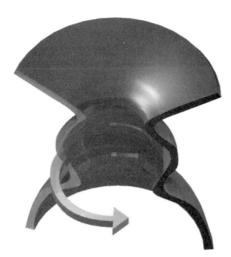

**Figure 5.23.** Continuing the lathing.

**Figure 5.24.** The final lathed object.

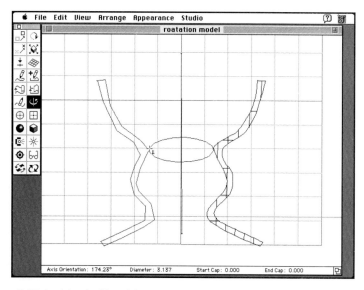

**Figure 5.25.** Lathing in Sketch!

---

**Tip**
As a rule, if an object has a consistent cross section that is
not circular, the object can be created by extrusion. If its
cross section is round, the object can usually be made by
lathing. An object with a regular cross section that follows
a crooked path (such as a garden hose) is made by extrusion on a path.

---

# Lathing techniques

Lathing an object, builds an object by sweeping a profile around an
axis in space. If you change the position or orientation of the axis
relative to the profile, you will get very different shapes. For example,
if the axis of revolution is parallel to a straight line, you will create a
cylinder. If the axis intersects the line at an angle, you will get two
cones, point to point. If it intersects an endpoint at an angle, you will
create a single cone.

Here are examples of simple lathed objects:

- Cylinder
- Vase
- Lamp shade
- Bearing
- Coffee cup
- Donut
- Pencil eraser ring

Partial lathes (a lathe of less than 360 dcgrccs) include the following:

- Dome (a quarter circle lathed 360 degrees or a half circle lathed 180 degrees)
- Coffee cup handle (180 degree lathe)
- Arch (180 degree lathe)

# Axis of rotation

Two things—the line or 2-D object being lathed and the position and angle of the axis of rotation—determine what you'll get when you lathe. The following example illustrates the difference between a diagonal and vertical axis of rotation. Note that in both examples, you begin with the same squiggly line. The resulting shape, however, changes dramatically depending on what you use as an axis.

1. Begin with a line drawn on the Sketch! working plane (see figure 5.26).

2. Select the lathe tool, click on the line, and drag the mouse down and to the right (see figure 5.27). Notice that this sets the "direction" of rotation. The axis of rotation is perpendicular to this direction, and appears as a straight diagonal line.

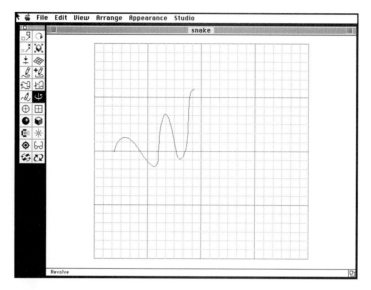

**Figure 5.26.** The line used to create the lathes.

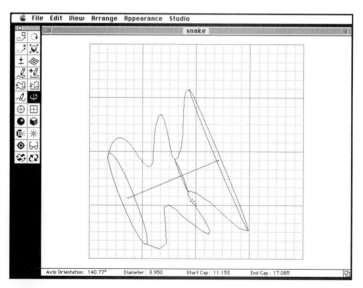

**Figure 5.27.** Setting the axis of rotation.

3. Release the mouse to draw the shape (see figure 5.28).

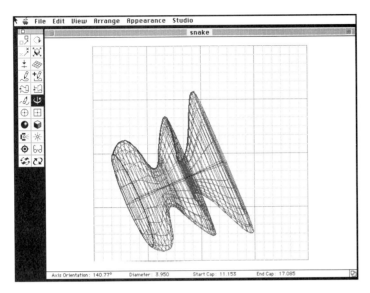

**Figure 5.28.** The lathed shape.

4. Undo the previous lathe command to get back to just a line on the grid. This time, click and drag straight to the right a short distance (see figure 5.29).

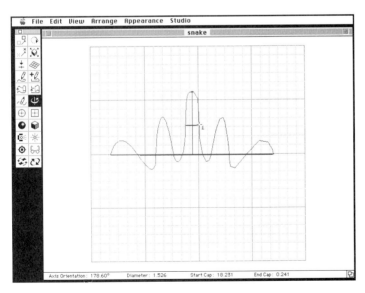

**Figure 5.29.** Defining a different axis of rotation.

5. Release the mouse to draw the new shape using the new axis of rotation (see figure 5.30).

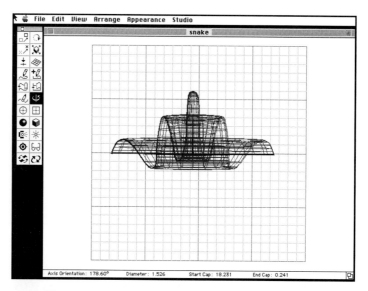

**Figure 5.30.** The same line, rotated about a different axis, creates a very different shape.

## A cylinder

Though many 3-D programs include primitives for cylinders and other simple shapes, it may be convenient at times to make your own primitive shapes. A cylinder is the simplest shape to lathe. It consists of a line rotated around an axis. You may want to lathe a cylinder instead of using a ready-made one if you want to use a specific line rotated around a specific axis or point in space. The following example illustrates lathing a cylinder in Sketch!

1. Draw a line on the working plane (see figure 5.31).

2. Choose the lathe tool, click on the center of the line and drag away from it (see figure 5.32). If you hold down the option key, you can rotate the lathe axis to align it.

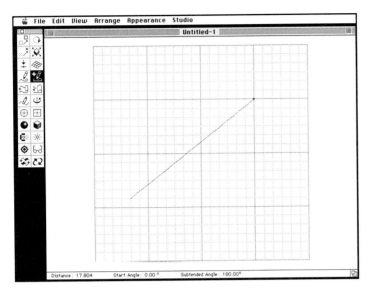

**Figure 5.31.** Drawing a line.

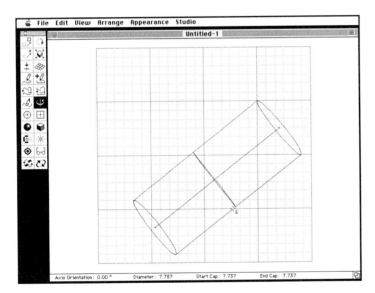

**Figure 5.32.** Defining the axis of rotation.

3. When the preview wireframe achieves the right shape, let go of the mouse button (see figure 5.33).

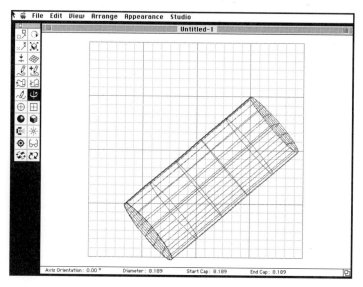

**Figure 5.33.** The lathed cylinder.

# Partial lathe

The following illustration shows the lathing of an irregular shape in MacroModel (in this case, a bearing profile) around a partial circle. Instead of lathing the shape all the way around the axis of rotation, this lathe goes only half-way around and stops, resulting in a semi-circular shape.

1. Begin by drawing a profile shape in MacroModel using the arc and other drawing tools (see figure 5.34).

2. Select the lathe tool, click on the drawing to tell MacroModel you want to lathe it. In the lathe degree settings box at the bottom of the window, enter a value of 180 degrees.

3. Drag the mouse to draw the axis of rotation on the screen (see figure 5.35).

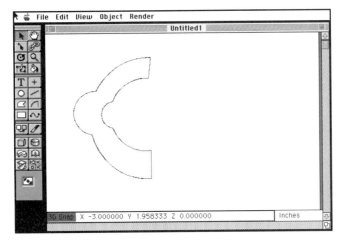

**Figure 5.34.** Creating the profile shape.

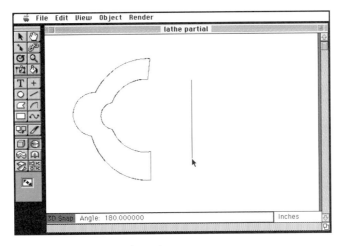

**Figure 5.35.** Creating the axis of rotation.

4. Release the mouse to finish the lathe and generate a 3-D shape (see figure 5.36).

5. Rotating the model slightly gives you a better idea of what you've created (see figure 5.37).

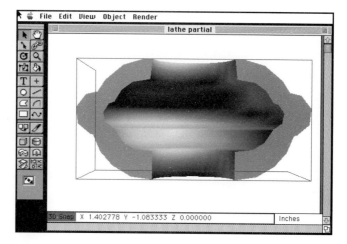

**Figure 5.36.** The shape creating by lathing the profile around a partial circle.

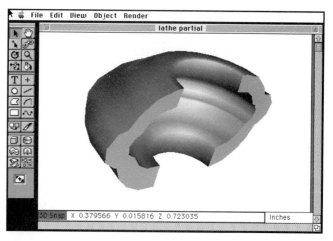

**Figure 5.37.** The same shape viewed from a slightly different angle.

# Other lathed shapes

The following three pairs of images show some typical lathed objects
and how they were made in MacroModel.

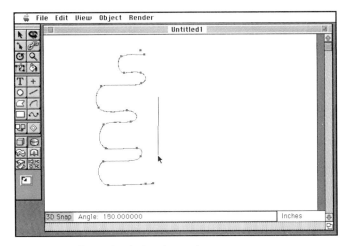

**Figure 5.38.** The profile and axis for shape 1.

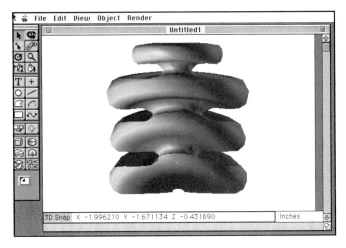

**Figure 5.39.** The lathed shape 1.

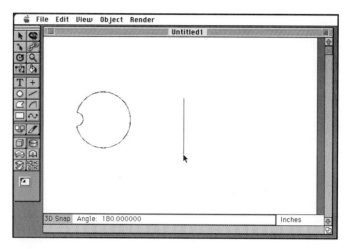

**Figure 5.40.** The profile and axis for shape 2.

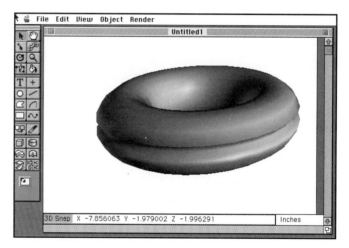

**Figure 5.41.** The lathed shape 2.

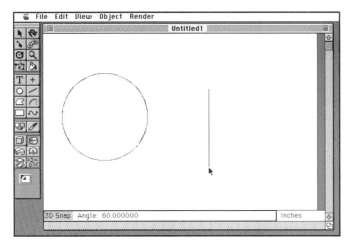

**Figure 5.42.** The profile and axis for shape 3.

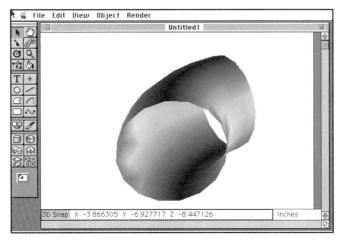

**Figure 5.43.** The lathed shape 3.

# Swept & tapered extrusion

Swept extrusion is a combination of extrusion and lathing. Essentially, you designate a number of steps to extrude the object, but for every step, you also specify a distance to offset the next end face, and

133

how much to rotate it from the previous step (imagine pulling a piece of taffy and twisting as you go). You may also be able to specify a resize ratio for subsequent steps, so that each step is slightly larger or smaller than the last.

VIDI's Modeler Professional takes this approach one step further, enabling you to reduce the distance to the axis of revolution proportional to the amount you are decreasing the size with each step. This allows you to create smoothly concentric spirals, such as those found in nautilus and snail shells and at the top of Greek columns. In this example, an oval is swept around the x-axis. Figure 5.44 shows the basic oval that will be used for the sweep.

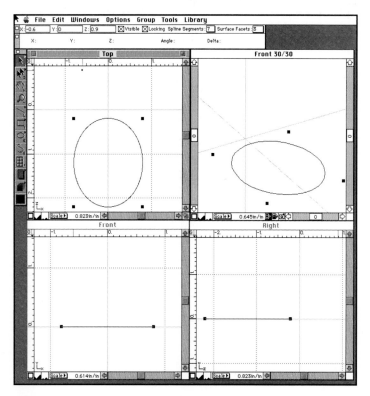

**Figure 5.44.** The oval that will be used for the sweep.

Figure 5.45 shows the dialog box used in VIDI to specify the parameters for the sweep; all dimensions are reduced slightly with each step. The oval goes through 23 steps, rotating 20 degrees each time and shrinking by ten percent (of its new total) each time. Note that the radius of the rotation also changes proportionally to the size of each step.

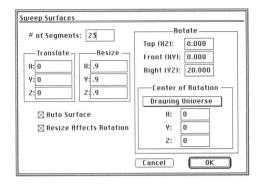

**Figure 5.45.** The VIDI dialog box used to define the parameters for a sweep.

The final image is that of a nautilus or snail shell (see figure 5.46).

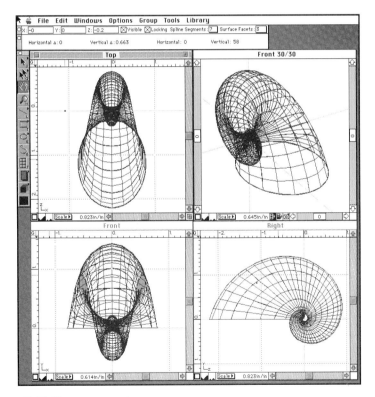

**Figure 5.46.** The swept oval.

There are many other common objects which are examples of swept objects. They have varying degrees of complexity, and some are beyond the capabilities of most modelers.

- Twisted gear

- Screw

- Threaded light bulb base

- Wrought iron

- Spring

- Corkscrew

# Groups

One of the most important devices offered in 3-D applications is the convention of *groups*. For those familiar with groups and layers in 2-D illustration programs such as Aldus FreeHand and Adobe Illustrator, groups should be pretty familiar. Primarily, grouping allows the user to work on several objects at the same time. Let's take the example of a human body. We know that there are three joints of the right forefinger, each belong to the same group called "right index finger." This group, along with "pinky" and "thumb," is part of a group called "right hand," which in turn is part of a group known as "right forearm," which is itself part of a group called "right arm." The right arm of course, is part of the "upper body" group, which in turn, is part of the "body." Each group is a collection of related parts. It's much easier to say "the right hand" than to say "the right index finger, and the right middle finger, and the right ring finger,..." listing every part of the hand.

Groups come in handy when it comes time to perform operations such as applying textures or animating. In our example, you could move the "right hand" group, and the fingers would remain attached in the proper relationship to the hand. If you were then to move the "right forearm," the hand would keep its position in relation to the forearm, while the forearm maintains its proper relation to the "upper arm," which could then be moved relative to the "upper body." The following images show a human figure in Macromedia's MacroModel, imported from Macromedia's Life Forms. Note that choosing the Right Foreleg in the groups window selects the foreleg and all the groups attached to it (see figure 5.47). This group and then the foot group are rotated to make the leg straight; then the thigh group is selected and rotated (see figure 5.48). Also note that the placement of the rotation point of every object in this model allows it to pivot at the natural joint.

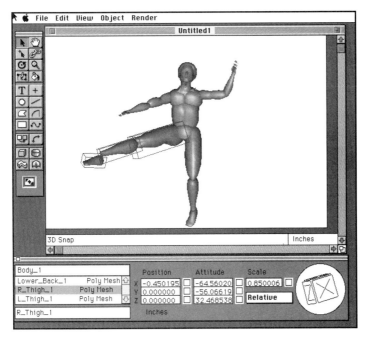

**Figure 5.47.** Selecting the Right Foreleg selects all the groups attached to it.

Another important use of grouping is the capability to hide and show specific objects. When you're working on a large collection of objects in a single model, it is often virtually impossible to see what you're doing, and the screen redraws can take forever every time you make a change. This can make it frustrating—if not impossible—to work. By hiding all non-essential groups, you will see only the elements you're working on, without distraction from the others.

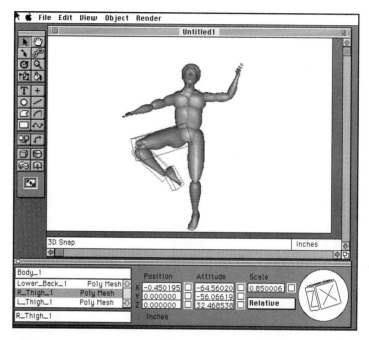

**Figure 5.48.** Rotating the Right Foreleg maintains its relationship to the other parts of the leg.

Group views also enable you to select objects even if their wireframes are overlapping. Grouping enables you to select the cube in figure 5.49, even though its wireframe overlaps the cylinder. You simply select the "cube" group from the groups window. In Sketch!, as in many other 3-D programs, end caps are treated as separate groups, enabling you to select and modify them individually (see figure 5.50). Grouping is also critical in applying textures to objects. If you have many objects grouped together, you can apply a texture to all of them in a single stroke (see figure 5.51).

Imagine that you have a jeweled gold crown. You can put the diamonds in one group, the emeralds in another, and the gold parts of the crown in a third. Then when you apply the appropriate textures to the crown, you only have to apply three of them—one for each group—instead of applying the texture to each diamond, emerald, and piece of gold individually. This becomes critical when you're working on very large projects. For example, a model of a high-rise building may have 200 discrete blocks of concrete and 300 panes of glass. Using groups, you only have to apply textures twice; without groups you'd have to do it 500 times!

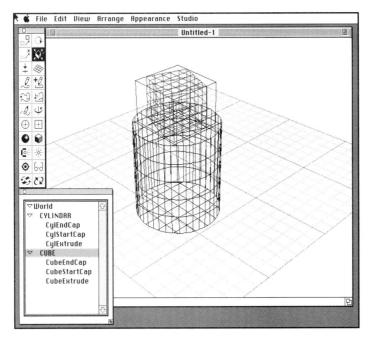

**Figure 5.49.** Grouping enables you to select just the cube, even though it overlaps the cylinder.

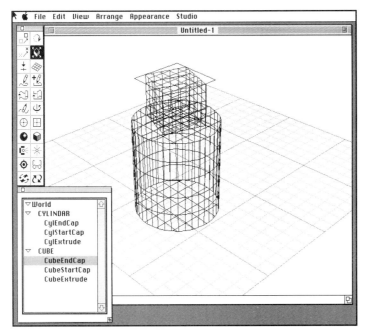

**Figure 5.50.** In Sketch!, end caps are treated as separate groups.

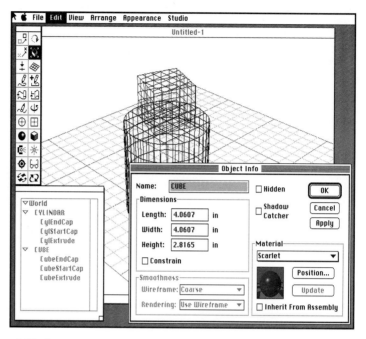

**Figure 5.51.** Groups enable you to apply a texture to a collection of objects in one step.

Grouping is even more important for animation, because you often want an entire assembly to move—for instance, a spaceship—while parts of the assembly have their own motions going on (space shuttle probes coming and going, doors opening, and so forth). Electric Image Animation System takes the grouping concept to an extreme. Each group can be part of other groups, arranged in a hierarchical fashion, and every group can have different motion, rotation, scale, color and other factors at any moment in time (see figure 5.52).

Grouped objects are also very useful in dealing with variations in materials and shapes.

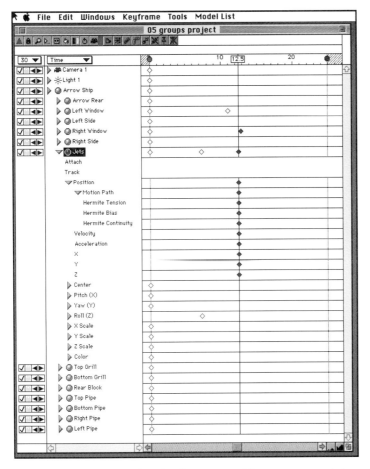

**Figure 5.52.** Electric Image Animation System provides a very complete system for grouping objects in an animation.

# Materials

Materials are another reason for making objects out of discreet parts. In real-world manufacturing, objects are usually made out of many different materials.

In a bicycle, the frame may be made out of light-weight titanium alloy, while the gears are machined from hard carbon steel and the tires are synthetic rubber. Since color and surface texture are considered "materials" in 3-D, even a change in color can call for a new part (as is often the case with manufactured objects). For example, a ball point pen may be made out of different colors of the same type of plastic, but each colored piece, the cap, the end, and the bezel around the tip are discreet parts, even though a they are all part of the same basic cylindrical shape.

Lathing a single line is a convenient way to make complex round objects. However this technique results in a single object which can only have one texture. Imagine a modern French coffee pot. It is actually composed of several parts: a glass container, a metal frame and legs, a chrome top, a plastic plunger, and a handle. It is possible to create the cylinder shape of the glass, the metal ring around the circumference, the lid, the metal disk of the plunger, and even the round knob on top, all by lathing a single complex line (see figure 5.53). However, this will create an object with only one texture (see figure 5.54).

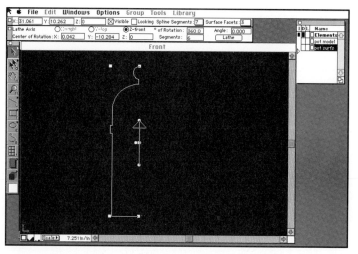

**Figure 5.53.** One complex line could be used to lathe a coffee pot...

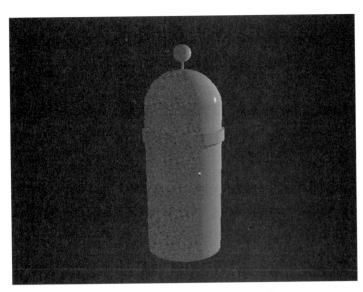

**Figure 5.54.** …but that would create a very simplistic coffee pot.

In order to make each of these parts out of the appropriate materials, you're far better off creating them individually. Creating a model out of many parts (see figure 5.55) allows you to employ many different materials and textures—an important part of realistic renderings (see figure 5.56).

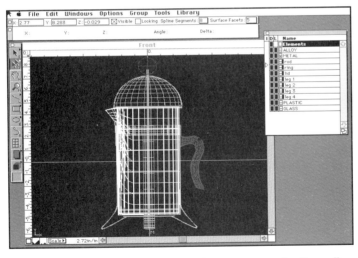

**Figure 5.55.** Using several different lathed shapes to comprise the coffee pot…

**Figure 5.56.** ...makes for a much more realistic coffee pot.

# Shapes

It would be very difficult, if not impossible, to carve most shapes out of a single block—particularly if the block needs to be comprised of many different materials. The same is true in a 3-D surface modeler. It is far easier to create the constituent shapes and add them together to form the whole.

With experience, it is easy to recognize the component shapes in everyday objects. For example, you will see that a stereo is a rectangular solid, with more solids for buttons, and a few cylinders for knobs. While it may not be obvious at the outset, a film roll is made by extruding a shape like the letter "Q" around a cylinder. A baseball bat, as in real life, is made by lathing the bat's outline. The banister of a spiral staircase is made by extruding a single cross section of molded wood along a spiral path.

Most 3-D applications offer only a subset of the many possible tools for creating complex shapes. In many instances, however, the shape you are after can be improvised with a combination of techniques.

Some shapes are not created easily. Organic forms are the most difficult, because they shun the geometric order people impose on manufactured goods. Creating these complex shapes requires special techniques. The irregular trunk of a maple tree, like the graceful curves of a wing, can be created by *skinning* a series of outlines. (Unlike the traditional use of the word, this implies putting a skin on, not taking it off.) The outlines are assembled in a specific order, and the surface is created by connecting the sequential outlines—just like a model airplane wing is created by stretching tissue paper over a series of balsa ribs.

Solid modelers are uniquely powerful in their ability to *carve* one shape with another, and they overcome many of the limitations of surface modelers. Even then, however, you begin with basic shapes which are additively and subtractively combined to form a single object.

But how do you create the diaphanous swirls of a puff of smoke? Some things still can't be adequately modeled with existing software. It's one thing to create a spiral or a helix—it's quite another to create the curling fronds of a fern.

Some complex objects can be "scanned" using special digitizing tools that record an object's shape in three dimensions (see "3-D digitizers" in chapter 2, "Getting Started"). In fact, this is the way many Hollywood animators work: an artist will sculpt a finely detailed model out of clay; the model is in turn painstakingly digitized into 3-D using a hardware digitizing tablet. The resulting models are then articulated and animated in the 3-D software. At the end of this chapter is the section "Exploding a train," which shows how many of the most common modeling techniques are used to assemble a single complex model.

# Primitives

As painters and sculptors have long known, most objects, even the soft, organic forms of humans, are suggested by primitives. *Primitives* are the simplest of geometric shapes: spheres, cylinders, cubes, and cones. Flatten a sphere and it becomes an ovoid; square a cone and it becomes a pyramid; stretch a cube and it becomes a rectangular solid; squash a cylinder and it becomes a disk. Most 3-D programs offer simple, quick ways to create primitives, as well as ways to mold and combine them into the shapes you need.

Because primitives are mathematically very simple, many 3-D programs are fast at modeling and rendering these shapes, offering an incentive to the modeler to use them whenever possible.

# Block

A block is formed either by drawing directly using the application's primitives tools, or by extruding a rectangle or square perpendicular to its original plane.

To create a beveled cube or rectangular solid, you'll have to use the bevel extrude command offered by the 3-D application, or you alternately use a path extrude command to trace a rectangle with a beveled line.

# Cylinder

A cylinder is like a round block. Instead of beginning from a square extruded upwards, it is formed by extruding a circle upwards. If you extrude a circle a short distance relative to its diameter, you'll get a flat disk. Extrude it a long distance relative to its diameter and you can create a rod or straight wire.

Additionally, you can form a cylinder by lathing a rectangle around one of its edges. To form a cylinder without end caps, you can lathe a straight line around a parallel axis.

To form an open-ended cylinder with thick walls, lathe a thin rectangle around an offset axis.

# Sphere

A sphere is formed in 3-D either by drawing directly, from a tool menu choice, or by lathing a half-circle around its straight edge. To create a half-sphere, lathe a half-circle 180 degrees.

# Ovoid

You can squash a sphere in one or two dimensions to form an elliptical solid (an egg shape). If you need an ovoid shape that is narrower on one end than the other, you can lathe an outline of the desired shape around a central axis (see figures 5.57 and 5.58).

# Cone

A cone is created either directly through drawing from a toolbox, or as a line lathed diagonally around an axis. If you lathe a right triangle around one of its 90-degree axes (see figure 5.60), you'll get a closed cone (see figure 5.59). Lathing a diagonal line creates a cone with an open end, like an ice cream cone.

# Torus

A torus, more commonly called a "donut," is sometimes provided as a primitive, where it has two pairs of pertinent variables: its major axes, which define the height and width of the big circle; and its minor axes, which define the diameter of the "tube's" cross section. Figures 5.61 and 5.62 show how a torus can be created by lathing a circle around an axis outside the circle.

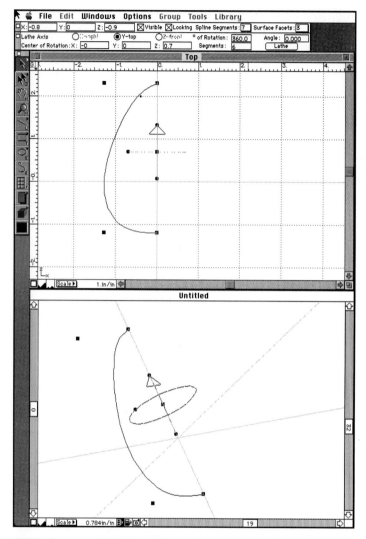

**Figure 5.57.** The outlines used to lathe two ovoid spheres.

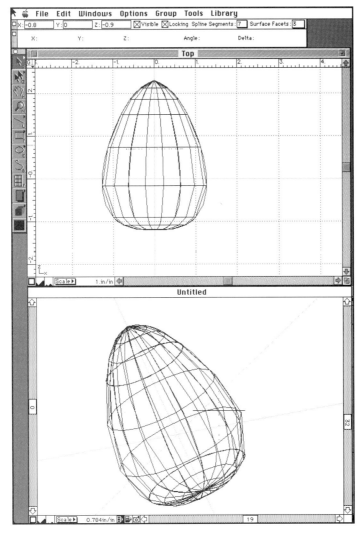

**Figure 5.58.** The lathed ovoid spheres.

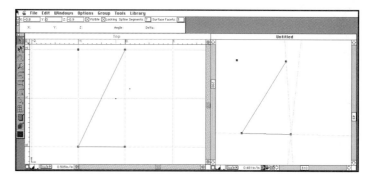

**Figure 5.59.** A right triangle can be used to lathe a cone.

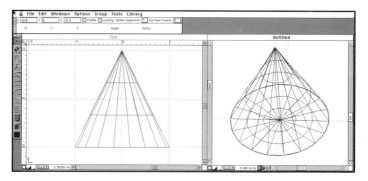

**Figure 5.60.** The cone created by lathing a right triangle around its side.

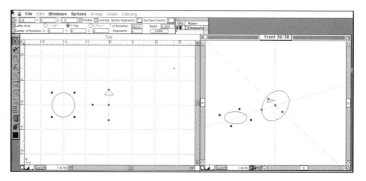

**Figure 5.61.** Defining the cross section and axis of rotation for a torus.

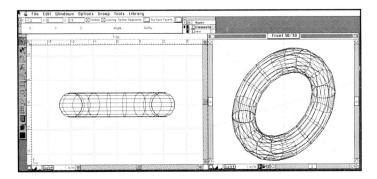

**Figure 5.62.** The lathed torus.

A standard torus is formed by lathing a circle around an offset axis, but similar shapes can be formed by revolving non-circles, such as squares, triangles, or the grooved outline of a bearing (see figures 5.63 and 5.64).

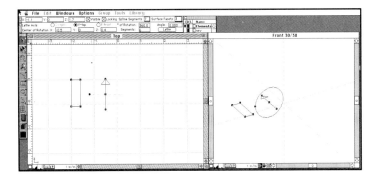

**Figure 5.63.** Lathing a rectangle around an offset axis creates a torus with right-angle edges.

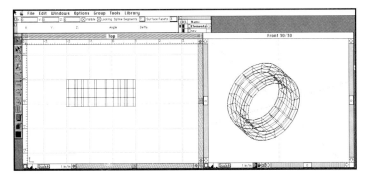

**Figure 5.64.** A lathed torus with a rectangular cross-section.

# Pyramid

Some programs support the creation of three- and four-sided pyramids, some don't. If a primitive tool isn't offered for building these shapes directly, you can try extruding the base shape, then shrinking one end to an infinitely small size.

In Alias Sketch!, the face of a cube is selected and shrunk using the scale tool (see figures 5.65 and 5.66). Sketch! responds by automatically bending its edge splines in to match (see figure 5.67).

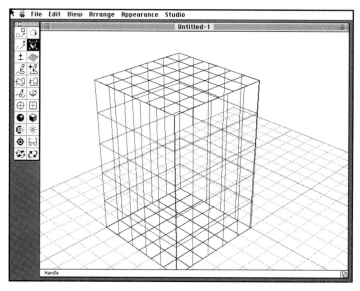

**Figure 5.65.** Selecting the face of the cube.

Some programs that support cones as primitives allow you to specify a number of sides for a polygonal base—instead of a circle—as a way of generating pyramids.

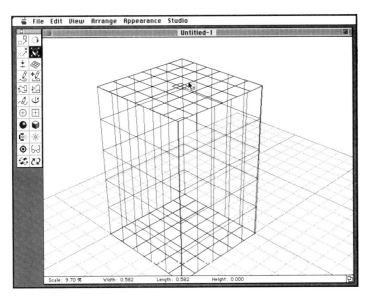

**Figure 5.66.** Shrinking the face of the cube.

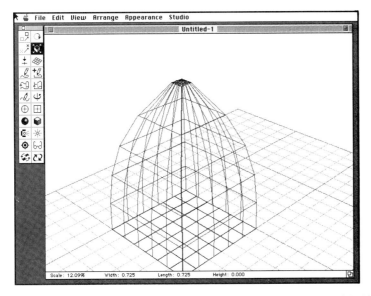

**Figure 5.67.** Sketch! automatically bends the edges to create a pyramid with curved faces.

# Bevels

Most manufactured objects are beveled. The reason for this is simple enough: sharp edges. If television sets, stereos, furniture, and even jewelry were made with perfectly hard geometric edges, people would constantly be cutting themselves on everyday objects. Craftsmen long ago discovered that softening the edges of objects is a good idea, so if you want to make your creations look realistic, you'll have to come to grips with the need for bevels. Wooden furniture is particularly hazardous if it has sharp edges because it splinters. Carpenters often use intricate bevels on the edges of furniture for this reason.

In 3-D, bevels serve another important function: they catch and reflect light. If you were to place a black cube against a black background it would virtually disappear. However, if you bevel the cube's edges, the cube will suddenly stand out against the background because the bevels are curves which scatter light in all directions, guaranteeing that the edges of the cube are visible.

Another consideration in creating bevels is that they help to make objects look aged. If you look at pictures of Greek or Roman ruins, you will see that the edges of great marble blocks are all worn down by weather (and lately by acid rain). If you were to model a recreation of the Parthenon and use hard (rather than beveled) edges, it will have the appearance of being very new.

Another common use of bevels is in glass. Bevels in glass catch and reflect light refracting it in many directions, like a prism. While 3-D is not yet sophisticated enough to diffract light into a rainbow, beveling glass and mirrors will enhance the sparkle and realism in your scenes.

# Bevels in animation

Bevels are particularly important in animation, where highlights glinting off moving bevels greatly enhance the sense of motion and sparkle in a scene. With the careful aiming and moving of spotlights, or with creative reflection mapping, you can make highlights "travel" along a beveled edge.

Many animators choose to apply a separate texture to bevels, which enhances readability as well as the sense of depth in 3-D text. However, this requires using a program that supports bevels as separate objects, such as Electric Image's Mr. Font.

# Lofting (or skinning)

*Lofting* (also called *skinning*) is like stretching a rubber sheet over two or more 2-D surfaces. The sheet will have the shape of each rib at the rib, while smoothly blending to the shape of the next rib as you go. (Just how smoothly the sheet blends depends on the smoothness setting you choose.)

This is precisely analogous to the construction of airplane wings and boat hulls in the real world, where a series of ribs or cross sections are covered with a smooth curving skin of metal or fiberglass.

Surfboard designers have a convention whereby they indicate the dimensions of a board by its width and elevation one foot off the nose and one foot off the tail, as well as its width at the widest point and how far forward or back this point lies. With these measurements and a general idea of the profile of the board, they can recreate almost any surfboard, essentially skinning the known outlines by eye as they build.

Lofting is the best method for creating many complex organic shapes that defy description as extrusions or lathes. For example, a bird's wing is narrow and round where it joins at the shoulder, it is wide and curved as you proceed out towards the tip, and then it is narrow and pointed at the end. By skinning these along with a few more intermediate cross sections, you can get a close approximation of a bird's wing. Of course, the more cross sections you have, the more accurate will be the final shape.

A series of concentric circles (see figure 5.68) was skinned to create the jet engine in figure 5.69. Note that MacroModel stretches the skin in the order that you click on the objects.

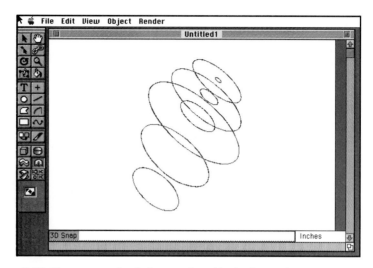

**Figure 5.68.** The concentric circles used to skin the jet engine.

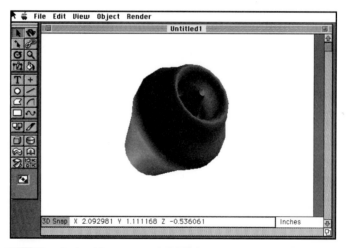

**Figure 5.69.** The jet engine was skinned from a series of concentric circles.

The following are other examples of skinned objects:

- Airplane wing

- Boat hull

- Leg

- Surfboard

# Molding

A growing number of modelers (including Modeler Professional, MacroModel, Playmation, Sketch! and Shade II) enable you to modify parts of objects created by conventional additive and constructive modeling techniques. Just as a glass blower might create a perfectly round pitcher, then bend a small lip outward as a pouring spout, 3-D designers often need to modify otherwise perfectly geometric shapes in small ways. Slight bends and distortions to perfectly straight and flat objects often lend a sense of realism. In manufactured goods, this is not frequently called for, but in real-world models, it's almost required to create realism. Organic forms, in particular, are almost never perfectly symmetrical geometric shapes.

There are several approaches to molding forms in 3-D. In vogue with spline-based modelers is the technique of modifying splines in 3-D via Bézier-type control handles. This works just like modifying curves in 2-D illustration programs such as Adobe Illustrator or Aldus FreeHand, except the handles can modify a curved surface in 3-D, rather than just a flat line.

Simpler modelers have tools which allow you to modify a shape in 2-D. Infini-D, for example, uses System 7's Publish and Subscribe to use Adobe Illustrator as an editing tool for modifying curves.

Polygonal modelers, such as Sculpt 3-D, allow you to modify "patches," which are basically 2-D polygons that make up the surface of 3-D objects. By pushing, pulling and otherwise changing the shape of a patch, you can affect the nearby surface of the object, because every patch shares points with adjacent patches.

# Solid modeling

> The following programs all offer solid modeling tools.
>
> - form•Z
>
> - Sculpt
>
> - ZOOM
>
> - Turbo 3D
>
> In addition, many CAD systems, such as MiniCAD+,
> Autodesk's Advanced Modeling Extension for AutoCAD,
> and Ashlar's Vellum 3D, offer solid modeling.

Solid modelers, which can carve one shape from another, are an exceptional type of software that combine standard 3-D techniques with mathematical modeling, often called "Boolean operations."

The image in figure 5.70 was made from a few primitives in form•Z: a block, three cylinders, two spheres and a plane. The block was "carved up" with the various primitives, then sliced with the plane. It was rendered in StrataVision 3d.

Booleans are simply a group of simple formulas along the lines of "subtract sphere A from cube B." The result of this operation would be a cube with a spherical hole in it. It is also possible to fuse objects together with addition—for example, "add columns A and B to arch C" to produce a complete architectural arch.

This kind of modeling is impossible in surface modelers because everything is hollow. Surface modelers can keep track of surface intersections, but not internal relationships.

**Figure 5.70.** Solid modeling enables you to create very complex shapes.

The following images illustrate the concept of Boolean modeling. The first image shows a block with four cones arranged at and intersecting the corners (see figure 5.71). (This arrangement would be equally easy to create in a surface modeler.) The second image shows the results of subtracting the cones from the block (see figure 5.72). The third image shows the results of the Intersection Boolean. This leaves behind only the parts the objects have in common (see figure 5.73). The final image shows the results of subtracting the block from the cones (see figure 5.74).

There are several great advantages to the solid modeler approach. Objects can have more of the properties of real objects, such as mass and volume. You could, for example, create a complex model of an engine, and determine from the model exactly how much the engine will weigh, and the inertia of its pistons.

Another advantage of solid modeling is that you can view portions of your model as cutaway sections: slice a building design down the middle, and see a cross section of offices, floors and utility shafts.

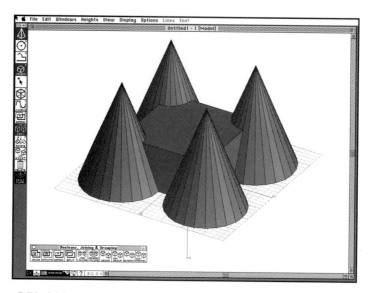

**Figure 5.71.** A block with four cones intersecting the corners.

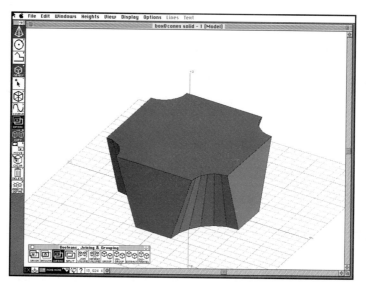

**Figure 5.72.** The result of subtracting the cones from the block.

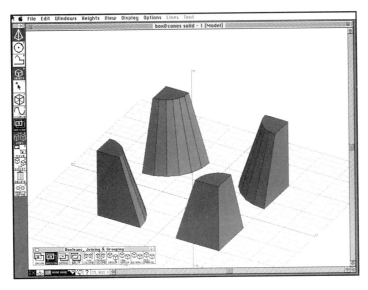

**Figure 5.73.** The intersection of the block with the cones.

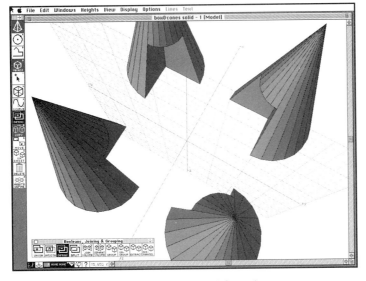

**Figure 5.74.** The result of subtracting the block from the cones.

Another Boolean operation is possible in this configuration, but not shown: Difference. The difference between the block and the cone looks exactly the same from this view as the first image; the operation leaves hollows inside both the block and the cones where they intersect.

161

Suppose, for example, that you need to create a single object that is partly extruded, partly lathed, and partly molded. The surfaces of all three parts need to flow smoothly together, with no interruptions or nonconformaties, and because the objects will be semi-transparent, they can't have overlapping protrusions that might show up in rendering. Solid modelers easily handle these kinds of situations, while surface modelers run into a variety of problems.

The Boolean approach to modeling is particularly powerful in its ability to carve up one object with several others. This closely mimics the real world, where an object may be lathed, punched, drilled, stamped, and routed on its way through the machine shop. The following sequence (figures 5.75 through 5.78) shows a single sphere being carved up by two objects.

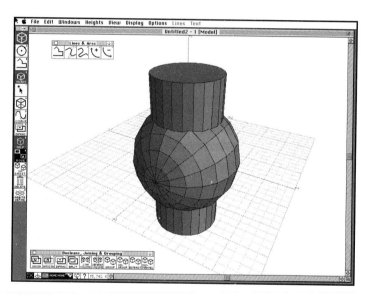

**Figure 5.75.** The sphere and cylinder are carved simultaneously with the Split command. This cuts intersecting objects with their intersecting surfaces, but leaves the resulting parts unhidden.

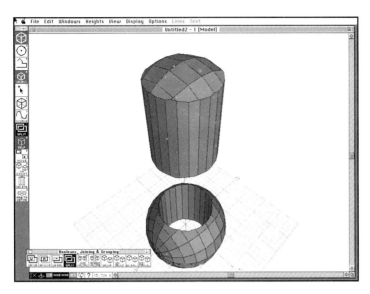

**Figure 5.76.** Note the hole in the sphere and the "plug" with spherical end caps (the original cylinder ends are hidden).

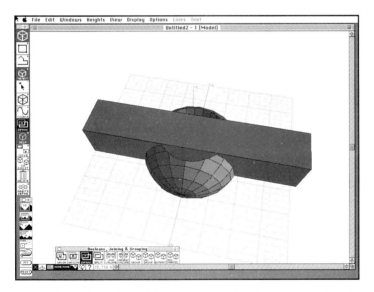

**Figure 5.77.** The rectangular solid will be subtracted from the remains of the sphere.

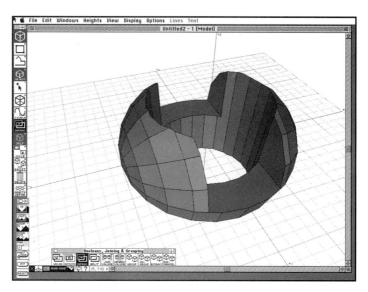

**Figure 5.78.** Subtracting the rectangular solid from the remains of the sphere results in this complex shape that would be nearly impossible to create any other way.

# Sharpening a pencil

In another example, let's take a simple shape from earlier in this chapter, the pencil. In a surface modeler, you have to model the octagonal length of the pencil as an extrusion, and the smoothly sharpened end as an octagon skinned with a circular point. The resulting shape is not totally realistic because there are no ridges where the sharpener nicked the corners of the hexagon but missed the flat spots. With a solid modeler, you can subtract the intersection of a sharpener-shaped object from the end of the octagonal shape, and get a perfect representation of a sharpened pencil, as in the following example.

1. To create a highly realistic pencil in form•Z, begin by building the raw shapes. In this case, create a long extruded cylinder—the lead—inside a long, thin extruded hexagon. Group the two together once you have them completed. These shapes are created with standard extrusion techniques (see figure 5.79). Note that this is exactly like a real, unsharpened pencil you could buy at Wal-mart.

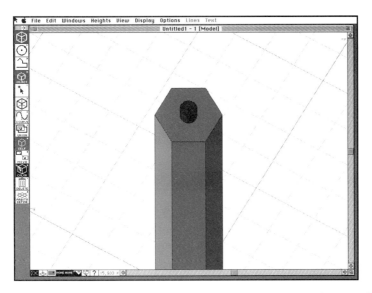

**Figure 5.79.** Extrude a cylinder inside a hexagon to create the unsharpened pencil.

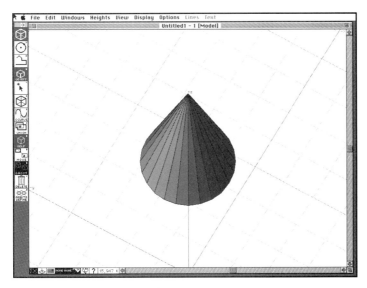

**Figure 5.80.** Creating the shape of the sharpener.

2. The "sharpener" is nothing more than a simple cone. Take care
to make it large enough around that it will fully enclose the end
of the pencil, and pointy enough that you'll get the pencil sharp
(see figure 5.80).

3. Align the cone so that the tip is enclosed by the lead and the wood (see figure 5.81).

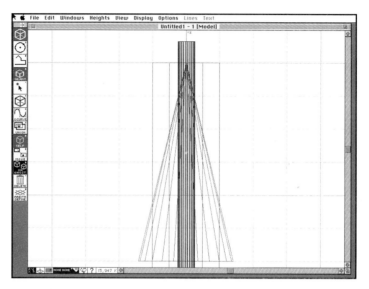

**Figure 5.81.** Aligning the cone with the pencil—just as if you put the pencil in a sharpener. The cone will "carve away" the wood and lead to form a point.

4. Finally, using form•Z's Boolean palette, select the Intersection tool to keep only the intersecting parts of the two groups. This will keep only the cone-shaped pencil tip with the nicked corners. form•Z hides the remainder of the part from the originals. In this case, unhide the rest of the shaft of the pencil (see figure 5.82).

5. Since form•Z distinguishes between the many surfaces of any object, make the "painted" sides yellow, the wood brown, and the lead black. You can preserve these distinct groupings when exporting to a realistic renderer, such as Electric Image's Animation System, which enables you to apply more realistic textures to each surface.

For many purposes, surface modelers are the preferred tool, because they are simpler to use and more economical in terms of file size and speed. But some solid modelers are beginning to approach the simplicity and speed of surface modelers, while some surface modelers are beginning to take on the powerful concept of Booleans.

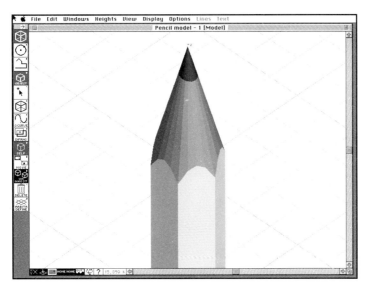

**Figure 5.82.** The sharpened pencil—note the edges where the point meets the hexagonal sides. If a cone was simply joined to a hexagonal solid, they would join on a straight line—and wouldn't look as realistic.

# Living forms

There are a few programs on the market specifically designed for modeling realistic living objects. There are a number of clip model collections which offer some natural models, but these are more limited in usefulness.

# Animal forms

Macromedia Inc.'s Life Forms, originally designed for producing choreography, produces realistic animations of human figures which can be exported to other modelers and animation packages. This program, however, is limited to a single "model," which means your renderings will all begin to take on a familiar look if you frequently use this somewhat androgynous "person."

Life Forms is really more of an animation package than a modeler, and it's covered it in greater depth in chapter 9, "Animation."

Of course, everyone would like to be able to create "Terminator II" on their Macintosh. In truth, the studios that accurately model human figures down to the twitch of a finger are using banks of high-end UNIX workstations and sophisticated digitizing stations that can handle human-sized subjects. This, more than any other reason, is why so many 3-D animators concentrate on space themes. Everybody would like to be able to model the animals marching two-by-two onto the Ark, or Lincoln delivering his address at Gettysburg, but it's really much more practical to create geometrically-shaped robots and vaguely human-like androids.

For creating realistic organic objects, such as people and animals, you'll almost be forced to turn to a spline-based modeler, and even then, no one has ever satisfactorily animated human expression. Although the realistic animation of spline-based objects made in-roads with the recent Macintosh release of Will Vinton's Playmation, Macintosh software currently can't compete with workstation-level programs like Wavefront from Alias.

# Playmation

Will Vinton's Playmation is a fabulous product on Microsoft Windows machines, and the recent port to the Macintosh shows promise. It works on the concept of spines, muscles, and skin to create extremely organic and natural-looking characters in 3-D. It also uses sophisticated event-based animation.

Unfortunately, the Macintosh version of the program was nearly unusable at the time this book was written, because of bugs and quirky problems with hardware. It is also limited to ray tracing, which for an animation package doesn't make much sense. It didn't have any export options at the time this book was written, so users will have to settle for its also-quirky texture mapping and slow rendering. Hopefully, a more Macintosh-savvy version will show up soon.

# Plants

AMAP is a "plant generator," by Abvent, in France, and available from View by View Corporation in the United States. It's used to build realistic 3-D models of many different kinds of plants, primarily for architectural renderings and animations.

**Figure 5.83.** Palm tree generated in AMAP and rendered in Electric Image.

The interface is childlike in its simplicity—a good thing, since when it showed up for inclusion in this book, the complicated key disk copy protection and all-French installation directions and interface left the author a bit grumbly by the time the trees started growing. After several minutes, the program generates a ready-to-import-and-render DXF model of a lifelike plant. The program costs more than the most exotic garden-variety shrubbery, but the trees and shrubs the program creates add amazing realism to 3-D scenes.

# What not to model

Modeling can be a painstaking, time-consuming process, especially if you're just learning! But fortunately there are many tricks and short-cuts.

Take the example of a dimpled golf ball. This shape is not only hard to classify—it's a sphere with lots of perfectly regular hemispherical dents—but it would be virtually impossible to model with a surface modeler. Even with a solid modeler, which could conceivably be used to subtract dozens of dimples from the surface of a sphere, creating a golf ball as geometry would be a challenge. So how come you see all of those realistic golf balls flying out of the TV on Sundays?

# Bumps and textures

The answer is textures—in this case bump maps. *Bump maps* can be thought of as "texture modeling." That is, they don't affect the geometry of objects to which they're applied, but they appear to. Bump maps are invaluable for adding texture detail to otherwise flat, plastic-looking surfaces. You can apply a grid bump map to a floor to simulate tiles, or you can bump map type on stone to create the effect of etched or raised lettering. Bump maps are extremely effective when combined with visual textures. You can also combine a ripply bump map with a glass texture to create the effect of waves on water.

Many textures, aside from bumps, can adequately substitute for all kinds of painstaking modeling. Surface textures, such as a photo-graph of an intricate metal grate, a procedural texture, or wood grain, can provide much more detail than you'll ever want to model. Other texture effects can also substitute for many of the shortcomings (like transparency) of modeling.

# Background details

Backgrounds, similarly, don't need to be modeled as long as it's okay if they remain a flat part of your scene. Often, photographic or painted backgrounds are used along with modeled backdrop elements to create a sense of depth and realism. For programs that support alpha channels (discussed later in this book), backgrounds sometimes are not even a consideration in the 3-D environment. A 32-bit rendering with alpha channel information can be very simply composited in Photoshop or a similar program with a backdrop of any image.

Animators may need to provide some level of modeled realism in their backdrops, particularly if long shots where the camera moves call for background objects to shift their relationships. However, animated flat backgrounds can do much of this work.

On the other hand, if objects are far enough off in the distance, you won't notice a lack of depth—mountains, for example, don't need to change position against the distant sky. In this case, only still images are required. In chapter 6, "Scene Building," we even discuss how you can match the perspective of your rendering to fit into a 3-D image, and how to cast shadows onto objects in the background.

> **Tip**
> In animations, you can often use sparing levels of detail when modeling background and other non-essential objects. Since the viewer's attention will be keenly focused on the main subject, your time would be better spent on providing detail there. Often, animators use multiple copies of the main subject model (for instance, a flock of pterodactyls in flight). But, to speed up rendering and reduce the level of complexity in your scene, you may be able to hide or even delete finely-modeled details in the "extras."

# RenderMan options

Users of Pixar's RenderMan system benefit from Boolean rendering as well as "displacement shading," which both offer modeling features at the rendering level. RenderMan's Boolean rendering allows you, for example, to specify that an object appear to be riddled with round holes, without having to model the holes.

Unlike bump mapping, whose illusion vanishes at the edges of objects, displacement shading allows RenderMan to actually move and sculpt a surface during rendering. For example, a sphere with a gravel texture will have clearly-defined pebbles appearing to cling to the edges. In animation, displacement shaders can be used to make surfaces appear to ooze, ripple or breathe. These effects would be nearly impossible to model.

# CAD

Manufacturing- or architecturally-accurate design requires the use of sophisticated CAD (computer-aided design) software. This type of software has many specialized tools for forming joints and creating parts, even where they are not visible to the eye. Files created by CAD programs can even be used to drive manufacturing machinery or to produce blueprints. Because CAD programs are desinged more for the creation of working drawings than for conceptual design and the production of realistic images, they focus as much attention on 2-D drawings as they do on 3-D work, and many of the tasks are open to automation through programming and macros. For this reason, CAD packages are beyond the scope of this book.

One of the things that distinguishes CAD applications from general modelers is a vast degree of mathematical precision. Autodesk, the maker of AutoCAD, demonstrates its Mac software by zooming from the moon, all the way to the front door of a building in Italy, without recalculating coordinates.

There are a number of CAD applications which are important contributors to Macintosh 3-D. Some programs, like MiniCAD+ combine powerful 2-D drawing tools with tools for lifting floor plans into the third dimension.

CAD users can often benefit from the simplified tools offered by general modelers. For example, an architect may use a CAD program such as Microstation or ArchiCAD for creating an initial design of a new office building, but furniture, lighting, and other fixtures may be much easier to create in a general modeler. Using CAD and modeling applications that communicate their files easily makes it simple to export the architectural model to a program such as StrataVision 3d, where the architectural model can be combined with models of fixtures, lit and photorealistically rendered.

On the other hand, users of general modeling packages will sometimes need to create a very accurate or complex shape that is beyond the scope of a general modeling package. These users may be able to turn to a CAD package to solve their needs. For example, an animator who needs to create a western ghost town may do well to turn to an architectural application like MiniCAD+, where there are simplified tools for quickly creating walls, doors, windows, and roofs.

# Splines vs. polygons

There is a trend in 3-D surface modelers to forgo polygons in favor of splines. Modeler Professional, Shade II, Sketch!, MacroModel, Playmation, StrataStudio Pro, and form•Z all offer 3-D spline tools. Even polygonal modelers have bowed to the drawing power of spline curves, and programs like StrataVision 3d, Designer, and Showplace offer constructive modeling with Bezier (Illustrator-style) splines.

Polygonal systems, however, remain the industry standard. Autodesk's AutoCAD (along with its DXF file format), Electric Image's Animation System, Sculpt 3D, and StrataVision 3d are all based on polygonal models, as are all of the older 3-D applications.

At the simplistic level, splines are smooth curves and polygons are straight-edged facets. For beginning users, the differences are transparent; a sphere, for example, is a sphere no matter the underlying geometry. The advantages and pitfalls of the two competing approaches become apparent with serious use.

Polygons, by their nature, are extremely efficient at representing straight-edged geometry, such as that which makes up the bulk of architectural design. Polygons run into trouble in the representation of curves, such as the forms which define most living creatures. In order to represent a smooth curve, a polygonal modeler has to draw many short segments or facets.

The user can specify how smooth the curves will be by specifying that a circle should be drawn with a given number of facets—for instance, 64 facets instead of 32. The more facets, the smoother the object—and the larger and more complex the resulting file. This results in increased RAM requirements and longer rendering times.

Splines, on the other hand, are extremely efficient at representing curves. A mathematically precise circle requires only four spline segments, each with a pair of control points which determine tension on the lines. You can enlarge a spline-based object to any size without a loss of resolution—that is the circle will continue to look like a smoothly rounded circle, no matter how large you make it or how closely you look at it.

The difference between splines and polygons is very similar to the advantage PostScript line art has over its bitmapped counterpart. Bitmaps resemble polygonal systems, in that they are both resolution-dependent, while splines in both the 2-D and 3-D world are resolution-independent.

Splines, however, have problems when you create objects that are primarily polygonal shapes. For one, they are harder to control than simple straight segments. Splines also impose an overhead in that they are not as efficient as polygonal systems at creating simple polygonal geometry. They take up more space and take longer to render when used for objects such as simple cubes.

Splines come into their own when you have to do a lot of surface distortion. Because each spline point exerts a tension on adjacent segments, you can pull on one point and expect the surrounding curves to bend and change accordingly. In a polygonal modeler, in contrast, pulling on a single point will tend to leave others in place (depending on the modeler), creating a sharp point or spike.

Imagine a lizard's tail. If you pull sideways on the tip of the tail, you want the whole tail to bend smoothly, along a "spine." This simply isn't possible in a polygonal modeler.

# Exploding a train

Figure 5.84 shows an old-fashioned steam locomotive modeled entirely in VIDI's Presenter Professional and rendered with RenderMan. This is an extremely complex model, involving over two hundred groups (although you might not guess it by looking at it). Fortunately, none of it was particularly difficult to build. In these examples, where we've exploded various groups for illustration, the parts have been moved around somewhat, so you can see what's going on.

**Figure 5.84.** The finished, rendered steam engine.

All of the objects in the following image are simple primitives, including blocks and cylinders (see figure 5.85).

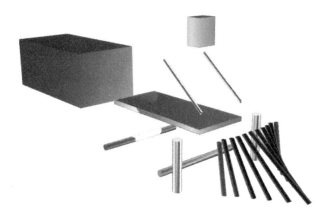

**Figure 5.85.** Some of the primitives used to create the steam engine.

The objects in figure 5.86, which comprise the cabin of the locomotive, were actually the most difficult parts of the model to produce.

**Figure 5.86.** The parts that comprise the cabin of the locomotive.

The roof is a simple front-to-back extrusion of an arc shape with the curvature of the roof. The front and side walls are each created in the same way. Start by drawing the outline of the wall, then draw the window shapes inside the wall. Finally, surface the group of objects. (Actually, only one side wall is modeled; it is then duplicated and moved to the other side.) The hardest part of this assembly is beveling the joints between the font and side walls. In order to avoid a very hard, jagged looking edge at the corners, the front and side wall are offset by one-quarter inch (to scale) front and side so that there is a gap between them. Viewing from the top, this gap is spanned by an arc (called a *fillet*). This curve is extruded vertically, to entirely fill the gap between the two surfaces. This bevel is barely visible in the finished rendering, but it would be extremely useful in any close-up shots of the cabin.

The objects in figure 5.87 are all simple extrusions.

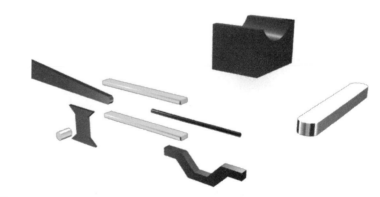

**Figure 5.87.** Simple extrusion was used to make many of the components.

Note that each one has a consistent cross section and two flat surfaces at either end. The only difficult one to build is the large block-like object at top used to support the locomotive's main tank. To build this object, view the tank from the front and draw the cross section so that the arc part of the shape closely matches the curvature of the tank. Then extrude the object parallel to the tank.

The wheels of the locomotive pose two problems: one is the large number of identical spokes evenly distributed around a point; the other is the rim of the wheel itself, whose cross section (if you cut through the rim) is roughly an "L" shape (see figure 5.88).

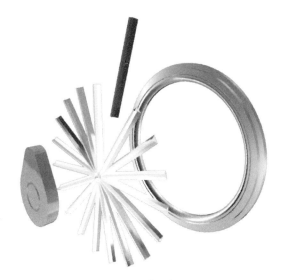

**Figure 5.88.** The parts that comprise a wheel.

The wheel rim is a simple lathe of the cross section. The rotation point of the lathe is located at the precise center of the wheel. The spokes also have an odd cross section, but they're straight, so the first one (shown out of its original position) is a simple extrusion. Creating the other spokes is very easy in Modeler Professional—you simply choose the Duplicate command and in the dialog box, instruct the program to make 19 copies evenly distributed around the point that was used for lathing the rim. The bearing is a simple extrusion of an object with a hole in it around a short cylinder.

Lathed objects make up the bulk of the locomotive (see figure 5.89). The main tank is actually three lathes: the big tank, the brightly colored, reinforced front end, and the ringed end cap on the front.

**Figure 5.89.** Many lathed objects are used in the locomotive.

Note that the rings (which fit around the tank) were made by lathing small rectangles around the tank's central axis. The smokestack is the most complex object in this group, because of the complex outline used to lathe it.

The objects in figure 5.90 are all path extrusions. If sawed through a certain way, each one has a consistent cross section no matter where you cut.

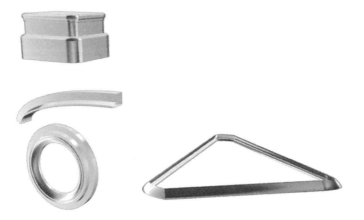

**Figure 5.90.** Path extrusions are used to create some very complex shapes.

The base of the cow catcher was made by extruding a small irregular shape along a triangular path. The front wheel rim, unlike the rear rim (which was lathed) is a shape extruded along a circular path. The fender is a simple shape extruded along a gently sloped curve. The heavily beveled object at top is actually two objects. The end cap on the top surface is merely a round-cornered rectangle. The sides were created by extruding a line with two bevels in it around the outside edge of this rounded rectangle.

# Summary

- Additive modeling is the assembly of pre-built pieces.

- Constructive modeling uses simple shapes to construct a more complex shape. Techniques include extrusion and lathing, as well as sweeping and lofting.

- Extrusion is the extension of a simple 2-D object into 3-D.

- Lathing is the revolution of a 2-D shape around an axis to form a shape from the sweep of its lines.

- Groups are critical to working with and animating models. They are often used at the modeling level.

- Primitives are the simplest form of models.

- Bevels are an important part of modeling man-made objects.

- Molding is the pushing and pulling on parts of a model as if it were soft clay.

- Solid modeling offers Boolean operations (the adding and subtracting of volumes).

- Several programs are designed for modeling living forms.

- Not all details should be modeled.

- CAD differs from standard 3-D in the complexity of tools and the high accuracy and precision of the applications.

- Splines and polygons offer distinctly different modeling features.

6

# Scene building

A nyone who has ever played with electric trains, a doll house, or toy soldiers understands the essentials of scene building. This is the phase of 3-D where you place your models on a stage, dress them up in textures, add lights, and adjust your camera so that everything appears in the proper perspective. While modeling is the most technically demanding part of creating Three-D graphics, scene building is the most creative.

*Scene building* in the creative application of textures, lights, and cameras so that the compelling 3-D rendering rises above the merely realistic.

Because scene building is such a specialized part of 3-D graphics, there are a number of programs specifically devoted to the task. These include animation programs such as Macromedia Three-D, Electric Image Animation System (EIAS), as well as programs that create only still images such as Pixar's ShowPlace. In addition to providing tools to assemble and light the scene—as well as applying textures and environments—these programs include the rendering interface and engine used to create final images.

# Setting the stage

The first order of scene building is the placement of models in a scene. In the cases when the modeler and scene builder are the same application, this is merely an extension of the modeling procedure. We've already described the basics of navigation; they are essentially the same in modeling and scene building—in some 3-D programs they are indistinguishable.

# Using snaps and grids

Scene builders, like modelers, rely on the use of snaps and grids: reference points that help the user place and align objects. Sketch!, form•Z, and MacroModel, for example, use the concept of a "working plane." When using a floor as a working plane, you can place furniture as you would place real furniture in a real room.

# Constraining and linking

Most scene builders—particularly those designed for animation—enable you to create physical relationships between objects. These relationships can be as simple as group hierarchies, or they can include complex spatial relationships, such as specifying how a ball joint can move within its socket. Typically, links can be established outside of the constraint of group relationships established during the modeling stage; although a foot originally may be part of a leg group, you may want to establish a link to a ball and chain: every time you move the ball and chain, the foot will move with it. In this example, the leg and the rest of the body may be linked to the foot so that when they move, it does.

In programs like EIAS, Infini-D, or StrataVision 3d, group hierarchies are maintained when you import a model, but these can be rearranged. You can break a child off from a parent and link it to another object instead. Maintaining hierarchies is sometimes a trial and error process. How well hierarchies are maintained depends on how well your modeler and scene builder work together.

# Parents and children

There are many instances when you will want to create parent-child relationships. Essentially, you use these relationships any time you want to move a parent and you want the children to move with the parent without changing their relationship. At the same time, moving the child will not effect the parent. You may want a car's wheels free to rotate independently of the car body, but you also may want the wheels to move when the car moves. If you were to merely group the car and wheels, rotating the wheels will also rotate the car! Even a light can be the child of an object or camera; you can attach a spot light to a camera, for example, so that when you move the camera, the spotlight moves with it.

The difference between a simple group and a link is that links allow for the independent motion of child-groups, while grouping objects is like gluing them together: where one moves so does the other. By implication, when a parent moves so does its child—but the child is free to move without the parent.

# Rotation

Rotation of a child group in this scenario is relative to its original orientation to the parent group. This is important to consider when numerically transforming an object's position. If it is linked to another object, this transformation—unless otherwise specified—is relative to the parent, not to the world axes. Local rotation enables you to spin a propeller, for example, even while an airplane banks and turns through space. If you rotate the airplane, the propeller's orientation changes along with the plane.

Figure 6.1 shows the Orientation dialog box from Infini-D.

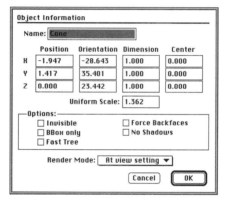

**Figure 6.1.** Orientation, position, and dimension can be set in Infini-D's Object Information dialog box.

> **Tip**
> When positioning an object in 3-D space, you must know where its reference point is located. A reference point is the point that is actually referred to when you look at an object's numerical position, and it is the point that the object rotates around (unless otherwise specified). Some programs, such as StrataVision 3d and StudioPro, make it easy to move this point in relationship to the model.

# Joints

Joints are special cases of parent-child constraints. Common examples of joints in the real world are the axles and bearings in bicycle wheels, the ball and socket in a hip joint, sliding drawers, and common door hinges. In all of these joints, the rotation and movement are constrained within certain limits (see figure 6.2). For instance, a hinge uses two pieces of metal folded around a pin. Each leaf of the hinge can rotate freely around the axis formed by the pin, but is prevented from rotating along other axes. Assuming one of the leaves of the hinge is affixed to an immovable object (such as the frame of a house), the entire assembly also is constrained to a single location in space. Of course, there is little need for joints in still images; you simply position objects and leave them in place for rendering. Joints come in handy as an easy way to create convincing animations of constrained movement. Some of the types of links and constraints found in high-end animation applications are shown in figure 6.3.

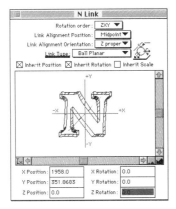

**Figure 6.2.** This image shows EIAS' constraint window. The current object is constrained to move only as a ball joint relative to its parent.

**Figure 6.3.** EIAS offers many types of links and constraints. This selection is similar to that found in Swivel 3-D Professional.

# Stretching and squashing

Most scene builders enable you to enlarge and shrink, or stretch and squash an object. Uniformly resizing an object changes its dimensions relative to other objects in the scene, while stretching or squashing the object changes the dimension of an object along a single axis (you could flatten a cylinder to a disk). The difference between stretching or squashing an object versus resizing an object is that stretching takes place along a single axis, while resizing is applied uniformly to all axes at once.

# Backgrounds

Few things in life appear against a perfectly black or white background. For this reason, all 3-D programs have some degree of support for importing or creating interesting backdrops for 3-D models. Aside from the fact that it's easier, the advantage of an imported background—rather than a rendered 3-D set—is that backgrounds do not require complex calculations of light and shadow. You simply drop them into place.

On the other hand, rendered background scenery lends a strong sense of realism to an image (particularly if foreground lights and objects cast shadows into the backdrop). The most common types of rendered background sets are rooms and landscape or terrain.

Imported backgrounds often look flat and "chroma-keyed" (much like the phony backdrops in movie scenes). This is because the object does not reflect or, if it is transparent, it does not transmit the background image. However, it is also a fact that imported backgrounds often have different lighting than the foreground model. You can make up for this, to some extent, by careful lighting of the scene.

Often the best course is to combine nearby background objects modeled in 3-D with an imported background image to get the best of both worlds.

A variety of very interesting options exist for creating unusual modeled backgrounds and scenery. This includes fractal terrain generators which create convincing 3-D mountains, and bitmap-to-3-D converters that can turn a grayscale bitmap into a continuous surface model.

# Rendered backgrounds

Rendered backgrounds are often as simple as a floor and a wall (with a strip of molding between them for realism). The advantage of this setup is that objects placed on this set will cast shadows onto both the floor and wall (assuming you placed your lights correctly). You can add a strong sense of realism to this scene by using a shadow gel on your key light to cast shadows onto both the foreground and background objects (see chapter 8, "Lighting"). To create even more realism, it often helps to apply appropriate textures (such as wood or tile to the floor, stucco or wallpaper to the walls). To add a little clutter to rooms (to make them look more realistic), you may consider modeling or purchasing clip models of chairs and other furniture.

> **Tip**
> Keep in mind that background scenery usually doesn't
> need to be as detailed as that in the foreground. In fact, it's
> often better to maintain very simple, uncluttered back-
> grounds to help focus attention on the main subject. In
> these cases, the background serves to set the mood for
> foreground objects.

In cases where you need to add details to a 3-D space (but you
don't want to model them), it is often possible to strike a compromise between rendered and imported backgrounds. For example,
you can texture map an air conditioning vent to the floor of a
room—which is much easier than modeling one.

# Bitmaps to models

Outdoor scenery requires a bit more work when creating backgrounds. Several programs, such as Infini-D, StrataVision 3d, and
StrataStudio Pro will generate fractal terrains or other organic-
looking objects for use in 3-D. Fractal terrains are particularly well
suited to rough-looking cliffs and mountains. If you're after more
subtle creations, Knoll Software's CyberSave (a plug-in filter for
Photoshop) can turn any grayscale bitmap into a 3-D model of
unusual terrain that you even can wrap around a sphere.

In addition to creating terrain, these tools are ideal for quickly
extruding a scanned-in logo or other piece of artwork. Unlike an
Illustrator outline (which will be extruded to all one height), extruding a grayscale bitmap enables you to extrude an image to multiple
levels.

## StrataStudio Pro and StrataVision 3d

Both StrataStudio Pro and StrataVision 3d enable you to open an
image file and to have the image's brightness values automatically

converted to 3-D geometry. One of the best aspects of this approach is that you also can import the image (or its "negative") and use it as a texture map. This allows you to map colors that correspond to the terrain onto the terrain model.

You can create the feathered polka dots, as shown in figures 6.4 and 6.5, in Photoshop.

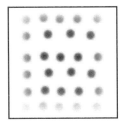

**Figure 6.4.** An inverted version of the map is converted to grayscale, then turned into a negative with the Map Invert command in Photoshop. Fill the entire image with five percent white to soften the black areas to a dark gray (otherwise they will disappear completely in StrataStudio).

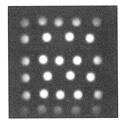

**Figure 6.5.** Import the inverted image into StrataStudio Pro which will automatically convert it into a model based on its gray values. Dark areas are extruded as high points while light areas are shallow. With the image selected, select the Make texture command, and select the original color texture as a color map. This is automatically mapped to the model.

# Infini-D

Infini-D has a very fast and easy tool you can use called "Terrain" which generates convincing 3-D models from 2-D images. In addition, it enables you to generate fractal terrains from Mandelbrot or Julia sets, as well as automatically generating a variety of other interesting 3-D models from 2-D imagery. The fractal models are particularly useful for creating interesting mountainous landscapes (see figure 6.7). Another use of this tool is the creation of terraced contour landscapes. It is also useful when you want to generate a "bump model" that defines an actual volume to generate more realism than a bump map. For example, you may want to turn a scanned logo into 3-D art.

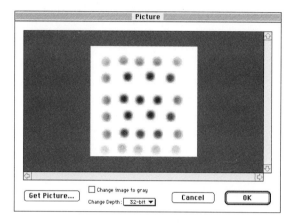

**Figure 6.6.** Rotate the model to get a better perspective and render it.

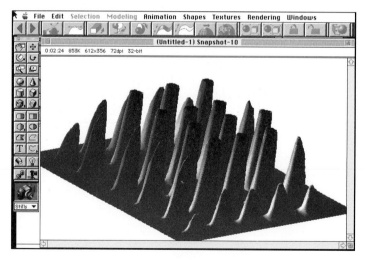

**Figure 6.7.** Mountainous projectiles created in Infini-D.

Like StrataVision 3-D and StrataStudio Pro, you can use an image you have used to create a model and apply it as a texture to that model (see figure 6.8 and figure 6.9).

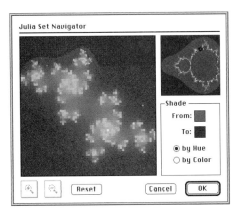

**Figure 6.8.** This interface enables you to select a small segment of the Julia Set to use as a model generator and texture in Infini-D.

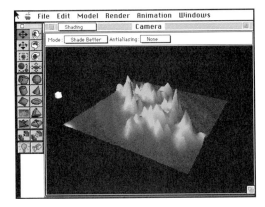

**Figure 6.9.** The result after rendering.

## Showplace Terrain

Pixar's Showplace has a Terrain generator much like that of Strata's and Specular's products (see figure 6.10). However, you do not have the option of importing an image to generate terrain. You generate bump models from algorithmically generated pictures instead.

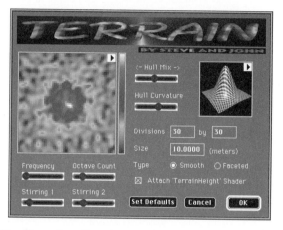

**Figure 6.10.** The Showplace Terrain generator.

## CyberSave

CyberSave is a remarkable, low-cost utility created by John Knoll (one of the original creators of Photoshop). It works as an Adobe Photoshop plug-in filter. Its sole purpose is to convert grayscale bitmaps into 3-D models. It does this much like a bump map: by interpreting the bright values as "tall" and the dark values as "short." The difference is that CyberSave converts this information to CyberWare- or DXF-format geometry that you can import into almost any 3-D application. By creatively producing texture maps that correspond to "bump models," you can precisely map colors and other surface qualities to different parts of a scenery model.

# Imported backgrounds

As we mentioned, every 3-D program allows some degree of background importing. This means you can have a model of a spaceship against a starry sky without modeling a starry sky. (You simply draw one in a paint program or scan one from a public-domain NASA photo.)

Even though an imported background renders much faster than a modeled background, you will pay a significant time penalty for including it in your rendering. All renderers take a good deal of time calculating the appearance of a background—even if it is completely unaffected by the foreground image.

# Transparent backgrounds

A solution with many advantages over importing an image prior to rendering, is to render the image using the 3-D program's alpha channel setting which creates a transparency matte. You can use this method for seamlessly integrating the rendered foreground with a background image. (The alpha channel is described in chapter 10, "Rendering," in much greater detail. A discussion of the alpha channel can be found in chapter 11, "Working with images.")

One of the primary advantages of this approach is speed. Renderers take a long time just to move the data in a background image through the system (when you're really not gaining anything by doing this in most cases). On the other hand, creating an alpha channel barely slows down the rendering process. Combining images using the alpha channel in a program like Photoshop takes only a few seconds.

Another advantage is that you can try out many different background images until you find just what you are after. You also can move a rendering around over the background until you get it in just the right position.

In addition, alpha compositing enables you to assemble many individual parts of a scene in one place. You can matte a 3-D logo over a 3-D backdrop, for example, without rendering them at the same time. This allows you to build and render a perfect background and composite it with the ideal logo (created separately) to get just the right effect.

# Perspective matching

One of the most useful techniques in 3-D is creating and rendering a model so that it fits exactly into a pre-existing scene. Imagine that you plan to build a new structure in the midst of existing buildings. Ideally, you would photograph the existing site, scan the photo in, and create and render a model that will fit seamlessly into the scene. Perspective matching is a technique that lets you do this.

## Sketch!

Alias' Sketch! has a simple mechanism for perspective matching. You can use a perspective matching tool to drag the corners of an object to the corners of a corresponding object in the image. This changes the point of view of the camera so that the entire scene aligns to corresponding objects in the image.

When you are ready to render, you import the scanned photograph of the background and, using the perspective matching tool, stretch the corners of the drawing grid to the corners of the vacant lot in the photo. This changes the perspective of the 3-D world to match exactly that of the photograph. When you render the model, it will appear to fit perfectly into place in the photo.

For example, you may build a model of a house on a rectangle known to match the lot dimensions in the photo. When you stretch the corners of the rectangle to match the corners of the lot in the photo, the model of the house and everything else in the scene are moved into this new perspective.

## General perspective matching

Any program that lets you view a background while you build a scene, can be used to match the perspective of a photographic background.

The way you do this, without Sketch!'s tricky tool, is to model an object that corresponds to a known object in the background scene. You then drag your view around, zooming, panning, and rotating until the model lines up with the scene. This can take a bit of trial and error, but it is not too difficult.

If accuracy is crucial, you can photograph the site from a measured distance, taking careful note of the camera lens length and the angle and elevation from which you are shooting. Programs that support moveable cameras allow you to recreate the camera's position in your model. This technique takes careful planning and a lot of time.

> **Tip**
> One company in California photographs a site with a video camera mounted on a dolly along with an expensive, highly-accurate Global Positioning Satellite receiver. Once the time-coded video is digitized and the data from the GPS computer is synchronized, they can generate a positionally-accurate 3-D perspective movie of a model on a site by animating their 3-D camera to match the motion of the real video camera.

# Shadow casting on backgrounds

Sketch! has a unique facility for casting shadows into an imported background so that they appear to belong in the scene. For example, if you want to place a trophy in a scene with a book shelf and you want the trophy to cast a shadow onto the shelf, you first model a simple version of the shelf with the trophy standing on it, and match the modeled shelf's perspective to that of the photograph of the shelf. You then make the modeled shelf an invisible "Shadow Catcher." When Sketch! renders the scene, it makes the modeled shelf invisible, but casts the trophy's shadow (in perspective), onto the photo of the shelf which is already in perspective. You can make Shadow Catchers out of any modeled object, so you can have shadows realistically cast onto all kinds of background scenery. This is important to realism because shadows wrap around curved objects or bend at intersecting planes (such as where a floor meets a wall).

# Cameras

As discussed in chapter 3, "Navigating in 3-D," cameras can be used to provide new views into 3-D space. When creating a final scene or animation, lens length (zoom), orientation, and sometimes depth of field become particularly important.

## Lens

The longer a camera's lens, the more it will "zoom." A telescope is nothing more than a very long lens. A zoomed lens has the effect of bringing very distant objects close, while narrowing the field of view. (Imagine focusing a telescope on a dime a hundred miles away.) Conversely, a short lens has a very wide angle of view. (Picture squeezing an entire football team standing only a few feet away into the frame.)

## Orientation

The orientation of the camera is critical to getting the picture right. You can aim a camera at any object, but you also will need to concern yourself with the roll of the camera (how much it's tilted left or right), as well as its elevation.

## Depth of field

Some renderers are sensitive to depth of field. This is an effect found in cameras, whereby the "f-stop" or opening of the lens determines how much of the scene will fall into focus. Things that are too close or too far from the camera are increasingly blurred as they fall out of the focal range. As you open up the lens, the depth of field decreases. This effect is primarily useful when you want your rendering to mimic the appearance of a photograph.

The default setting for 3-D software is usually infinite depth of field (which mimics the way our eyes focus on objects in the foreground or background).

# Atmosphere

Atmosphere is a difficult thing to create in 3-D. Most of the time, atmosphere is thought of as clean, invisible air—until you think of terms like pea-soup fog, drizzle and haze. All of these are visible examples of atmosphere and there are many others.

It is possible to model a tornado seen from a distance. (Make sure you use lots of random objects flying around.) Modeling an effect like smoke is more problematic: smoke twists and curls as it rises and at some point in its ascent from the source, breaks up into mist. This is an extremely difficult model to build to say the least. You could try building a texture—part transparent, part smoke colored—and applying it to a twisted object in the scene, but this is a tricky solution, particularly in animation. Take the example of rain; we all know what a rainy day looks like; but what does rain itself look like? You could build thousands of tiny droplets and scatter them throughout your model, but this is likely to overwhelm a renderer. As with smoke, a more effective solution may be to "paint" these effects into an image with a program like Photoshop.

# Fog

One of the few atmospheric effects adequately simulated by 3-D programs is fog. It can be used to portray foggy days, but more importantly it provides *depth cueing*. When objects disappear into a distant haze, it is a strong visual clue that they are really far away; this effect enhances the sense of depth in a scene.

Unlike real fog—which is subject to the irregularities of clouds—3-D fog is an even blurring of the scene as you move further away from the camera. The fog uses a color which is increasingly dominant as you move farther away in the scene until the background is uniformly colored (see figure 6.11). Usually you can set the amount of fogginess as well as the point at which you want the fog to begin affecting the scene. Thus, if your modeled airplane is twenty "feet" away in the 3-D space and you want the fog to begin just behind it, you can set the fog to begin at 30 feet. This will cause anything behind the airplane to be lost in fog: the farther away, the more it will be obscured. This is an extremely effective technique for creating the effect of distance—especially when you have scenery such as a mountains which in real life are often partially obscured by the atmosphere. Most high-quality 3-D renderers offer fog.

**Figure 6.11.** This image was rendered, with lots of fog in Electric Image Animation System.

---

**Tip**

Unlike real fog, 3-D fog is not affected by lights in a scene. You cannot, for example, shine a red light into a fog bank and have a red streak show through the fog. On the other hand, fog does have a color. So, if you're showing fog at sunset, you can give it a pinkish cast; fog in the afternoon will tend to be an even light gray or white; and fog at night fades to black.

---

# Summary

- *Scene building* is where all the parts are put together prior to rendering an image or animation. These parts include models, textures, lights, and atmospheric effects.

- *Constraining* and *linking* enables you to establish relationships between objects in a scene.

- There are many approaches to backgrounds, including: modeling and rendering background props, importing images prior to rendering, and post-compositing an image with a background.

- Bitmap-to-model converters can extrude the gray values of a bitmap into a 3-D model.

- Terrain generators, like bitmap-to-model converters, use a bitmap or other information to generate realistic modeled terrain or "bump models."

- Perspective matching enables you to render a model so that it appears as a natural part of a scene.

- Cameras control your point of view through lens length, orientation, and depth of field.

- Atmospheric effects like fog add realism and depth cueing to a scene.

7

# Materials

I n this material world, it's no wonder that 3-D programs give you so many exotic substances to work with. It was the alchemists' calling to turn lead into gold, but 3-D enables you to do so without sorcery.

Many factors affect the surface appearance of an object; the following is only a sampling of the major ones:

- **Surface quality.** This includes color, reflectivity, transparency, smoothness, shininess, and glow.

- **Surface texture.** This includes variable colors, position, direction, and scale of objects "mapped" on a surface. Typical textures include materials such as bricks or fish scales. In addition to covering the entire surface of objects, textures can be precisely mapped to specific locations. You can, for example, place a wine label on a bottle, or a photograph in a picture frame.

- **Solid texture or grain.** Picture a cut piece of wood. Along its length, the grain is straight and roughly parallel; on the ends, the grain is in concentric circles. This quality is also found in some stones, such as marble.

- **Surface projection.** This property controls the manner in which surface textures are applied. Like latitude and longitude lines on a globe, they may shrink as they approach the poles; or like the label on a cola can, they may remain proportional all around; it's also possible to map a texture flat onto an object, so that it sticks to it like wallpaper, or to apply it in flat rectangular faces, as to the surface of a cube.

- **Bumps.** If the whole world were smooth and glossy, everything would look like plastic. Bump maps give surfaces a tactile texture or roughness. Without a bump map, if you were to wrap a photograph of bricks around a perfectly smooth surface, the smooth uninterrupted gloss of the surface would appear like brick-colored plastic shelf paper. Bump maps can be very regular, like the spaces between kitchen tiles, or irregular, like pebbles or stucco.

Most 3-D programs make it fairly easy to use materials. Normally it's merely a matter of selecting an object or group and making a few menu selections or clicking on a palette of texture thumbnails. Many textures lend themselves to detailed editing and control, but often turning lead into gold is as simple as waving your magic wand and saying "Poof! You're gold." In most cases, you can import PICT images for use as textures, so it's easy to scan a photograph of a real-world surface for addition to your materials palette. There are also many commercially available texture collections.

The exceptions to this rule are the PostScript 3-D programs which enable you to map PostScript line art—but not bitmapped artwork—onto a surface.

# Surface quality

Have you ever wondered why it's possible to look at an object and know with relative certainty what it's made of? We have come to associate certain surface qualities with particular materials. For example, a glass vase may have a very deep blue color. But if we look at it more closely, we'll find a more complex assemblage of qualities. Overall it is very dark. It doesn't reflect much of the ambient light in the room, and its deep blue color only shows in very bright light. There are very bright, sharp reflections of windows and other bright objects in the room, but we can also see some of the internal structure of the vase, as well as some of the main details on the other side of the glass, which seem bent and deformed as if seen through a lens. The vase is very smooth and glossy, but it does not give off any light of its own, so it can't be said to glow. (However, if we heated it to a very high temperature, it would glow bright red, then orange, and finally white hot.) All of these properties make up the surface quality of an object. While we usually don't think about these properties, their presence or absence provide us with the clues we use to tell what objects are made from.

When building objects in 3-D, you'll have to give some thought to the surface qualities of real-world materials, so that you can mimic them to create realistic textures. The surface qualities of an object define how it reflects light. These include color, diffuse reflection, specular reflection, ambient reflection, glow, and transparency.

Every material has a distinctive set of surface qualities that makes it unlike other materials. (This is independent of texture, which will be discussed in detail in the next section.) Consider that there are hundreds of kinds of plastic, dozens of variations of glass, and paints that achieve many different qualities. By experimenting with surface quality settings, you should be able to achieve the surface properties you're after.

When children first learn to draw and paint, they begin to identify materials by their color—a tree is green, a house is brown, a dog is black and white. But even most adults will have a hard time telling you what color chrome is. (Try asking a friend to identify the color of a mirror or of clear glass.) In fact, such objects are colorless, or nearly so. Their surface qualities are defined by other characteristics, such as reflectivity and transparency.

# How we see

We see most objects in virtue of the light they reflect. Light from a source, such as the sun, strikes a surface, is changed to some degree, and is reflected towards the eye, which reads the light and sends the information to the brain. The 3-D world is modeled after this simple process; the only difference is that the process is calculated in reverse. The computer doesn't calculate where all the light from a given source goes. Most of that light would be reflected away and would never reach the viewer anyway. Instead, the computer traces the light rays in reverse, calculating exactly what the eye sees and tracing the reflections backwards to the light sources. However, the end result is the same either way.

The way that light is reflected from a surface, and the degree to which it changes in the process, ultimately determine the appearance of a surface. Imagine throwing a rubber ball at a 45-degree angle to the ground; a person positioned to catch the ball after it bounces would "see" the ball's reflection. The angle at which light is reflected is relative to the surface *normal,* an imaginary line that is exactly perpendicular to the surface at the point of impact.

In the case of a perfect mirror reflection (see figure 7.1) the angle that light makes relative to this line as it is strikes the surface is the same both coming and going away. With other materials, this angle can change as light is scattered or deflected.

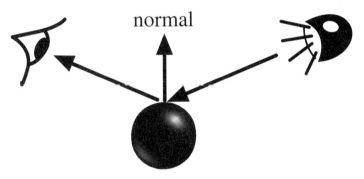

**Figure 7.1.** Light from a light source, such as a lamp, or light reflected from a distant object, strikes a surface and reflects toward the viewer. We see this reflected light.

# Color

Color is the most basic surface property. The color of a surface usually is described as the light it reflects when lit by diffuse white light (see figure 7.2). Since white light is made up of all the visible colors in the spectrum, a material's color is usually the sum of all the colors that it doesn't absorb.

In situations where the light is of a single color other than white, the object may reflect no color at all, appearing black or nearly so. The color of a material is sometimes obscured by reflection of directional light or diluted by transparency. Thus, it's not always easy to determine the true color of a surface by looking at it. For example, a wafer-thin plate of dark blue glass may appear to be very pale blue, while a thick plate of the same material may appear almost black in equal light. Meanwhile, blue plastic with a matte finish that is non-reflective and completely opaque will look "blue" in most lighting conditions.

Astronomers and chemists, in fact, know that materials reflect and emit many different colors of light, depending on what's happening to them. They use spectrometers and other color-sensitive devices to locate and identify different materials—in both outer space and in test tubes.

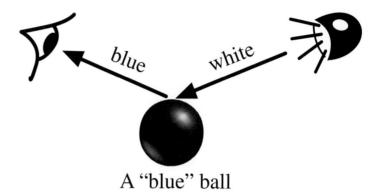

A "blue" ball

**Figure 7.2.** White light strikes a surface and blue light is reflected. This, by definition, is a "blue" surface.

# Mirror reflection

*Mirror reflectance* (often called just "reflection") is a special case of directional reflectance: when light is reflected at the same angle and intensity relative to the surface normal, and when the reflected light is non-diffuse, the result is a mirror image (see figure 7.3). Unlike dull-finished metal, a mirror is very smooth, and even weak directional light rays bounce off in an orderly fashion. Mirror reflection is the extent to which all light is reflected in a coherent manner from the object's surface.

An object with a very high degree of mirror reflectivity will reflect even dimly-lit objects, while an object with low mirror reflectivity may reflect only the brightest parts of objects. Objects with high reflectance tend to be highly polished and hard, although some liquids, such as water, can also be highly reflective under certain conditions. Usually you can express mirror reflectance in terms of a percentage: a looking glass reflects very close to 100% of the light that strikes it, while a plate glass window (which isn't coated with silver on one side) reflects around 10%.

Some surfaces are highly reflective at oblique angles—water, for example. If you look straight down into a fountain, you are likely to see all of the pennies at the bottom, but if you look towards the far edge of the fountain, you may see only a reflection of blue sky. Though the physics are different, this is like skipping a stone on water—if you throw the stone straight down, it will splash and disappear, but if you skim it across, it will glance off the surface and sail back into the air.

Some materials alter the color of light, even as they reflect it. A mirror made of polished copper, for example, will reflect a scene accurately, but will give the scene an orange cast.

Highly reflective materials include mirrored glass or plastic, smooth chrome and silver, polished wood, and silver mylar (see figure 7.4). Objects with only a small amount of mirror reflectance include polished marble, white china, a television tube (when it's turned off), and glossy Scotch tape.

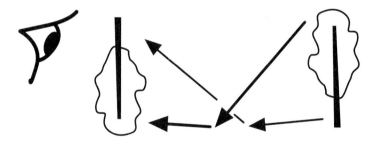

**Figure 7.3.** Light striking a mirror is reflected in a coherent manner. The path of light to and from a reflective surface accounts for the fact that reflections are inverted when they reach the observer.

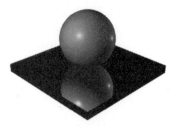

**Figure 7.4.** Making a surface reflective causes it to appear hard and smooth.

## Specular reflection

*Specular reflection* (sometimes called *glint*) is the directional reflection of a directional light source, near to but not quite in the mirror direction (see figure 7.5). The effect is that of a more or less blurred mirror reflection. This is why light sources such as square windows will cause a square specular highlight on a metal surface.

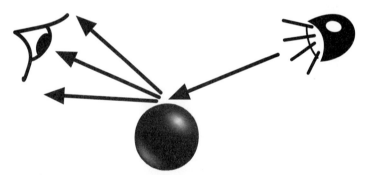

**Figure 7.5.** Specular reflection reflects light in directions slightly different from the mirror reflection.

Some surfaces, such as glass and plastic, have a specular quality that reflects light in its original color. In these materials, shining a white light on the surface results in a white highlight. Metals, on the other hand, have specular highlights that reflect the base color of the metal. Shine a white light on a 24 karat gold sphere and the specular reflection will be brilliant yellow. This is one of the distinguishing properties that defines the appearance of metals. Shine a white light on carbon steel (often called "blue steel") and the specular highlight is pale blue. To some degree specular reflection retains the shape of the light source distorted by the reflecting surface. A square light, for example, is reflected as a square highlight. This effect is often seen in photographs of people, where one or more small round lights are reflected in the model's eyes. The smoother and shinier the surface, the smaller and more perfect the specular reflection (see figure 7.6).

**Figure 7.6.** Specular reflection is responsible for the size and accuracy of the highlight reflection.

While specular reflection is a disorderly case of mirror reflectance, even renderers that don't use ray tracing allow for some degree of simulated specular reflection, usually in the form of a round highlight for each light source. Without specular highlights, surfaces tend to look soft and dull, while specular highlights are a strong visual clue to the identity of a surface.

# Diffuse reflection

*Diffuse reflectance* describes the amount that a surface scatters directional light in all directions (see figure 7.7). This gives objects the appearance of dullness or softness.

This type of reflection occurs when light penetrates a surface slightly, then is scattered back out in a random fashion, often with a new color. Objects with a high degree of diffuse reflectance are very evenly shaded from highlight to shadow. Objects with low diffuse reflectance appear hard and smooth and have a very abrupt transition from highlight to shadow. Low diffuse reflectance usually accounts for "dark" surfaces. Chalk, concrete and leather are all examples of high-diffuse materials. Black velvet and polished ebony are examples of low diffusion textures. Diffuse reflection is primarily responsible for the apparent color of objects.

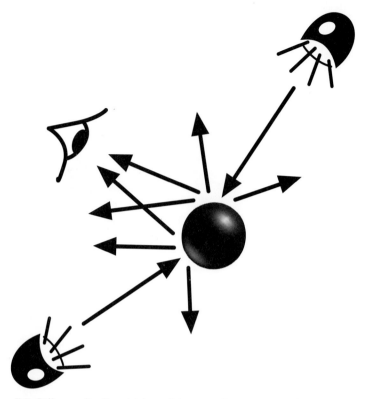

**Figure 7.7.** Diffuse reflection. Light striking a surface is widely scattered. At every point on a surface, the observer sees light reflected from many different directions. The result is a uniformly blurred or "diffuse" surface. Diffuse reflection is primarily responsible for what we see as the overall color of a surface.

# Ambient reflection

*Ambient reflectance* is the degree to which a surface reflects incidental light coming from every direction (see figure 7.8). An object with high ambient reflectance will tend to have soft shadows, while one that does not catch ambient light will have deeper, hard shadows.

In the real world, particularly during daylight hours, there is a tremendous amount of ambient light being scattered around. That's why you can see clearly in the shade of a giant elm tree on a sunny day. Some objects, such as the pages of the book you're reading under the tree, have a very high ambient reflectance, that is, they easily scatter and reflect even faint indirect light. On the other hand, some objects show their colors only when lighted by strong direct light.

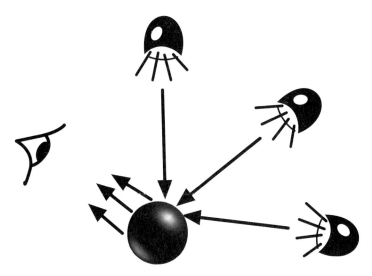

**Figure 7.8.** Ambient reflectance is the degree to which diffuse light is scattered away from the mirror direction. The more ambient reflectance, the higher the likelihood that light coming from many different directions will reach the viewer.

If very even, incidental light coming from every direction can light the surface, it has high ambient reflectance (paper, cotton, and acrylic paint are common examples). On the other hand, if the object is nearly black unless held in direct sunlight, it has a low ambient reflectance (for example, deeply colored glass, or glossy black paint).

# Transparency

*Transparency* is the capability of light to pass through a surface (see figure 7.9). Glass, air, and water are all highly transparent. Some plastic is also transparent, as are many gemstones, including diamond. A material that is somewhat transparent but is too opaque or deeply colored to transmit light clearly is called *translucent*. A tree leaf is translucent; so is a sheet of paper, colored plastic, glass, and the skin between your fingers, if you hold them up to a bright flashlight.

**Figure 7.9.** Transparency is the tranmission of light through a material.

As with reflection, transparent materials often change the color of light as it passes through. Stained glass is an attractive example of this effect. Try holding a colored bottle between a white wall and a white light and note the color of the shadow that strikes the surface. (In real life, the glass absorbs certain colors and transmits others; renderers simulate this effect by changing light's color and intensity as it's transmitted.)

Like reflection, transparency can be specified as a percentage, with air being 100 percent transparent and plate steel being totally opaque or 0 percent transparent.

> **Tip**
> In nature, total reflection and total transparency never exceed 100 percent of the total light striking a surface (unless it is glowing). In an extreme example, you can't have perfectly clear glass that also reflects like a perfect mirror. Some 3-D programs let you get away with this, but it isn't realistic. Sometimes, however, the trick can be used to interesting effect.

# Refraction

*Refraction* is the bending of light as it passes through a transparent surface (see figure 7.10). This quality is responsible for the optical properties of a lens or magnifying glass. Refraction is also apparent when you look at a room through a glass of water. Light is bent once as it passes through one side of the glass, again as it enters and exits the water and again as it passes through the far wall of the glass.

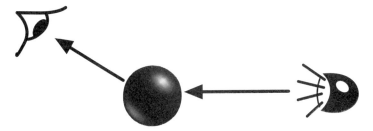

**Figure 7.10.** Refraction changes the direction of the light.

The amount that light bends as it passes through any given material is defined by a standard number called the "index of refraction." Air has an index of refraction of 1.0, meaning it doesn't refract at all; glass has an index of refraction of 1.2 to 1.9; water has an index of 1.33 (1.30 for ice); and diamond has an index of 2.4. Refraction is a fairly subtle effect, but it is an effective clue to a material's composition.

Because of its nature—the bending of light rays—refraction is only calculated in ray-traced renderings. It is not supported in Gouraud or Phong shading.

Refraction is an over-simplification of the bending of light. Transparent materials to some degree also *diffract* light—that is, different colors of light bend different amounts as they pass through a surface. This is how a crystal prism works, with the result that white light passing through the prism is split into a rainbow. Even sophisticated ray tracers, to date, don't attempt to recreate this effect.

# Glow

*Glow* is the degree to which a surface appears to emit light (see figure 7.11). This light is added to the light reflected from the surface, often to the point where the reflected light is overwhelmed. In 3-D applications a glow is not the same as a true light for the simple reason that it does not cast light onto other objects.

In Electric Image Animation System, the only Mac 3-D application with visible lights sources, you can set a light to glow, but not cast light; or to cast light, but not glow. It can also be set to do both, in which case it looks like a sphere (or tube) brightly lighted in the middle and fading towards the edges. EIAS, like other 3-D programs, does not support glowing models casting light onto other surfaces.

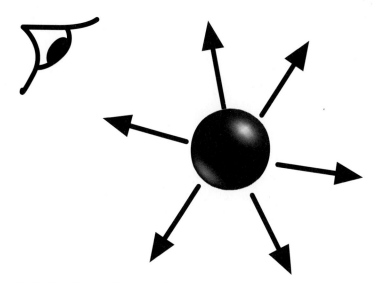

**Figure 7.11.** Glow is not a form of reflection at all. Objects that are heated to great temperatures, excited by electricity, or radioactive emit light of their own.

# Texture maps

While some materials, particularly plastic and paint, have a uniform appearance across a surface, it is much more common for objects to have great variations in color: veins of marble, grains of granite, blades of grass, ripples of water, spatters of paint, or swirls of oil on water. Often a single "texture" is made up of many small parts (such as ceramic tiles) or an agglomeration of material (such as granite) that would be impossible to model separately. These textures exceed the descriptive power of simple color and reflectance. Even seemingly uniform surfaces like painted wood have a texture when viewed up close; the brush strokes and the imperfections in the mixing of paint conspire to make a finely detailed surface. Brushed aluminum, dented chrome, and smoke-damaged paint are all surfaces that benefit from details and textures that go beyond simple surface qualities. Consider a brick wall. It is possible to model hundreds of bricks and to stack them up, with mortar, one by one, as does a real brick wall. However, this would be terribly time-consuming. (In fact, it would probably be quicker to go out and lay real bricks!)

Three-D programs offer a combination of techniques, loosely called *texture mapping,* which can accurately describe complex surfaces. In its simplest form, texture mapping stretches a photographic image as if it were a rubber sheet stretched around a object, so that it fits to every curve and corner. This makes the object appear to be composed of the materials in the texture image.

But texture mapping involves more than choosing an image and pointing at the object to receive the texture. Bricks aren't four feet long, nor are they laid on end; and a photo of bricks may contain only eight bricks, while the object being texture mapped needs hundreds. These considerations call for the control of position, scale, direction, and tiling of textures.

In some cases you will want the bricks to wrap around a cylinder, while on a sphere you may want them laid in concentric circles like the latitude lines on a globe; or you may want them simply laid out like a sheet. These different methods are defined by mapping projections.

# Seamless textures

A seamless texture is a scanned photograph or painted image whose top edge precisely matches its bottom edge, and whose left edge matches the right. This enables you to place many tiles edge-to-edge without a visible seam between them. Typical seamless textures are bricks and other masonry, grass, carpeting, or hammered metal. Any surface that has a regularly repeated pattern (or such a complex pattern that you can't tell that it's repeated) is a good candidate for a tiled texture. Another advantage of this approach is that you can use a relatively small image file to cover all of a large model without a great loss of texture quality.

Using Adobe Photoshop and other image editing programs with a "cloning brush," it's fairly easy to create your own detailed seamless textures (see "Creating textures," in this chapter). Kai's Power Tools, from HSC software, provides an unlimited source of abstract seamless textures.

There are a number of seamless texture collections available on CD-ROM, such as Wraptures, from Form and Function, and the 3-D Expert Collection, from the Alpha Channel.

The Mac 3-D Workshop CD-ROM contains a collection of seamless textures from Alpha Channel Multimedia that include matching bump maps.

# Color mapping

The simplest form of texture mapping is to simply wrap an existing 2-D image around a 3-D model. This image can be a bitmapped illustration created in a paint program, a scanned photo, or even a mathematically generated image created on the fly.

You'll use color mapping any time you want a modeled surface to have a "skin" of more than a single color. The following is a small sample of things you could use color maps for:

- Painting details on a wall.

- Adding stripes, polka dots or other regular patterns to a surface.

- Placing labels on boxes, cans, and other package designs.

- Putting rivets on the edges of steel panels.

- Painting a banana.

- Putting a "skin" on a surface, such as fur, scales, spots or stripes.

- Putting grass in a front yard or moss on a rolling stone.

## Position

Most scene builders allow you to apply a texture beginning in one location on a surface and ending at another (see figure 7.12). Imagine that you have a texture resembling a tapestry hanging on a wall. It wouldn't do to have it wrapped across the corner between two walls, or draped over the top of the wall like a towel on a rack.

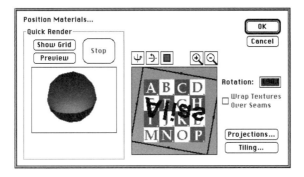

**Figure 7.12.** Alias' Sketch! Texture mapping dialog enables you to set direction, projection, scale and tiling of textures.

A common example of the need for positioning textures is in industrial product designs. You need to be able to place a label precisely on a shampoo bottle, or a logo in the right spot on a stereo's front panel.

For the illustrator or animator, creative positioning of textures can put rust on a pipe joint, or rivets on the seams of a ship. These details go a long way towards adding realism.

# Scale

The scale of textures in 3-D is as important as the size of fonts used in book publishing. Kitchen tiles are normally about six inches square. You'll get a strange looking counter top if you surface it with tiles that appear to be two feet square. Likewise, gravel the size of boulders or bricks the size of postage stamps will cause confusion. Most 3-D programs that support texture mapping allow you to set the scale of the texture so that it matches the scale of your models (see figure 7.13). In some cases, scale is handled by adjusting the tiling. For example, if you specify that there should be 40 copies of the brick mapped to fill the wall, the brick texture will automatically be scaled to fit.

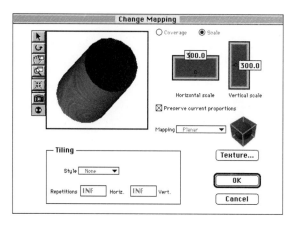

**Figure 7.13.** StrataStudio Pro has a graphical interface for positioning, scaling, tiling, and orienting textures.

# Tiling

It's common to use a single "seamless" texture of limited size, and to place it, over and over, edge-to-edge. *Tiling,* as this technique is called, is akin to laying many tiles on a floor or counter. This is useful if you have a texture that isn't big enough to cover a surface at a certain scale; you can tile it several times so that it covers the object completely with multiple repetitions. A tiled texture could be as simple as a single polka dot, or it could be an elaborately disguised seamless texture repeated over and over on the surface. Tiling is an extremely fast and effective method of texture mapping because the image being mapped is small and it only has to be loaded into memory once.

# Direction

A common use of textures is to map a label onto a package. It's possible to map this same label in many orientations: standing on either end, upside down, or backwards. Obviously, it's important to align it in the right direction. A more subtle application of direction is wood grain. The grain of wood always runs lengthwise. It would look awfully strange to have it run in the short direction. With wood and other *procedural textures,* this is particularly crucial because these textures have a grain that resembles that of real wood—that is, they are different on the sides than on the ends.

Fortunately, most 3-D programs have some sort of alignment preview which enables you to pinpoint and change a texture's alignment before you create a final rendering. Generally, a texture is applied using the position of the object in the current window as a reference, mapping the texture in normal upright orientation, but this varies from program to program.

# Projections

There are many different ways to apply a texture to a surface. Essentially, techniques have one thing in common: the texture is either applied as a flexible sheet or projected as if from a slide projector. This is analogous to what map makers do when they build a globe of the earth. The rubber sheet metaphor takes several forms; the more complex projections, like cylindrical, cubic and spherical, treat the map like shrink wrap that is uniformly shrunk from every direction until it sticks to the model. Usually, these different techniques are used for texture mapping correspondingly-shaped objects. For example, you would use spherical mapping if you wanted to apply a texture to a grapefruit, while you would use cubic mapping to apply a surface to all the sides of a box. A combination of careful design when building a texture and the use of the right mapping technique makes it possible to very precisely apply surfaces to objects. In the example of a cereal box, more powerful 3-D programs make it possible to create a texture with the appropriate cut-outs so that a single texture will precisely cover all the surfaces of the box.

While projections are usually used to map surfaces onto corresponding shapes (for example, cylindrical mapping is used mostly for cylinders) it's possible to use the "wrong" mapping techniques to achieve interesting effects. Planar mapping a label onto a sphere, for example, will stretch the label onto the round surface of one side of the sphere.

# Planar mapping

The simplest form of texture mapping is *planar.* This uses a flat sheet through which the model is pushed (see figure 7.14). Imagine doing this with a cube: the front face will receive an undistorted projection of the texture, as if you were projecting a slide on a screen. In general, planar mapping is reserved for putting flat objects onto more-or-less flat surfaces. It is often used for labels, as well as for basic mappings such as putting a painting in a frame.

**Figure 7.14.** Planar mapping enables you to apply texture onto flat surfaces without distortion, as on the front face of the cube, but it can also be used to create interesting effects on surfaces that aren't flat.

**Tip**
Planar mapping enables you to very precisely apply fine details to a model, such as a wall. You begin by generating a rendering of the surface from an orthogonal projection. Then paint over this rendering in a 2-D paint program. If you then import the image back into the 3-D program and map it to the wall using planar mapping, you should be able to match details precisely to the shape of the object.

# Making a box label

This example uses planar mapping to apply a label to a candy box. The hexagonal candy box in this example was created in StrataStudio Pro and the texture map was generated using a combination of Adobe Illustrator and Adobe Photoshop.

1. Draw a hexagon in Adobe Illustrator (version 5.0 has a filter that will do this automatically) (see figure 7.15). Save this plain shape as an Illustrator outline for later use, then decorate the shape with a border and artwork and save this.

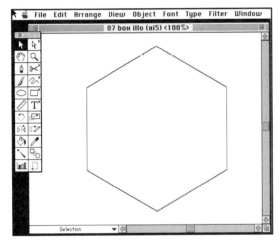

**Figure 7.15.** Create a hexagonal outline in Illustrator.

2. In Adobe Photoshop, place the decorated artwork in a new image file and render it in to the image. Crop it close to the edges and save it as a PICT file (see figure 7.16).

3. In StrataStudio Pro, import the hexagon, convert it to a filled shape, and extrude it with a bevel. Add a table, if you'd like something to catch shadows in the image, but make sure to switch views to rotate postion instead of rotating the model.

4. Switch back to the front view and open the Textures editor and select New Texture (see figure 7.17). Click on the Color Map button; this will open the Get Picture dialog box (see figure 7.18). Import the PICT file you created by rendering your Illustrator document in Photoshop.

**Figure 7.16.** The finished PICT that will be used for the label.

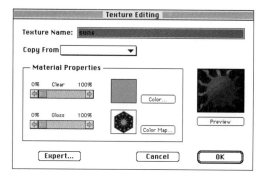

**Figure 7.17.** Creating a new texture in StrataStudio Pro.

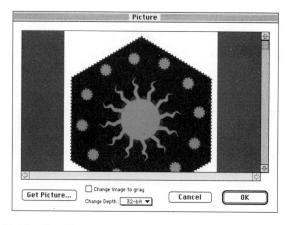

**Figure 7.18.** The Get Picture dialog box.

5. Open the Projections dialog box (see figure 7.19) to make sure the texture is mapped with planar projection and covers the box surface. This is also your chance to change the positioning of the texture, if necessary.

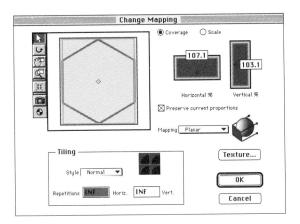

**Figure 7.19.** The Projections dialog box enables you to ensure that the texture will cover the box surface.

6. Position the model, set lighting, and render the image (see figure 7.20).

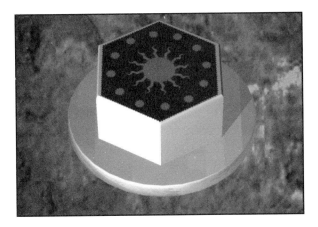

**Figure 7.20.** The final image.

# Cubic mapping

In *cubic* mapping, the texture is applied in the shape of a box (see figure 7.21). This is usually used for mapping textures onto boxes and other cubic box-shaped objects, such as the walls of a house.

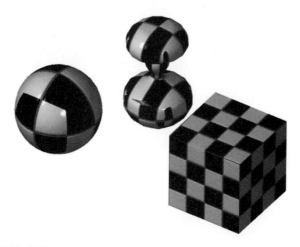

**Figure 7.21.** Cubic mapping applies the texture to all sides of a box. Compare with planar mapping, shown in figure 7.15.

# Parametric mapping

*Parametric* (sometimes called *proportional*) mapping attempts to adjust the texture to the shape of the object in different locations (see figure 7.22). This mapping method is best when you're texturing a surface that has lots of variations in size and you want the details of the texture to vary with it.

# Cylindrical mapping

*Cylindrical* mapping wraps the texture around the object like a label around a cola can (see figure 7.23). Some programs let you specify cylindrical mapping with end caps, meaning that the texture is mapped around the surface in a circular fashion, and round cut-outs of the texture are placed on the ends.

**Figure 7.22.** Sketch!'s unusual parametric texture mapping. Surfaces are stretched to fit various parts of the models.

**Figure 7.23.** Cylindrical mapping wraps a texture around an object.

# Spherical mapping

*Spherical* mapping is like that which is used to put the surface of the earth on a globe (see figure 7.24). In this method, textures shrink at the ends (or poles) and stretch at the center (or equator). This method is useful for mapping textures onto spherical or otherwise rounded objects.

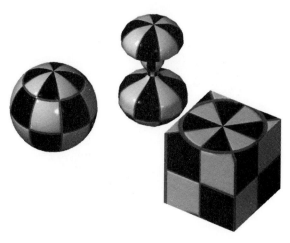

**Figure 7.24.** Spherical mapping applies a texture evenly around a sphere.

# 3-D painting

Two 3-D programs have new approaches to texture mapping: StrataStudio Pro enables you to "paint" on a model as it's being rendered; RayDream's Designer allows you to draw and paint on a model's surface in real-time.

## RayPainting

Strata's new StrataStudio Pro offers a new kind of rendering, called "RayPainting." Instead of realistically rendering objects in a model, RayPainting renders objects with simulated strokes of paint. This is much faster than ray tracing or Phong shading, because the technique uses fairly wide impressionistic strokes to render an image (see figure 7.25). One of the unique effects of this technique is that the edges of objects are displaced by the brush strokes, creating the effect of procedural fur and other rough textures.

RayPainting uses ray tracing as its starting point, so images you create with the technique can have mirror reflections and transparency as part of the effect.

**Figure 7.25.** These "fur" bananas were rendered with StrataStudio Pro's RayPainting system. Notice that the edges of the objects are displaced, unlike with normal rendering methods.

# Designer's painting

Once you have defined a shape in RayDream Designer, you can easily paint or draw directly on its surface. If you draw a rectangle on an irregular surface, for example, you can export the rectangle to a program like Photoshop for the addition of fine details. Designer automatically re-imports this modified image into its original position on the model.

You can even use Photoshop-compatible plug-ins in Designer. For instance, you could have Kai's Power Tools textures automatically applied to the surface of a model (or within the boundaries of a painted texture map.

This is currently the closest thing to painting a real model with real paints.

# The G-buffer

One thing that RayDream is evangalizing since the introduction of Designer 3.0 is a file format that incorporates a "G-buffer." Just as an alpha channel can be used to carry transparency information along with an image, an 8-bit grayscale image could also be used to carry depth information. If a paint package such as Photoshop or Painter, or an animation program such as After Effects, makes use of this depth information, it would enable a user to paint in between objects, or to have painting affect a 3-D image differently as you paint over different "depths" of the image. You could easily add realistic fog using an airbrush tool, for example, or use a blur filter to create depth-of-field effects.

The G-buffer may even be able to carry lighting information through to a paint package, so that you can paint on an object's surface while maintaining realistic shading. Time will tell whether the creators of paint and animation programs will embrace this new format.

# Bump maps

Bump maps are a special type of texture map, which are often used in unison with regular texture maps. A *bump map* creates the effect of bumps on an object's surface. Bump maps begin as simple grayscale images, such as a series of soft-edged black polka dots on a white background to simulate a golf ball texture. When you use this texture as a bump map, the renderer interprets the dots as depressions in the surface of the object. Light will reflect and cast shadows as you would expect if there are actually dents in the surface. Usually, you can choose to have either the light or dark areas rendered as depressions. But even if the application forces you to use one or the other, most image editing applications will let you create a negative (inverted) image to step around this problem.

Figures 7.26, 7.27, and 7.28 show a texture, its associated bump map, and the result of using them in a rendering.

Imagine mapping an image of kitchen tiles onto a 3-D countertop. If this is accompanied by a bump map of a grid of lines where the grout between the tiles should be, the surface will not only have the qualities of the tiled surface, but it will appear to have grooved depressions between each tile.

**Figure 7.26.** A texture used to create a bump map.

**Figure 7.27.** The bump map created from the texture in figure 7.26.

**Figure 7.28.** The bump map from figure 7.27 as applied to a sphere.

In many instances, you won't need a color map at all if you use a bump map. Stucco on a wall, for example, is a continuous color of a rather flat material. By applying a bump map that simulates the rough texture of the surface, you can achieve a very realistic stucco imitation.

Renderers rely on the direction of the vectors that define a surface ("normals") to determine the quality and direction of reflected light. Bump maps trick the renderer by changing the direction of the surface normal based on the bump map (see figure 7.29). While the actual surface normal of a point on a countertop aims straight up, a bump map sets the normal to tilt more or less to one side (the actual direction is determined by comparing one point on the bump map to a small square of adjacent points). When the render goes to shade this point, it does so based on the tilted normal.

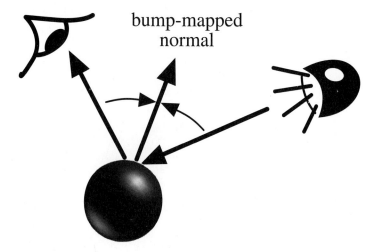

bump-mapped
normal

**Figure 7.29.** A bump map tilts the surface normal, causing light to be reflected in the wrong direction. This causes an optical illusion of a bump in the surface.

For some subtle effects, the result of a bump map is every bit as realistic as rendering a modeled bump (since the renderer, in effect, doesn't know the difference). The primary limitation of bump maps compared to modeling details is that bump maps lose the illusion of modeled texture at the edges of modeled surfaces, and at the edges of the "bumps" themselves (see figure 7.30). Where you would expect to see a serrated surface at the edges of a golf ball, a bump-mapped surface instead appears perfectly smooth.

The CD-ROM contains a sampling of ready-made bump maps you can try out in your 3-D application. These include pitted metal, brushed aluminum, golf ball dimples, riveted plates, and non-skid floor.

**Figure 7.30.** Even though this bump-mapped sphere looks bumpy, its smooth edges belie the fact that bump mapping is a trick.

# Bump mapping type on a plain surface

One of the simplest and most effective uses of bump mapping is the rendering of embossed or stamped type on a surface. This example uses Photoshop and StrataStudio Pro, but most 3-D programs that offer texture mapping also allow for bump mapping. The procedure for using a bump map is almost the same as for any other texture map.

1. Begin by creating a grayscale image of black-on-white text in Photoshop (see figure 7.31). Use the **Blur More** filter to blur the image. This will give the bump mapped object a soft beveled edge, instead of hard corners. Save this image as a PICT.

2. Open StrataStudio Pro and build a simple model by drawing an outline in the front view, clicking the extrude button, setting an extrusion depth, and clicking OK (see figure 7.32).

3. Create a new texture in the Textures window. Give the texture a medium gray tombstone color. Click on the **Expert** button (see figure 7.33) and enter 20 in the **Bump Amplitude** box (this scales the degree to which the bump map affects the image). Click on the **Bump** box in the scrolling effects window. In the Load Image dialog box, select the PICT file you created in Photoshop. Exit the Textures dialog box.

# R.I.P.
## HERE LIES
# CASEY JONES
## NUTHIN' LEFT
## BUT THESE HERE
## BONES

**Figure 7.31.** Create the text in Photoshop and save it as a PICT. The soft edges will give the bump map a beveled edge.

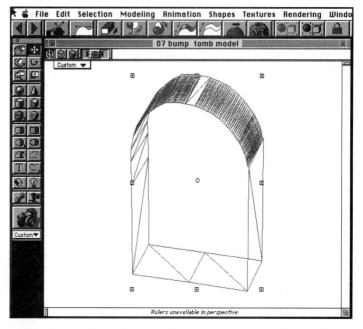

**Figure 7.32.** Creating the object to which the bump map will be applied.

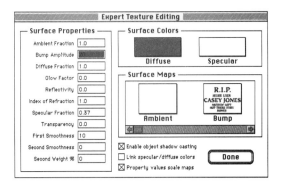

**Figure 7.33.** Give the bump map an amplitude of 20.

4. With the model still selected, open the **Projections** dialog box and set the projection to **Planar**. Adjust the scale so that the ghost figure of the texture fills an appropriate area on the model (see figure 7.34).

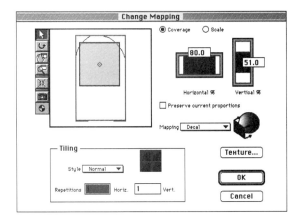

**Figure 7.34.** Position the ghost figure of the bump map on the model.

5. Exit, set your lights and viewpoint, and render the image (see figure 7.35).

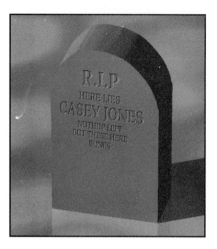

**Figure 7.35.** The rendered image. Note how the bump map gives the appearance of chiseled letters.

# Surface maps

Just as you can apply an image to a surface to create a texture, more powerful 3-D applications enable you to apply a texture that does nothing more than modify one or more of a surface's qualities. These textures are usually in the form of grayscale images. The brightness values in the image are used to increase or decrease a given quality in the object. For example, you can map a piece of black and white type onto a sphere's surface, and everywhere the type is mapped to the surface it will be highly reflective; where the map is white the surface won't change at all. You could apply this same map to the glow channel of the object, and the surface will glow brightly everywhere the type is mapped onto the surface.

Effects maps are used the same way as bump maps, in that they affect the degree to which a surface property is emphasized.

You could use this technique to create a globe where only the continents are opaque and the rest is transparent. Mapping type as a reflection map can create the effect of foil or mirrored type. In some programs, it can also be used for transparency, specular reflectance, and glow.

There area a number of programs that support surface-quality mapping, including:

- Infini-D
- Sketch! (transparency)
- Electric Image Animation System
- StrataVision 3d
- StrataStudio Pro
- Sculpt 3-D

# Glowing neon

To create the effect of light emitted from a neon sign in StrataVision 3d, you can map a soft-edged glow map onto a wall or other object near the neon light. It will appear as though the glow is light cast by the glowing light.

1. In Photoshop, build a black on white logo, as shown in figure 7.36 (its shape should roughly match the size of the wall you'll map it to). Save this for later use. Invert the image so you have a white-on-black type logo and save it. (This image is 300 pixels square.)

**Figure 7.36.** Creating the logo in Photoshop.

2. Blur the texture map extensively so that the white shape has a soft edge all around, and save it at the same resolution (see figure 7.37). This will be used as the glow map on your backdrop wall.

**Figure 7.37.** Blur the logo in Photoshop.

3. In StrataVision 3d, build a simple model of a wall in a front view and give it a dark color. In the same view, import the black on white PICT. When you import it, it will automatically be converted to an extruded model. Switch to a side or top view to move this model in front of the wall (see figure 7.38).

**Figure 7.38.** Importing the glow map into StrataVision 3d.

4. Select the wall model and create a new texture. Give the texture a dark color (the darker your texture color, the more the glow map will appear to glow) and use the blurred PICT file as a glow map (see figure 7.39). Set the glow factor to a value of 5.

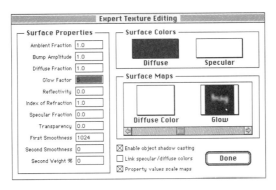

**Figure 7.39.** Use a glow factor of 5 for the glow map.

5. Render the scene (see figure 7.40).

**Figure 7.40.** The rendered scene.

237

# Labels

A label is nothing more than a texture map which covers part of another texture. This is commonly used for packaging designs, where you want a surface applied over another surface.

---

### Progams that support texture layers

The ability to layer multiple textures, one atop the other, is extremely useful and powerful. For example, you can create a label out of gold foil type that can be overlaid on a granite surface. In programs that don't support multiple textures on a surface, you'll have to create a separate model to accomodate the gold type—and this may not work if the underlying model is very complex. To date, only a handful of 3-D programs allow you to do this. They include:

- Electric Image Animation System

- Infini-D

- Sculpt 3-D

- Presenter Professional

- RayDream Designer

---

For programs that support surface quality maps, but not multiple texture layers, you can create a single texture out of composited images, then create surface quality maps to modify parts of the texture. For, example, you might use a reflection map to make part of the texture mirror-like.

To use an illustration created in a program like Adobe Illustrator, Aldus FreeHand or Deneba's Canvas (or other 2-D illustration programs) as a label, you'll first have to save it in a format that can be used by the 3-D application. (See "Making a box label," in this chapter.) In general this means PICT, although as described in the section on 3-D PostScript, addDepth and Dimensions enable you to use an Illustrator-type EPS file as a label. To use a PICT in Electric Image Animation System, you have to first use the file translator, Transporter, to convert the PICT into an "Image" format file.

# Procedural shading

*Procedural shading* is more sophisticated than simple images wrapped around surfaces. Wood, for example, has a long, wavy, relatively straight grain along the long cut of a board. On the ends, the grain is a section of concentric circles—the growth rings of the tree (see figure 7.41). Marble has a similar effect, in that the grain along the side of a piece of marble is continued from the front face to the sides of a piece of the stone. Because procedural shaders act on volumes, rather than surfaces, they are sometimes called *volume shaders* or *solid shaders*.

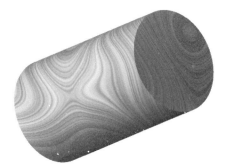

**Figure 7.41.** The grain of procedural wood shaders adapts to the geometry of an object. This wood, renered in StrataStudio Pro, has continuous grain around the object's corners.

## Procedural shaders

The following renderers have procedural shading options:

- RayDream Designer
- StrataVision 3d
- StrataStudio Pro
- Shade II
- Presenter Professonal
- Sculpt 3-D
- MacRenderMan

Fortunately, 3-D programs do not require you to understand the underlying procedures; those that support procedural shading come with a simple editing interface which allows you to modify and orient the texture. Most wood shaders allow you to modify the base and grain colors, as well as the tightness and waviness of the grain (see figure 7.42).

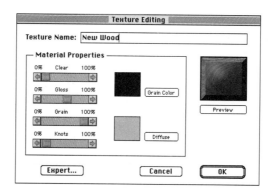

**Figure 7.42.** StrataStudio Pro's configuration controls for a procedural wood shader.

Pixar's RenderMan specializes in the use of procedural textures more diverse than wood and marble. RenderMan shaders exist, for example, for dragon skin, flaking paint, and gravel. Unlike bump maps, these procedural shaders create real displacement (see RenderMan, later in this chapter).

# Adding textures

Most 3-D applications that support sophisticated texture mapping also ship with a library of textures. Typically, these will include bricks, marble, glass, granite, chrome, and a few other stones and metals. It's inevitable, however, that you'll want to add new textures to the mix. For instance, if you're creating an outdoor scene, you may want to add crab grass, tree bark or frog skin. None of these is likely to come with the standard package.

There are several options for adding textures to your library shelf: you can purchase texture libraries from 3-D and clip-art vendors, modify existing textures to get new effects, or create your own textures by scanning, painting or synthetically generating them.

---

**Tip**

It's important to consider the size and resolution of the textures you plan to use. If you are creating a 640-by-480-pixel image, the largest texture map you're likely to need is one that's as large, in pixels, as the background (640 by 480). However, many models take up only a fraction of the total image, and there's little reason to use a large, high-resolution image for tiling onto your model at very small sizes, as this will take up lots of extra computer resources and result in long rendering times. Since the Macintosh QuickDraw and most renderers work at 72 dpi, you'll want your texture maps to be 72 dpi in resolution, or just over it. Ideally, you'll also want them to be just slightly larger than their finished rendered size, although for 3-D objects, this often becomes a game of guessing. A small extra margin of size and resolution ensures that the texture will fill the intended space without being stretched and "pixelizing." However, different 3-D programs treat the size and resolution settings of a PICT graphic differently, so you'll have to consult the software documentation and vendor for specific recommendations. Creating an environment map for reflections also requires a bit of experimenting. Often, you can imitate the size and resolutions of textures and environments provided with your 3-D application.

---

# Texture libraries

Most 3-D vendors sell add-on texture libraries which supplement the basics. Often these will combine surfaces with bump maps, so you get a complete texture rather than just photograph to wrap around the subject. Seamless textures sold for use as background fills are particularly well suited to the task and can save you a lot of preparatory work. Simple photographic background collections make excellent backdrops for 3-D scenes but they can also be called into service as the starting point for building textures. By editing supplied textures, you can create your own variations.

The CD-ROM that's included with this book contains a sample collection from The Alpha Channel's 3-D Expert Series. These include a selection of complimentary backgrounds, textures, bump maps, and environment maps which will enable 3-D users to create a huge variety of 3-D images.

# Creating textures

There are several ways you can create you own 3-D textures. You can begin with a scanned-in photograph of a material, you can paint or draw a texture in a program such as Fractal's Painter or Adobe Photoshop, or you can use a texture generator such as Kai's Power Tools (a Photoshop plug-in) to create a texture for you.

## Textures with bump maps

If you plan to create a bump map to go with an image texture, you'll often want to make them at the same time, as the information they contain is usually closely related. For example, if you are scanning in a photograph of a leaf pile to use as a texture, you may want to save a high contrast, grayscale version of the same image to use as a bump map. This will allow you to map the dark spaces between leaves as depressions in the texture's surface.

# A seamless texture for Sketch!

To create your own seamless textures in Photoshop, the goal is to make an image whose left edge is the same as its right and whose top edge is the same as its bottom. This is easy if you're putting a single shape on a solid background and the shape doesn't touch the edge of the image, otherwise, use the following technique:

1. In Photoshop, create a square texture of 200 by 200 pixels. This can be a painted image, a scanned-in image, or a texture from a CD-ROM. Displace the entire image 20 pixels down and 20 pixels over (using **Filter, Other, Offset**). Be sure to use the **Wrap Around** option (see figure 7.43).

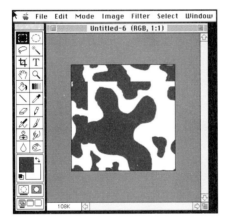

**Figure 7.43.** Use the **Offset** filter with the **Wrap Around** option to displace the texture.

2. Use Photoshop's Rubber Stamp tool to clone away the seams created by displacement (see figure 7.44). Be sure not to touch the edges of the texture. Save this image as a PICT.

3. Open a model in Sketch!. Choose the **Materials** command, and select **New Texture**. Click on the color box and load the new PICT you've created (see figure 7.45).

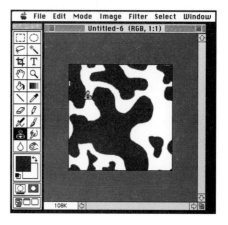

**Figure 7.44.** Use the Rubber Stamp tool to remove the seams—but don't alter the edges!

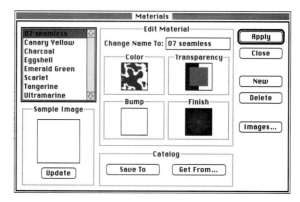

**Figure 7.45.** Load the PICT as a new texture.

4. In the **Position Material** dialog box, choose **Mapping** and select **Spherical** from the pull-down menu (see figure 7.46).

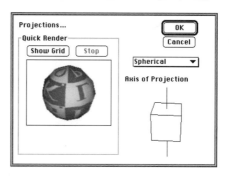

**Figure 7.46.** Selecting a spherical mapping for the texture.

5. Render the image (see figure 7.47).

**Figure 7.47.** The final rendered image. No seams!

# Kai's Power Tools

Kai's Power Tools (KPT) is an accessory product that runs within Photoshop (or other programs that support Photoshop plug-ins, such as Equillibrium's DeBabelizer). It's one of the most useful tools available to the 3-D user. The collection of tools enables you to easily create a huge variety of seamless textures, environments, and backgrounds. It also has the controls needed to create bump maps that neatly complement textures. Most useful among the tools is the Texture Explorer. This is a program with a unique "gene-tree" interface which allows you to create a virtually unlimited number of natural- and supernatural-looking seamless textures without painting.

To use the KPT Texture Explorer:

1. Create a new document in Photoshop, setting the vertical and horizontal size in pixels to a multiple of 96—in this case 192 pixels square. (This will create the highest-resolution textures when using the Texture Explorer.) Choose KPT Texture Explorer from the Filter menu, which brings up the unusual texture picker (see figure 7.48). Choose a base texture from the menu at the bottom of the screen, in this case "brown lattice work."

2. Click on the buttons on the "gene tree" at the left of the screen to mutate the textures until a texture appears that approximates the one you're after (see figure 7.49). (Clicking near the top of the tree causes great variations, while clicking low on the tree causes more subtle changes.) The color button, to the right of the gene tree, will change the color schemes of the textures in the texture ring without changing the selected pixel geometry.

**Figure 7.48.** The Kai's Power Tools Texture Explorer.

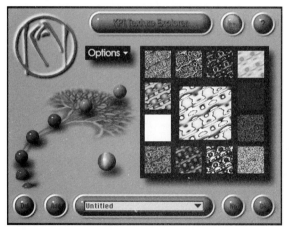

**Figure 7.49.** Mutating the chosen texture.

3. Click **OK** to fill the selected area in the Photoshop image with the new texture (see figure 7.50). Notice that the texture has tiled seamlessly twice across and twice down. Save the texture as a PICT.

The image in figure 7.51 was rendered in Sketch! using the PICT file as a texture. It was tiled with cylindrical mapping.

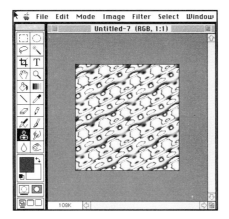

**Figure 7.50.** The KPT texture, as inserted into Photoshop. Notice the seamless tiling.

**Figure 7.51.** An image rendered with the texture created from Kai's Power Tools.

---

**Tip**

*Moiré patterns* are distracting grid-like patterns that result when you create a "screen" of an image that already contains finely-spaced lines or grids. This effect is often visible in printed material that reproduces previously-printed material, for example. Moirés can show up in

---

renderings when you use a texture with very finely-spaced
regular lines or patterns. Try to avoid this when you're
creating textures.

# RenderMan

Probably the most powerful and creatively flexible rendering system
available is Pixar's RenderMan. This system was originally created by
a group of artists and programmers under the employ of George
Lucas, the director who brought you *Star Wars*. The goal originally
was to create a rendering system that could run on super-high-
powered computers to create natural-looking renderings suitable for
use in motion picture special effects.

The result was the creation of a "device-independent" rendering
system—a language for 3-D graphics. Unlike other rendering systems, RenderMan is even independent of specific rendering algorithms; these are encapsulated in the *textures* applied to surfaces.
Essentially, RenderMan acts like a PostScript printer for 3-D software.
Any software that can produce RenderMan-compatible geometry and
rendering instructions can "print" a 3-D image using any version of
RenderMan, no matter what machine it's running on.

The heart of RenderMan is known collectively as Shaders, and (on the
Mac) their subset, Looks. These are textures, and at the same time,
they're more than textures (see figure 7.52). They are a method of
describing a surface, much the way procedural wood describes a
surface in other renderers. The beauty of RenderMan Shaders is in
their power for creating realistic images. The ugly side to Shaders is
that each one is like a separate program unto itself, and until recently, there was no easy what to see beforehand—or to control—
what you would get when you rendered. Rendering with RenderMan
was sometimes as much black art as numerical science. Fortunately,
the recent introduction of the Looks format has greatly simplified the
use of RenderMan for Mac users.

**Figure 7.52.** RenderMan's Shaders are extensions of the concept of textures.

## RenderMan support

Programs that have direct rendering support for RenderMan include:

- Showplace
- Typestry
- Presenter Professional
- Macromedia Three-D
- StrataStudio Pro (with the Rend•X add-on)
- StrataVision 3d and (with the Rend•X add-on)

Programs that export a RIB file which you can open, assign shaders to, and render in Pixar's Showplace include:

- Sketch!
- Swivel 3-D Professional
- UpFront

Of course, for the intrepid 3-D user, it's still possible to create your own RenderMan Shaders. While the specifics of programming RenderMan are beyond the scope of this book, many of the basic operations concerning the placement and control of textures are similar to other 3-D programs.

RenderMan is described in much more detail in chapter 12, "RenderMan."

# Environments

An environment may be as simple as a backdrop for rendered objects, or it may be an integral part of a scene. If you look at a reflective surface—a piece of chrome, a dinner knife, a polished brass doorknob, a china plate—what do you see? (If you do your dishes in a TV commercial, chances are you'll see yourself.) But objects reflect much more than the person looking at them; they reflect everything in their environment to some degree. In 3-D, if you were to put a sphere alone in a scene, and give it all of the surface qualities of chrome (high mirror reflectivity, a light blue color, high specularity and low diffusion), light it carefully, and render it, you may be surprised at the results. Namely, what you'll get is a dull gray flat looking ball (see figure 7.53). This is because the sphere is reflective... but it has nothing to reflect!

**Figure 7.53.** With nothing but a white table to sit on and an all-white environment, this chrome sphere looks flat and not much like chrome.

If you were to place a cube and render the scene the cube will be reflected from the surface of the sphere, and suddenly the sphere will begin to look like chrome (see figure 7.54).

**Tip**
Mirrors and chrome look like what they reflect. A mirror with only blackness to reflect will look black. Imagine standing in front of a mirror in outer space. Whenever you have a reflective object that looks too "flat," consider giving it a more detailed environment.

**Figure 7.54.** This sphere benefits from a busy environment and looks much more chrome-like.

# Environment maps

It's impractical to build a complicated set of 3-D models simply to provide something for a surface to reflect. An *environment map* is a picture—of the inside of a room, or another scene—that is wrapped like wallpaper on the inside of an imaginary globe surrounding your 3-D world. The environment image and the imaginary globe are invisible, except to the affected models. You only see the environment as it is reflected off the model's surface. Various 3-D programs handle environments somewhat differently. Some use a single global environment map for all models in the scene, while some allow different environments for individual objects or groups.

Environment mapping is sometimes used as an alternative to ray tracing for creating realistic scenes. All renderings require some degree of environment mapping for realism. While environment mapping requires some work on the user's part, it results in images that are realistic in appearance (if not in technical accuracy), in a small fraction of the time needed for ray tracing. For 3-D users limited to Phong shading, as well as for animators who can't take the time required for ray tracing, this is the only way to create realistic reflective surfaces.

It's possible to fake an environment map by simply texture-mapping an image to an object's surface, but this has drawbacks. When ray tracing, an environment map is in the background compared to other objects. This means that, in the example of the sphere and cube, the sphere will reflect the cube cleanly, unaffected by the environment map. In contrast, if you texture map a "reflection" to the sphere, the texture will interfere with the reflection of the cube.

Environment maps are crucial for animation. As an object turns and moves in space, an environment map stays still (unless it, too, is animated). This causes reflections to race across a moving model's surface, creating a very realistic sense of motion.

# Environmental reflections

Some programs, such as EIAS, can create an "automatic environment" for a model, based on the scene the model is in. Basically, because EIAS doesn't do ray tracing, it substitutes by rendering the scene from the point of view of the model, then using the resulting image internally as an environment map for that model. Every surface that receives this treatment requires another internal rendering, resulting in images that take many times longer than normal to render.

# Creating environments

Environment maps can subtly or dramatically affect your renderings. You'll want to create environment maps that fit the theme of your scene. For example, an image of a dark room, with windows lit brightly from the outside, makes for effective moody reflections. On the other hand, an environment map of a flat landscape with a few flat-topped mesas gives objects the appearance of floating over the desert.

For very curvy, detailed objects such as chrome type, the realism of environment maps is less important than a certain amount of "busi-ness." You'll want your chrome to have lots of things to reflect, so a simple black-and-white bitmap with lots of spaghetti-like squiggles works well.

# Polar environments

Environment maps, like texture maps, can use several different types of projections, but usually you'll want to use a spherical environment, because objects tend to reflect everything around them. The exception is a flat surface, such as a mirror, that you want to reflect a recognizable image. Here you would use a planar or flat projection.

Photoshop allows you to translate normal, rectangular photographic images with flat Cartesian coordinates into polar coordinates. This squeezes a rectangular image into a series of concentric circles, with the top row of pixels becoming the center point and every lower row wrapped in a circular fashion around it. A simple landscape photo converted this way looks like a bulls-eye with the sky in a circle at the center and the land in a ring around the outside. When you use this image as an environment map (with the center of the image at the "north pole"), it works as a perfect hemispherical dome and images are reflected off of spherical surfaces without distortion.

The CD-ROM contains many environment maps you can use in your own renderings. Some of these are fairly simple impressionistic images, but there is also a sampling of rectangular and polar environment maps, such as clouds, street scenes, and underwater images.

## Creating a polar environment

1. Open an image in Photoshop, such as the cloud photo in figure 7.55.

2. Apply the **Distort, Polar** filter to the image. Be sure to select **Rectangular to polar coordinates** in the dialog box (see figure 7.56).

3. Using Photoshop's Clone Tool, remove the "seam" between the edges of an environment map, so that it wraps seamlessly around an object.

**Figure 7.55.** This cloud photo will be used for the polar environment map.

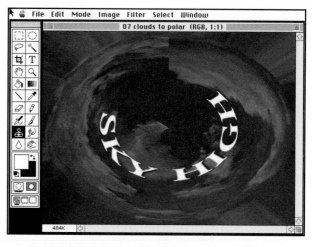

**Figure 7.56.** The results of applying polar distortion to the cloud picture.

# Backdrops

An important consideration in any 3-D rendering is the backdrop for the image. The best source of original material is scanned photographs. Hundreds of collections of these are avialable on CD-ROM in Photo CD, PICT, TIFF, and other formats. Impressionistic painted backgrounds or even other 3-D renderings are also a good source of background material.

Some programs, such as Sketch!, will automatically generate a background color gradation or other automatic color backdrop.

In general, the background image you use should be the same size and resolution as your finished rendering.

The CD-ROM contains many background images for use in your own renderings. This include scanned photographs and painted and mathematically generated images in 640-by-480 resolutions, suitable for multimedia and NTSC video.

# Summary

- Surface quality. This includes diffuse reflectivity and color, mirror reflectivity, specular reflectivity, ambient reflectivity, transparency, refraction, smoothness, shininess and glow.

- Surface textures are color maps which can be applied to the surfaces of objects like flexible sheets.

- Solid textures, such as marble or wood grain, are created by procedural shaders that calculate the appearance of a surface based on an object's volume.

- Surface projections are the techniques used to map textures onto an object. In general, projections correspond to an object's shape, though these can be modified.

- Bumps are used to trick the renderer into rendering bumps in an object's surface where none really exist. You can combine bump maps with color maps to create interesting textures.

- Surface quality maps allow you to change an object's surface quality values by applying a bitmap. For example, an image can be used to control the glow, mirror reflection or transparency values of a surface.

- A label is a texture map that's been overlaid on another texture, such as a label on a wine bottle.

- Environment maps are used to give reflective surfaces something to reflect.

- Backgrounds add realism to the final image.

# chapter

8

# Lighting

**M**acintosh 3-D—at least today—is virtual photography more than virtual reality. A person who understands the principles of photography is much more likely to succeed at creating interesting and evocative artwork than one who does not. And photography, above all, requires an understanding of light.

Light does more than just make objects visible. It sets the mood of a scene. Lighting reveals that which is important—hence the origin of the word *highlight*—and leaves in darkness that which should be imagined. Light provides contrast and color, and brings out form and texture (see figure 8.1). Without creative lighting, objects are rendered flat and textures become dull.

**Figure 8.1.** Rendered in Electric Image Animation System.

Think of the expressions in our everyday language: a "shadowy" figure, the "dark" ages, a "bright" future. In all cases, light—or the lack of it—is a powerful communicator.

The greatest painters, photographers, and filmmakers have long understood light. Rembrandt used "spot" lights to portray the moods of his subjects. Monet was infatuated with the color of light. Ed Weston toyed with the play of light on textures. And Ansel Adams obsessed over perfect contrast between light and shadow.

By the thoughtful placement of lights, 3-D lets you exploit the power of light to suit a particular task. Of course, most renderings should not look like masterpieces or dramatic productions. Often, placing an object in simple daylight or under a basic studio light arrangement is the best solution. Choosing the right lights brings a design to life; choosing the wrong lights can give new meaning to the expression "glaring error" (see figure 8.2). Imagine a table set for two, lit up by a hundred floodlights; or an office in the soft glow of flickering candles.

**Figure 8.2.** Underexposed. Not all lighting is good lighting.

Even sunlight is not as simple as it first seems. Compare the low, warm glow of early morning to the harsh overhead glare of mid-day. Successful 3-D artists spend far more time placing and testing lights than modeling. To perfect a single scene, you may do 20 renderings once you have finished modeling and scene building: placing, moving, and adjusting lights each time. The payoff is worth the effort. A well lit scene will either pop off the page or glow with the subtle mood that fits the moment.

To complicate matters, lights themselves are invisible in nearly all 3-D applications—only the light they cast is rendered. This makes it easy to place lights without having them clutter your scene; but it is problematic when you are trying to create a fireplace with a fire in it, or a flashlight with a convincing beam.

---

 The CD-ROM the comes with this book includes an interactive
lighting tutorial which gives specific examples of many types of
lighting.

# Daylight

Normal daylight is the most normal, natural looking light of all. The
question is, what does it look like? Direct sunlight is a distant directional light. (Directional lights have parallel rays, unlike a spotlight
which "spreads.") Sunlight, by definition, is pure white. (Other lights,
which deviate from the color balance of sunlight, are said to have a
color cast.)

Our brains tend to make up for what we cannot see by substituting
what we know from experience should be there. Therefore, even
though we may be in a room with very orange-cast tungsten light, we
tend to see white walls as white, red apples as red, and a blue rug as
blue. When it comes to pictures created by 3-D software, our eyes are
not so forgiving (or so easily fooled, depending on how you look at
it). If you put an orange light in your scene, you're going to get a
rendering where everything looks more or less, well, orange. This
would be fine if we were going to show the image to people whose
eyes are adjusted to orange light. But, usually, the people we intend
to show the image to will see the color cast for what it is because
their eyes are adjusted to normal light.

The most pleasing daylight renderings result from simulating early morning or evening sun. Here, you place a strong directional light low to one side, giving it a yellowish, or even pink or orange cast, and use a medium amount of blue ambient light. This will cause long blue shadows to fall on one side of the scene with bright highlights on the other. It is a very interesting lighting arrangement.

If you are trying to create the effect of direct afternoon sunlight (one of the worst conditions for photography and usually not highly recommended for 3-D imaging, either), put a strong white distant light overhead and use a large amount of ambient light.

# Studio lighting

Photographers and cinematographers have a long list of conventions they use as jumping-off points for creative work. One convention is the basic studio lighting setup: a combination of three lights that illuminates the subject, fills in harsh shadows, and provides a pleasing halo around edges (see figures 8.3 and 8.4). The *key light* is the main beam that provides most of the illumination in this setup. You usually position it in front of the subject about 45 degrees off the camera's line of view. Typically, you use a *fill light* to soften harsh shadows cast by the key light. (Vain actors appearing on TV talk shows often insist on one or more fill lights, hidden from view of the cameras, to soften their wrinkles.) In photography, the rule of thumb is to use a fill light that is half the strength of the key light. If the fill light is too weak, the key light's shadows will remain harsh. If the fill light is too strong, it will create its own highlights and shadows which appear unnatural. The final element in this triangular setup is the *back light*. Positioned directly behind the subject, this light picks up highlights on the back edges and enhances contrast between the subject and a dark background. Magazine models owe their glowing halos of hair to this trick, but it applies equally well to models of jet engines and particularly well to translucent objects.

**Figure 8.3.** The standard studio lighting setup. The light in the foreground is the key light and provides most of the illumination. The fill light, about half as strong, is in the left foreground; the back light is as strong as the key light, but placed directly behind the subject. All of the lights are a little over "head" high, except for the back light, which you sometimes place lower than the top of the subject.

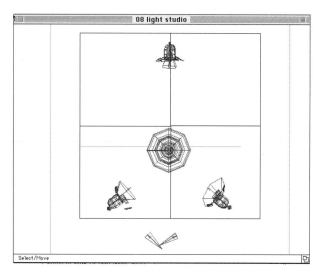

**Figure 8.4.** The lighting setup in Sketch! was used to create the previous image. Note the two highlight spots in the foreground (bottom) used to illuminate the light fixtures. A small amount of ambient light also was used overall.

# Night lights

Night lighting means artificial lights. You can simulate the output of almost any light in most 3-D programs. The one thing that you cannot recreate easily is the visible light itself (except in ElectricImage Animation System). Many 3-D users artfully suggest lights by placing them in shades or other places where—while you cannot see the light itself—you can see the effect of the light on adjacent surfaces. If you want your scenes to have a night-time feel, avoid overlighting them; turn lights down low and set the decay rate to high so they do not reach as far. For night-time scenes to have a night-time feel, it is important that you not use any lights that over-brighten the scene; also, avoid using ambient light. Try using dark matte textures on most of your objects, except for the occasional shiny trinket. Also use a bright environment map so shiny objects have something bright to reflect.

# Light types

There are many different types of lights in the real world and 3-D software enables you to work with most of the basic varieties. These include point, spot, distant, and ambient light. Some programs (such as addDepth and Dimensions), only support simple white lights set at a fixed distance. Typestry and StrataType 3d enable you to add color and shadow gels to multiple lights, but they are limited essentially to distant lighting. The more sophisticated 3-D programs add the important elements of point and spotlights, as well as the capability to control the level of ambient light. This kind of control is needed for creating photorealistic scenes. EIAS even enables you to create glowing lights, such as lasers and suns.

## Point lights

Point lights (sometimes called *radial* lights) are the most common type of artificial light in the real world as well as in 3-D. They work more or less like a light bulb. As the name implies, light emanates outward from a single point. Unlike a physical light bulb, these do not screw in, nor do they have hot or cold spots. You simply point and click with your mouse to place a light.

Point lights are useful wherever you need a light bulb. By putting them in a lamp or behind perforated stereo panels, you can create realistic day-to-day lighting effects.

Point lights can be employed as fill lights throughout a scene— putting low-intensity illumination near any troublesome dark spot.

Because they cast light in all directions, point lights are excellent at catching bevels and curves to provide highlights (see figure 8.5).

**Figure 8.5.** A point light illuminates objects in all directions.

In animation, point lights can be locked to moving objects (such as the wing lights on an airplane), attached to the camera (to provide constant illumination of a subject being followed), or moved through a scene to create highlights off beveled edges.

# Spotlight

A *spotlight* is usually placed and aimed in the same manner as a camera. It has a position in space as well as a direction. Illumination from a spotlight emanates outward in a cone with the point at the source and the wide "base" at the distant objective (see figure 8.6).

**Figure 8.6.** A spotlight is a directional cone. It begins at a point and ends in a circle.

Spotlights can be aimed at your subject and their cone angle can be adjusted to illuminate a wide or narrow area. Because they can be precisely aimed, they are the light of choice for picking up small details and placing specific highlights.

Because spotlights can be focused, they are also ideal for casting gel shadows (see below). Adjusting the drop-off of a spotlight affects the "fuzziness" of its cone; adjusting the decay determines how far the light will travel before it fades away.

Animators use spotlights in many ways, including tracking a subject (following an actor across a stage); locking to a subject (a car's headlights); or sweeping across a scene to effect a Hollywood movie opening, or to spot an airplane.

## Spotlights for highlights

Lights give shiny objects their glint and dull objects defined detail. At times, however, you won't want to over light a scene only to bring out a highlight or two, or to brighten the lights on a single subject in the scene. To bring out the highlights and detail on a spoked hubcap, for example, you can aim a small spotlight at the point of interest, but make it narrow enough to miss the rest of the car. The trick with spotlights is to position the light source accurately enough that it only catches the area you want to highlight.

In many cases, a 3-D rendering will lack a desirable highlight in small areas of detail (like the glimmer of gold off the bezel of a watch). You can position a spotlight very close to the object of interest and spread the spotlight's beam just wide enough to create the missing highlight.

---

**Tip**
Missing highlights are usually due to the lack of imperfections and minute details in 3-D models. A slightly imperfect object actually glimmers more brightly than one with very smooth angular surfaces and edges. It is often easier and quicker to create a few highlights manually in a program like Photoshop than it is to model imperfections, place new lights, and re-render the image. (In some modelers, it is impossible to create surface imperfections!) When adding highlights to small surfaces in Photoshop, use the eyedropper to choose the color from another highlight on the same surface; then lightly airbrush it in using a very fine brush size so that it blends with the image.

---

# Ambient light

The most common example of *ambient light* is that of normal daytime shade. Even though the sun isn't shining directly on your head, you are not groping in darkness because sunlight bounces and reflects off of everything it strikes, particularly the sky. Even on cloudy days, light is coming at you from everywhere (see figure 8.7).

**Figure 8.7.** Ambient light is general. It comes from all directions and strikes all surfaces.

Ambient light is important in natural scenes. In fact, most renderers default to some amount of ambient light. Single lights by themselves are rather harsh and give the distinct impression of indoor or stage-type lighting: a reading lamp at night, a spotlight on a stand-up comic, or even a vampire looming over a candle. Ambient light makes these scenes bright and more cheerful; it fills dark shadows and softens details (see figure 8.8).

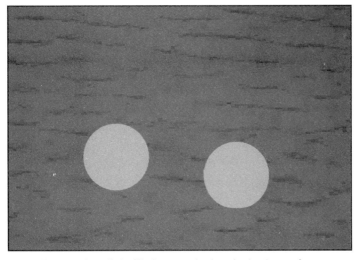

**Figure 8.8.** High ambient light fills in even the harsh shadows of a strong main light.

It doesn't make much sense to use ambient light only—since there is rarely an instance when you'll find yourself with no directional light. An example of purely ambient light is a "whiteout" snowstorm. In this case everything appears flat and lacking detail. In general, the more ambient light in a scene, the less contrast there is among objects.

Even though the vast majority of outdoor ambient light comes from the sky (which is pale blue), normal renderings call for white ambient light. As with a colored-fill light, colored ambient light will fill shadows with a subtle cast of color.

Monet often used purples and blues when he painted shadows—not a blacker version of "haystack color." While Monet was particularly adept at discerning the true colors of light, most people (the author included), have a brain that tricks them into perceiving shade as merely "darker"—and not necessarily of a different color.

Similarly, if you're rendering an interior scene where the walls of a room are bright orange, you can set your ambient light to a pale orange color. This gives a more realistic look for the scene than plain white light. If it is an all-shade scene, white ambient light appears more natural when rendered. To create the effect of a cloudy day, use plenty of ambient light and very little directional light. This will result in very flat renderings, with little shadow detail.

# Distant light

*Distant lights* are often referred to as "suns" for good reason: light rays coming from the sun are very nearly parallel. (The sun is a gigantic point of light so far away that Earth only gets a sliver of the rays it projects.) Placing a distant light creates the effect of a solid wall of light washing over your scene from a single direction (see figure 8.9). All shadows fall in a line and the effect is like direct sunlight. For early morning or sunset light, set your light angle low to the horizon, adjust the color to a soft yellow or pink (or orange for a blazing sunset), and turn down the intensity. Low light often calls for long shadows, so you may want to add a gel (also called a *shadow mask* or "*gobo*") to the scene (see below). Because of the shadows created when you use a distant light, you will want a fair amount of ambient light to soften them. For noon-time light, place the distant light directly overhead, turn up the intensity, and give the light a white color. In bright sun, the ambient light is closer to pure white than in morning and twilight hours.

**Figure 8.9.** Distant or "sun" light is directional—from infinitely far away—so it lights the whole scene equally.

# Pan light

Use *pan lights* when the goal is to generate a broad, highly-diffused light that casts few shadows. In the real world, they are extremely useful for lighting highly reflective subjects (such as glossy cars), where you don't want the lamp itself to be noticeably reflected in the image. Pan lights only light one side of a subject, but the light emanates in every direction from every point on the "pan," so shadows are extremely soft. While no Mac 3-D applications provide pan lights to date (since their lights are invisible anyway), you can simulate one by placing a grid of three or four diffuse point lights evenly spread behind a plane of brightly glowing transparent texture. While there is no such thing as a glowing, transparent texture in the real world, in 3-D this looks very much like the diffuse white glass of a frosted light bulb; the transparency allows the internal lights to shine through, illuminating the subject.

Some programs enable you to set the direction of ambient light, which will create pan-style lighting throughout your scene. Ambient light, however, does not generate specular highlights.

# Back light

Back lighting emphasizes the shapes and silhouettes of objects, rather than their surface appearance (see figure 8.10). Back lights placed above an object will emphasize its outline by putting a bright halo around a dark silhouette.

**Figure 8.10.** Back lighting can be used to emphasize an object's shape.

# Setting lights

In addition to positioning and changing the type and direction of lights, there are a number of other lighting options that can affect the appearance of your scene. While every scene-building application has somewhat different lighting options, the most common include:

- **Color**. Light color directly affects the appearance of rendered objects. A white key light, supplemented by a red-fill light used to light a blue sphere, generates a form that blends smoothly from blue to purple to red.

- **Intensity**. *Intensity* or brightness of lights affects the total exposure of the image, as well as the visibility of details. If lights are too bright, the image will be overexposed; objects will appear washed out and lacking detail. Without enough light, the image will render too dark. Shining multiple lights on an object adds their effects together. For example, if a model is properly exposed with one light shining on it, it would be overexposed with the addition of a second light.

- **Drop-off** (or fall-off). Affects how much a light blurs from the center of its beam to its edge. A spotlight with low drop-off has a very sharp edge where it strikes, while a beam with high drop-off is soft or blurry at the edges.

- **Decay**. Attenuation or *decay* is the distance from the source at which light fades. While in life this is determined by mathematical equations as well as elements in the atmosphere, 3-D lights operate in a completely transparent ether and the light's decay is proportional to the amount you specify. You will need to set a distance for this effect unless you want your lights to carry all the way to the moon.

# Setting lights in Sketch!

Sketch! has a unique and simple method for light placement.

1. Select either the Spot or Point Light tool and click on the target for the light. Drag the light away from the target along the surface of the working plane. The light automatically aims at the target as you drag it (see figure 8.11).

**Figure 8.11.** The effect of a spotlight aimed at the target.

2. At any time, you can press the Shift key to change the light's movement away from the working plane.

# Visible lights and lamps

With one exception (see "Electric Image lights," in this chapter), light sources themselves are invisible in 3-D. You can create a realistic light bulb with an unrealistic trick. Create a light bulb-shaped object with a transparent, glowing surface. Hide a point light or spotlight inside it. Because the surface is transparent the light will shine through. But, because it is glowing brightly, you cannot see through it.

Because light is such an important part of a scene, so are realistic looking lamps and other light sources. Your renderings will be much more convincing if you take the time to learn how to make visible lights.

# Glowing objects

Sometimes the need will arise to make an object (such as a strip of neon), act as a light. To do this, you must assign a glow surface quality to the object. The difference between a glow and a true light is that even though they may shine very brightly, glowing objects do not shed light on other objects. A neon tube comprised solely of a glow will not seem very realistic unless it casts a colored light on the wall where it is mounted. To compensate, you can make the glowing object "transparent" and hide an appropriate type of light inside it. You can apply a glow map to surfaces adjacent to a glowing object to create the effect of casting light.

If the realistic appearance of your lights is critical, you can use a more complicated but very effective compositing technique (see chapter 11, "Working with images"), to render parts of your image separately and combine them with manually created lighting effects. In the long run, this will probably save you time.

# Shadows

Light hitting an object is partially reflected and partly absorbed and in so doing the object "throws" a shadow onto objects behind it. (It is easier to deal with shadows if you think of objects blocking light, not "casting" darkness.)

In the real world, many objects can cast shadows from many light sources. But because the shadows from the strongest light source are the most visible, and because shadows are often as complex to render as objects, renderers sometimes limit you to a single shadow-casting light. On the other hand, high-quality ray tracers will generally let every light cast shadows. While overlapping lights and shadows can provide interesting effects, be aware that every shadow in your image will significantly increase the overall rendering time. The capability to turn off shadows is a clue to the trickery performed by renderers. Even though shadows are disabled, shading of objects is retained. In the real world, of course, you cannot have one without the other.

Gouraud and flat shaders cannot create realistic shadows; however, with an image editing program that supports masks, it is possible to simulate simple shadows.

You can create the most realistic shadows with radiosity (currently only offered by StrataVision 3d and StrataStudio Pro). However, this rendering technique is too slow to use regularly.

Typically, shadows have a soft indistinct edge. Most 3-D programs have an option to achieve soft edge shadows. Increasing the amount of drop-off also softens shadows.

# Gels and gobos

Gels allow you to throw mood setting shadows into a scene. Some applications (such as StrataVision 3d), enable you to map a texture to a light. For example, a silhouette of a window can be applied to a spotlight and projected onto a scene. The result is the realistic effect of light streaming through the window (see figure 8.12).

**Figure 8.12.** A *gel* is a mask applied to a light. It creates the effect of light streaming through a window.

If your scene builder doesn't offer gels, you can model a wall with a window (by creating a flat plane with holes cut out for windows) and place it just outside the visible part of your scene with the light shining through. Shining a light through a cut-out in this manner is called a *gobo* in stage lighting (see figure 8.13). The same technique can be used to create light shining through curtains, bars, stars, or Venetian blinds. By shining a light through panes of stained glass, you will cast colored shadows into your scene if you are rendering with a ray tracer. (See "Adding depth to PostScript art" in chaper 4, "Basic shapes and fonts," for a description of creating stained glass.)

**Figure 8.13.** A gobo is an object with a cut-out that you can shine a light through. Modeled and rendered in Sketch!.

When rendering for animation, you can put light behind a revolving ceiling fan for Casablanca-style lighting. For a Bugs Bunny cartoon effect, you can use a cut-out of a looming man in a hat and use it to cast a shadow that grows as the villain approaches.

## Using a gel in StrataStudio Pro

Using a gel is almost as easy as using a light alone. Essentially, you are attaching a texture to the light source.

1. Set up a model and aim a spotlight to illuminate it (this creates a stage-lit effect; for more natural lighting, you can use a point light instead). Double-click on the lighted object to bring up your setting options found in the Edit Global Light dialog box (see figure 8.14). Select a gel in the pop-down window. The mapping controls are the same as the texture projection controls. Use the default setting initially.

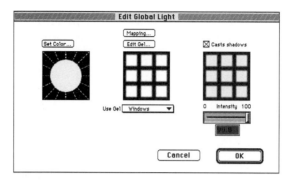

**Figure 8.14.** StrataStudio Pro's Edit Global Light dialog box for setting options.

2. Render the scene. This top view shows the effect of the gel from a distance (see figure 8.15).

**Figure 8.15.** The use of a gel from a distance.

Figure 8.16 illustrates a typical rendering with a light gel.

# Simulating shadows

One great time-saving measure is to reduce the number of shadows in a scene. In order to maintain realism, you can simulate shadows. Because of the amount of time it will take to do this, it is probably only worth the effort if you are producing animation, if you are planning to render a scene from many angles, or if your rendering application doesn't support shadows.

**Figure 8.16.** A rendered object using a light gel.

To simulate a shadow, you will need to use the same techniques used to create texture maps that fit a particular part of your image. (For more information on how this can be achieved, see "Making a box label," in chapter 7, "Materials.")

# Electric Image lights

Currently, the Electric Image Animation System is the only 3-D program that offers visible lights: a point light can glow like a bulb or you can use tube lights that realistically portray straight fluorescent tubes or laser beams.

Animation System uses an adjustable inner and outer light to create the effect of an intense light source with a fuzzy haze around it. This works for point, spot, and tube-style lights. Unlike glowing objects in other 3-D programs, EIAS' glowing lights *do* shine light on other objects.

The next incarnation of EIAS should offer automatic lens flare as a special effect. Macintosh renderers, to date, cannot produce the lens flare seen in photographs. A simple filter, Lens Flare (included with Photoshop), creates this effect automatically.

# Time-of-day lighting

One interesting technique—offered primarily by programs designed for the visualization of architectural models—is lighting that corresponds to a particular time of day on a particular day of the year. Alias UpFront is an example of such a program. When you build a model and orient it to the compass, you also can give it a latitude on the globe (see figure 8.17). The program is capable of calculating and displaying the lighting on the model based on the position of the sun at a given time of year. This enables a designer to see how a courtyard will be lit in the winter, or to see how the sun will strike the windows in the hottest part of a mid-summer's day. When generating an animation, you can set the program to calculate the sun's position at each frame so that you can see how the building looks over the course of a day.

Sculpt 4D also includes this capability.

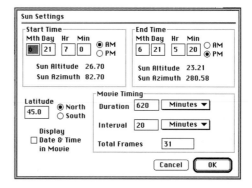

**Figure 8.17.** The time-of-day calculator in UpFront automatically calculates sun position for lighting a model.

# Summary

- Lighting is the key to successful renderings. For every hour you spend modeling and texture mapping, you are likely to spend several hours perfecting light setups and re-rendering.

- Basic daylight is the most common lighting setup and usually uses a single, distant light and a good deal of ambient light.

- Studio lighting begins with a 3-light setup. The key light provides most of the light. A fill light can be used to soften the shadows from the key light. A back light picks up highlights on the back of the subject and increases the contrast between the subject and the background.

- The basic types of lights include: spotlight, focused directional light, distant lights, point lights, and ambient light.

- Light settings can include color, intensity, drop-off, and decay.

- Glowing objects can be combined with lights to create the effect of visible lights.

- Shadow qualities vary with the renderer you use. Ray tracers and radiosity renderers produce shadows without trouble. Phong, Gouraud, and flat shaders can simulate only true shadow effects.

- Gels can be used to simulate a window or other object casting a shadow into a scene.

- Electric Image Animation System can render visible lights.

9

# Animation

W hile cell animation has been around for a century,
computer-based 3-D animation has many advantages
not available to animators using traditional film and cell
techniques. It is hardly a fair comparison. Two of the most important
differences are the infinite level of control available in 3-D, and the
fact that 3-D cameras need not bend to the limitations of depth of
field and film. Three-D animators are not necessarily bound to the
laws of physics, so cameras can fly through walls unscathed and
dishes can fly around a kitchen possessed. You can zoom in or out at
will, unconcerned with the pitfalls of changing exposures or blurred
foregrounds. In digital animations, an unlimited number of layers can
be superimposed without loss of quality of the images underneath.
Traditional animators, however, are limited to four or five layers
before visuals turn to mud under sheets of celluloid. Of course,
another significant bonus is saving time. Traditional animations are
the result of thousands of hours of tedious frame-at-a-time hand
drawings, while the Macintosh can do most of the work for you when
animating in 3-D. If you create a scene that needs changes, it is a
simple matter to go back, rearrange key parts of the animation, and
re-render it. This chapter will explain some special techniques for
animators.

# Animation basics

It is axiomatic that the shortest distance between two points is a
straight line. In the vocabulary of 3-D, the easiest way to create an
animation is also between two points. Suppose you want to create
a four-second animation of a hot-air balloon leaving the ground
and floating up and up until it rises out of the picture. By simply
defining the beginning and ending stages of the animation (the
balloon is on the ground and then the balloon is out of sight), you
have the two points needed to make a movie. Three-D animation,
in most ways, is identical to basic scene building. To make the
hot-air balloon movie, we build the scene with the balloon on the
ground, and then change the scene by dragging the balloon up and
off the screen. The software keeps track of where the balloon is at
the starting point, as well where it is at the end. The software then
does what you would rather not do yourself—it calculates the path

and position of the balloon in all the frames in between. This technique is called *key-frame animating* and it is the basis of even the most complex and creative 3-D animation. There is more to animation than moving an object in a straight line between two points; you also can animate surfaces so that skin turns to stone; or animate lights so that night becomes day; or even animate the cameras that provide the viewpoints of your scene.

# Uses of 3-D animation

There is a growing demand for 3-D animation, but the uses cannot be summarized easily in a sentence. Video and multimedia are two of the places where you are likely to find 3-D (although there are many uses that fit rather uneasily under these headings). Different types of users will have different demands from 3-D applications.

# Frame rate and resolution

One of the primary concerns for any animator will be producing animations at the right screen resolution and frame rate for the task at hand. The *frame rate* of an animation is the number of frames that flash onto the screen every second to create the illusion of smooth motion. Film, for example, uses 24 frames per second; video uses 30 frames per second; and a common rate for CD-ROM-based QuickTime animations designed for playback on lower-end Macs is 15 frames per second. Thus, a ten-second video animation contains 300 frames, while a ten-second QuickTime clip may have only 150 frames.

The resolution of an animation determines the size (in horizontal and vertical pixels) of the screen it occupies. The television standard, as well as the size of a Macintosh 13-inch monitor, is 640 pixels wide by 480 pixels high. This is constant—no matter how large or small the television (larger TVs just have bigger pixels). For CD-ROM QuickTime delivery, 320 by 240 pixels is barely manageable for slower Macs and CD-ROM drives. There are many other standard resolutions which depend on your intended output. Though film-resolution and upcoming HDTV animation is still primarily created on high-end dedicated systems, Macintosh 3-D programs can render resolutions as high as 4,096 pixels square.

## Video

Video animators are interested in creating animations of 640-by-480 (NTSC) resolution or better at 30 frames per second. Users in the video field have a large investment in equipment and demand high-quality output.

Field rendering and legalized colors are some of the concerns of the video producer. Field rendering creates two frames for every frame of video. One is an even field; the other is odd. When these frames are interlaced, they play back as an animation that is effectively 60-frames-per-second.

Because the color gamut (range of colors supported) of NTSC video is extremely limited compared to that which can be created and displayed on a 24-bit Macintosh system, many colors will not display properly when played back on an NTSC monitor (TV). This means you must settle for soft, muted colors if you plan to output your productions to videotape. Bright reds, for example, are notorious for *bleeding* when transferred to video; this means the large patches of red tend to blur out of their boundaries into other parts of the screen.

## Multimedia

Multimedia authors may create animations for video use in high-profile productions and presentations, or they may settle for smaller frames or lower frame rates, depending on the application. QuickTime—the standard platform for delivering digital animations on the Macintosh and one of the standards in use for Intel-based PCs—currently does not have the hardware support it needs to pump broadcast-quality video onto the Macintosh screen. New hardware from companies like SuperMac, Radius, and RasterOps, however, are bringing this capability very close to the Macintosh mainstream.

The medium of CD-ROM is an excellent delivery tool for smaller-sized video played at reduced frame rates. CD-ROMs are the current delivery tool of choice for commercial multimedia.

On the other hand, full-motion, full-frame video compression systems (such as the Radius VideoVision Studio and SuperMac Digital Film) are now available for the Macintosh, making it possible to create full-screen interactive 3-D animations for use in special kiosks and other delivery locations where hardware costs are a secondary concern.

Some multimedia authoring tools, such as Macromedia's Director and Passport Designs Producer Professional, allow you to use PICS files as an animation format. Unlike QuickTime which is time-based, this is a frame-based animation format meaning every frame of an animation will play no matter how long it takes. QuickTime, in contrast, "drops" frames to keep synch with sound and other timely events.

## Virtual reality

Three-D software has come along so quickly that virtual reality is virtually, well... reality. While the Mac has yet to fool anyone into thinking they are walking through another world, a number of applications now allow for real-time visualization of 3-D scenes. Virtus WalkThrough and WalkThrough Pro and the upcoming Strata Virtual 3d all allow you to navigate in real time through a 3-D scene. You can examine shaded models from any angle and walk through architectural designs to see concepts materialize before your eyes. Macromedia has previewed an upcoming program that will enable you to create your own virtual-reality games.

## Film

While 3-D on the Macintosh has the capability to produce renderings suitable for film, the high resolution and rapid turnaround times required in film production mean the Macintosh is generally too slow to produce segments for major motion pictures. However, Macintosh tools (such as Electric Image's Animation System), are pushing the envelope with techniques such as SGI rendering and it won't be long before Mac 3-D graphics regularly make their way onto the big screen.

# Key frames

Key-frame animation is based on the principle that you define the state of scenes and models at important or *key points* during the animation and the computer interpolates or "tweens" all of the states in between for every frame. This is an enormous time saver, allowing you to act as a director of action, with the computer doing all the busy work of calculating intermediate steps.

Key-frame animations are not limited to just the linear motion of models through a scene. You can define as many key frames as necessary to describe a scene. Depending on the software, you may be able to rotate, stretch, squash, or otherwise deform models; change lights and textures; and move the camera to follow and zoom in or out on the action. Virtually any property can be animated by defining its condition at the start and end points in time. Even special effects like morphing one model into another are possible in some programs.

There are a number of properties you may want to animate with key frames, including:

- Object position
- Object rotation
- Object dimensions
- Object texture
- Camera orientation
- Camera rotation
- Camera focal length
- Light intensity

- Light color

- Light direction

Not all animation programs support all of the possible animation variations, but the majority of the above types are supported by higher-end programs.

# A flying logo

The following sequence shows the creation of a simple flying logo in Pixar's Typestry. Nearly all of the techniques are identical to creating a static scene for rendering a still logo.

1. Generate a type logo by entering a text string. Specify the font, size, bevel style, and scale it to size. Also apply a texture and set a light source (see figure 9.1).

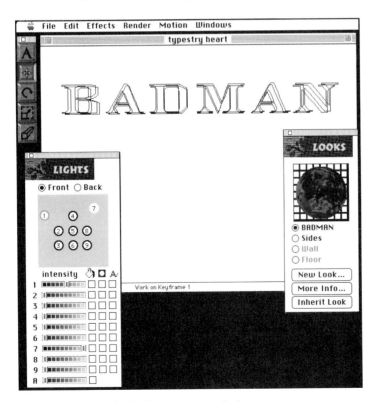

**Figure 9.1.** Entering text in the Typestry text window.

2. Rotate the logo approximately 90 degrees around the x-axis and 90 degrees around the y-axis so that it is lying on its side, aligned along the z-axis (see figure 9.2).

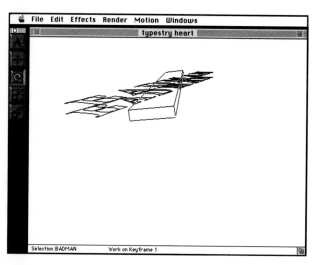

**Figure 9.2.** Rotating text for proper placement.

3. Drag the logo off the screen. Under the Motion pull-down menu, select Next Keyframe (see figure 9.3).

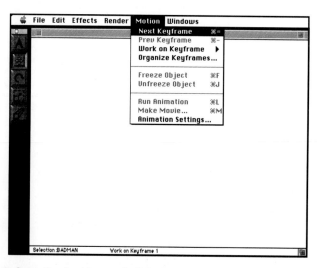

**Figure 9.3.** Selecting key frames in Typestry.

4. Drag the logo back onto the screen, center it, and rotate back into normal alignment (see figure 9.4).

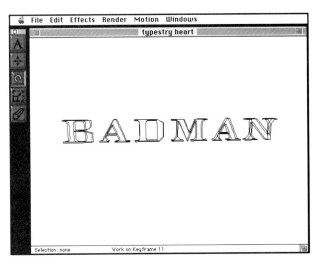

**Figure 9.4.** Rotating the text back into proper alignment.

5. Under the Motion menu, select Run Animation to preview the animation to check for problems. In the Preferences dialog box, set Typestry to render the background as transparent (see figure 9.5). Choose Make Movie under the Animation menu. Specify a file name and fill in the QuickTime settings box for Animation, high quality, 15 frames per second.

# Scene versus event key framing

There are actually two kinds of key animation available in 3-D programs. The most basic type is where a key frame describes the state of the entire world at a given time. More powerful 3-D animators enable you to create more complex motions by defining *key events*. Rather than defining the state of the entire world at a given point in time, event-based key framing offers separate time lines for each group and each object within the group. This enables you to establish motions for objects that are independent of what is happening in the rest of the scene.

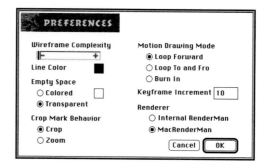

**Figure 9.5.** Setting preferences for creating your animation can be found in Typestry's Preferences dialog box.

With event-based key framing, a hot-air balloon pilot could fire his burner several times as the balloon rises off the screen. This kind of nested animation can be extremely sophisticated with gears turning, pendulums swinging, fish jumping, lights flashing, and the camera moving all at the same time.

Key frame animation is adequate for creating "fly-bys" and other simple animations. For example, you can have the camera fly around an object 360 degrees—all the while aimed at the object's center. This generates an animation as if viewed from the window of an airplane flying around the model.

Event-based animation allows one model to go one way at its own pace, while the camera goes another way along its own time line. This is the kind of animation you will need, for example, if you want to do a fly-by of a bouncing ball where the camera flies completely around the scene in 10 seconds, while the ball bounces on the ground several times and rolls away. The camera requires two key frames: one at zero and another at ten seconds. The bouncing ball, meanwhile, requires key events for movement up or down repeated several times at different intervals. This kind of animation is a huge hassle, and is often impossible without event-based key framing.

Another feature in some event-based animators is the capability to cycle parts of an animation. For example, you can select a group of objects such as a bicycle crank, and specify that it should rotate once every half second. By telling StrataStudio Pro to cycle this animation for ten seconds, the crank turns twenty times as the bicycle rolls across the screen.

Key-frame animators:

- Crystal TOPAS
- DynaPerspective
- Modelshop
- Presenter Professional
- Sculpt 4D
- Shade II
- StrataVision 3-D
- Swivel 3-D Professional
- Turbo 3-D
- Typestry
- UpFront!

Event-based animators

- Electric Image Animation System
- Macromedia Three-D
- StrataStudio Pro
- Playmation
- Infini-D

Virtual reality animators

- Virtus WalkThrough & WalkThrough Pro
- Strata Virtual 3d

# Electric Image Animation System

Electric Image Animation System has very detailed control over the animation parameters for each object. For example, you can change an object's acceleration at a given point. It also has a fine level of control over the animation of visible lights; you can even create a light that "flares."

Currently, EIAS offers far greater control over every aspect of animation than any other Mac 3-D program. Cameras and lights can point at, follow, and be attached to moving objects. Objects can appear and disappear at key points in time. The program also makes it easy to control the orientation and positioning of parent-child(ren) groups.

The program also has extremely sophisticated, but easy-to-use, spline-based velocity controls (see figure 9.6). You can change the shape of velocity curves to simply control the speed of an object or camera over time. The program automatically limits changes to fit within parameters that you have already set.

Electric Image has promised that version 2.0 of the Animation System will offer a wide range of new animation controls, some of which are not currently available elsewhere. These controls include:

- **Synch sound animation**. This puts a sound file on the same timeline as your animation, so you can synchronize visual events to events in time.

- **Model deformations**. These will enable you to twist, taper, bend, shear, ripple, and stretch models.

- **Particle animations**. You will be able to blow models apart and perform other particle animations.

- **Mesh object morphing**. This enables you to turn a flat plane into a sphere, for example.

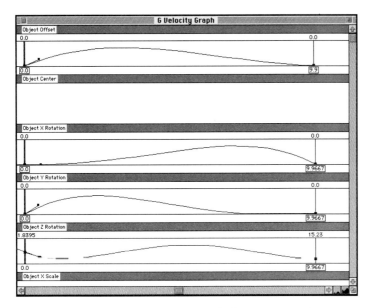

**Figure 9.6.** The Velocity Graph window in EIAS. Steep sections in a curve indicate acceleration and deceleration; level sections indicate constant change. If the curve is bottomed out, it means that parameter is not changing at that point in time.

# Macromedia 3-D

Another program with a high degree of control over the parameters of each element is Macromedia Three-D. Like EIAS, Macromedia Three-D enables you to modify most of the important parameters of a scene over time. This feature should be of particular interest to users dedicated to RenderMan rendering, since Macromedia Three-D enables you to modify individual shader parameters at the frame level (see figure 9.7).

| | 0 | | | | 5 | | | | | 10 |
|---|---|---|---|---|---|---|---|---|---|---|
| **All Values / All Tracks** | | | | | | | | | | |
| ◆ Camera 1 | | | | | ● | | | | | ● |
| ◆ Torus 1 | ● | | | | ● | | | | | ● |
| ◆ position | ● | | | | ◇ | | | | | ◇ |
| ◇ x position | 0 | -0.00112 | -0.00888 | -0.02940 | -0.06760 | -0.12657 | -0.20702 | -0.30706 | -0.42235 | -0.54678 | -0.67331 |
| ◇ y position | 0 | 0.001034 | 0.008185 | 0.027082 | 0.062268 | 0.116585 | 0.190684 | 0.282818 | 0.389014 | 0.50362 | 0.620154 |
| ◇ z position | 0 | 0.002567 | 0.020280 | 0.066742 | 0.151905 | 0.279767 | 0.446665 | 0.640864 | 0.843904 | 1.03364 | **1.18838** |
| ◆ orientation | ● | | | | ◇ | | | | | |
| ◇ x rotation | -90 | -89.9651 | -88.6945 | -82.7733 | -80.6863 | **-89.199** | -91.2357 | -96.2187 | -102.322 | -109.427 | -117.399 |
| ◇ y rotation | 0 | 0.008651 | 0.369462 | 2.19336 | 2.81387 | **0.09004** | -0.48518 | -1.7694 | -3.09838 | -4.29867 | -5.19277 |
| ◇ z rotation | 0 | -0.00563 | -0.40168 | -2.22205 | -2.59105 | **0.37525** | 1.11938 | 3.00442 | 5.42579 | 8.37193 | 11.7953 |
| ◆ scale | ● | | | | ◇ | | | | | |
| ◇ x scale | 1 | 1.00062 | 1.0049 | 1.01613 | 1.03676 | **1.06786** | 1.10873 | 1.1568 | 1.20791 | 1.25699 | 1.29901 |
| ◇ y scale | 1 | 1.01142 | 1.09022 | 1.29684 | 1.67535 | **2.24302** | 2.98267 | 3.84087 | 4.73405 | 5.56237 | 6.22833 |
| ◇ z scale | 1 | 1.00006 | 1.00056 | 1.00246 | 1.00831 | **1.02348** | 1.057 | 1.12138 | 1.23102 | 1.39941 | 1.63572 |
| ◆ attachment | | | | | | | | | | |
| ◆ shape | | | | | | | | | | |
| ◇ major radius | 1 | 1 | 1 | 1 | 1 | 1 | 1 | 1 | 1 | 1 | 1 |
| ◇ minor radius | 0.5 | 0.5 | 0.5 | 0.5 | 0.5 | 0.5 | 0.5 | 0.5 | 0.5 | 0.5 | 0.5 |
| ◇ phi min | 0 | 0 | 0 | 0 | 0 | 0 | 0 | 0 | 0 | 0 | 0 |
| ◇ phi max | 360 | 360 | 360 | 360 | 360 | 360 | 360 | 360 | 360 | 360 | 360 |
| ◇ theta max | 360 | 360 | 360 | 360 | 360 | 360 | 360 | 360 | 360 | 360 | 360 |
| ◆ shading | ● | | | | | ● | | | | | ● |
| ◆ color | | | | | | | | | | |
| ◆ specular color | | | | | | | | | | |
| ◇ visible | On | On | On | On | On | On | On | On | On | On | On |
| ◇ ambient | 1 | 1 | 1 | 1 | 1 | 1 | 1 | 1 | 1 | 1 | 1 |
| ◇ diffuse | 0.6 | 0.6 | 0.6 | 0.6 | 0.6 | 0.6 | 0.6 | 0.6 | 0.6 | 0.6 | 0.6 |
| ◇ specular | 0.4 | 0.4 | 0.4 | 0.4 | 0.4 | 0.4 | 0.4 | 0.4 | 0.4 | 0.4 | 0.4 |
| ◇ roughness | 0.1 | 0.1 | 0.1 | 0.1 | 0.1 | 0.1 | 0.1 | 0.1 | 0.1 | 0.1 | 0.1 |
| ◆ texture | | | | | | | | | | |
| ◆ reflection | | | | | | | | | | |
| ◆ bump | | | | | | | | | | |

**Figure 9.7.** Macromedia Three-D's Score window, showing the position and orientation parameters for a single animated object, "torus 1," over ten frames.

# Timelines

Every 3-D animator that supports event-based animation, uses something like a timeline or sequencer. This is a grid that represents time across the top, with objects forming the rows on the left. Markers representing key frames for each object can be placed on the grid itself. Every object has its own timeline and its own key frames (see figures 9.8 and 9.9). This approach is shared by Macromedia Three-D, Infini-D, StrataStudio Pro, and EIAS. Macromedia's object sequencer mimics Macromedia Director's multimedia sequencer. Animations can be "stretched" over time by changing the frame increment.

| | | 88 | 89 | 90 | 91 | 92 | 93 | 94 | 95 | 96 |
|---|---|---|---|---|---|---|---|---|---|---|
| ▽ Camera 1 | | | | | | | | | | |
| | Attach | None | None | None | None | None | None | None | None | None |
| | Track | None | None | None | None | None | None | None | None | None |
| ▷ | Position | | | | | | | | | |
| ▽ | Reference | | | | | | | | | |
| | ▷ Motion Path | Hermite ▼ | Hermite ▼ | Hermite ▼ | Hermite ▼ | Hermite ▼ | Hermite ▼ | Hermite ▼ | Hermite ▼ | Hermite ▼ |
| | Velocity | | | | | | | | | |
| | Acceleration | | | | | | | | | |
| | X | 809.0667 | 820.5334 | 832.0001 | 843.4667 | 854.9334 | 866.4 | 877.8666 | 889.3334 | 900.8001 |
| | Y | 356.6933 | 356.7467 | 356.8 | 356.8533 | 356.9067 | 356.96 | 357.0133 | 357.0667 | 357.12 |
| | Z | -304.5303 | -305.2636 | -305.9969 | -306.7302 | -307.4635 | -308.1968 | -308.9301 | -309.6634 | -310.3967 |
| ▷ | Roll (Z) | | | | | | | | | |
| | Focal Length | 2.0 | 2.0 | 2.0 | 2.0 | 2.0 | 2.0 | 2.0 | 2.0 | 2.0 |
| ▽ A | | | | | | | | | | |
| | Attach | None | None | None | None | None | None | None | None | None |
| | Track | None | None | None | None | None | None | None | None | None |
| ▷ | Position | | | | | | | | | |
| ▷ | Center | | | | | | | | | |
| ▷ | Pitch (X) | | | | | | | | | |
| ▽ | Yaw (Y) | | | | | | | | | |
| | ▷ Motion Path | Linear ▼ | Linear ▼ | Linear ▼ | Linear ▼ | Linear ▼ | Linear ▼ | Linear ▼ | Linear ▼ | Linear ▼ |
| | Velocity | | | | | | | | | |
| | Acceleration | | | | | | | | | |
| | Data | 180.0 | 180.0 | 179.8999 | 175.9467 | 171.7621 | 167.1663 | 162.0311 | 156.2749 | 149.8576 |
| ▷ | Roll (Z) | | | | | | | | | |
| ▷ | X Scale | | | | | | | | | |

**Figure 9.8.** Electric Image's animation sequencer.

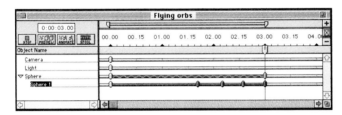

**Figure 9.9.** Infini-D's animation sequencer.

Will Vinton's Playmation has a unique approach to timelines, it offers separate graphs for every motion parameter (along the lines of Electric Image's), on which you can adjust an object's motion values by dragging handles on the graph against time.

Adding key frames in a sequencer is simple. You specify a position in time by dragging a slider or by clicking on a cell. Anything you then move or change you will get a new key event at that point in time.

# StrataStudio Pro's Animation Palette

StrataStudio Pro has introduced a new level of animation power to the high-end of Macintosh 3-D software. The high end includes Macromedia Three-D, and Infini-D; and EIAS (at roughly five times the price of any of them) hovers somewhere on the outer limits.

StrataStudio Pro's Animation Palette, similar to EIAS, is directly linked to the motion curves of objects. You can drag these curves around within your scene to quickly compose a satisfying motion (see figure 9.10).

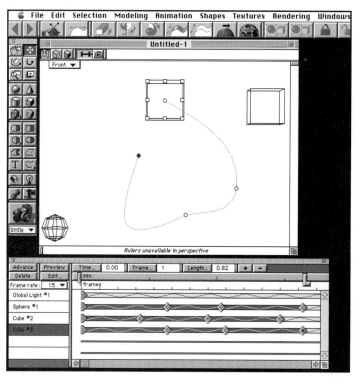

**Figure 9.10.** In StrataStudio Pro, you can drag curves to create motion.

# Action!

Just as a movie director tells his actors where to go, the director of a 3-D production has to position his models, lights, and other props over time. In the simplest animation programs (such as

Typestry), animation is limited to the movement of actors from one key frame to the next. Objects can float, fall, spin, bounce, and vibrate.

More common uses of motion are "fly-ins" and "fly-outs." Typically, a logo will fly onto the screen and stop, first attracting, then holding attention. It is important to confine or restrict the motion of supporting actors so that the object of interest is clear. A common technique is to use many layers of partly-transparent backgrounds, with the main actor hovering near the center of the foreground.

# Camera moves

Just as you can animate models, you can animate a camera—so any point of view is possible. This has an added advantage because 3-D cameras are not constrained by the limitations of film speed, changing exposure due to zooming, or depth of field.

It is possible to mimic the wildest actions of a cinematographer's movie camera: panning, zooming, and dollying side-to-side or front-to-back. It is also possible to have a camera float above a scene, follow an actor, or remain attached to an actor.

Keep in mind that perspective is your friend. Objects flying into and out of the screen, as opposed to just side-to-side, tend to create a better impression of 3-D movement.

## Flying camera logo

The following animation was created in Electric Image's Animation System. The result is a much more sophisticated example of a flying logo than the one created in the previous example. While the camera flies along to view different parts of the scene, objects within the scene are independently animated with different start and end points.

1. **0 seconds.** After you generate a logo model in Mr. Font and import it into the scene, position the camera for a top view so that it is aiming at the left end of the logo, but positioned far to the right. In the Camera Info dialog box, rotate the camera 90

degrees so that the logo forms the floor of the camera view (see figure 9.11). Rotate each of the letters 180 degrees around its own y-axis.

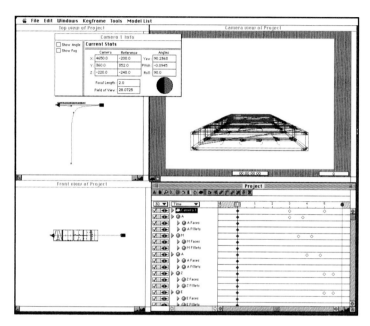

**Figure 9.11.** Positioning the camera in the Camera Info dialog box.

2. **3 seconds.** In 3/4-second intervals, the letters of the logo are revolved to their proper orientation. This gives the effect of the letters flipping into position one at a time. Move the camera so that it is nearly touching the focus point at the left end of the logo (see figure 9.12).

3. **3.5 seconds.** Move the camera away from the logo and rotate it back to its normal upright orientation and aim it at the center of the logo. This results in the logo swinging into proper orientation and the logo will fit completely into the camera window (see figure 9.13).

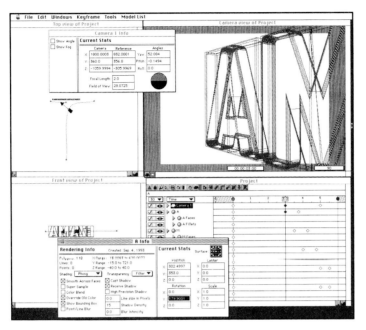

**Figure 9.12.** Moving the camera position again.

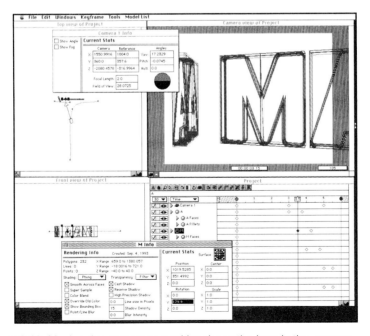

**Figure 9.13.** Moving the camera to position the entire logo in the camera window.

4. **5.5 seconds**. The final two letters of the logo settle into correct position, freezing the logo (see figure 9.14).

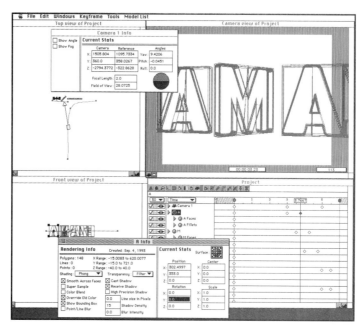

**Figure 9.14.** The final letters move into place.

5. **6 seconds**. The end.

A number of interesting 3-D animation techniques and samples are on the CD-ROM included with this book.

# Synching to sound

Serious character animators usually begin with a pre-recorded soundtrack. They then animate their characters to synchronize with specific events (such as dialog). In order to synch sounds when working in 3-D, you will need to generate an animation script that lists events by time. The standard measure of time in video and animation is called SMPTE Time Code, and it expresses video in terms of hours, minutes, seconds, and frames. Armed with this script, you can set key frames for each event on your 3-D software's timeline. (These may be as tedious as specifying "lips open," "lips closed," "eyebrows up," or "eyebrows down.") After you generate your animation, you can combine the sounds and video using standard compositing techniques.

The alternative is to generate an animation and then dub in a sound track, editing parts of the animation to fit the audio. In the long run, this is less efficient, but gives the editor more material with which to work.

Electric Image's Animation System is the first Mac 3-D program to offer built-in sound support, enabling you to automatically synchronize animations to a sound track. A QuickTime track is imported and displayed at the bottom of the frame. You can set key points on this track and then synch your animation to each of the key points.

# Deck II

OSC Software's Deck II is a particularly powerful sound editing application that handles full CD-quality audio in multiple tracks. For serious animators working with sound it is almost a must, although it requires DSP hardware on an accelerator or on the motherboard of Apple's AV Macs. It is a fairly expensive investment.

The program enables you to import a QuickTime movie and easily synchronize sound to specific video events. You also can generate a time sheet from a particular piece of music and use this as a reference for setting your key frames. So if you're building an animation for video overlay or if you want to mix your sound after you have generated an animation, this is an ideal solution.

> **Tip**
> Often when building animations you will find that you want
> to aim a camera near an object, but that you want the
> object to appear near the top right of the frame, not in the
> center. At other times, you will want to create an anima-
> tion cycle and have it repeat multiple times as you move
> the whole group around in the scene. The solution to both
> problems is simple: create an invisible object (a cube is
> good and small), and make it the parent of the object you
> want to aim at, or the cycling group you want to move.
> Since the object has parent status, anything it does will be
> reflected in its child(ren). If you aim a camera, the children
> will maintain their proximity to the "ghost," but remain
> outside of the center of the screen. If you attach a group to
> the ghost object (even if this group is going through
> motion cycles) you can move the ghost and everything
> else will move along with it.

# Ease-in and ease-out

One problem with animation is that it does not always account for
the natural acceleration, deceleration, orientation, and distortion
of objects as they stop and go and move around. For animators,
simulating these changes is an important part of realistic animations. In real life things do not go from 0 to 60 in 0 seconds. (There is
always an element of acceleration and deceleration when things
speed up or come to rest.)

Infini-D, for example, uses a slider control to determine the ease-in
and ease-out value of an event (see figure 9.15). To access the
slider, you double-click on an event mark (object key frame). You
can specify an amount you want the object to ease into its next
motion, as well as how long you want it to ease out. These capabilities are also offered by Macromedia Three-D, StrataStudio Pro, and
EIAS.

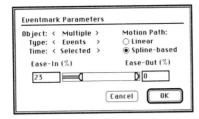

**Figure 9.15.** Infini-D's basic motion smoothing control.

# Smoothing motion

One of the problems of key frame animation is that you cannot see how objects will move in real time. Often you will end up with animations where the camera or objects move or turn unnaturally. Like acceleration, it's important to be able to adjust these parameters to smooth motions so they conform to our expectations of the real world.

Having an object maintain proper orientation as it flies is tricky. Cameras can generally be set to look at another object as they fly about. This means that if a camera is flying on a narrow oval track around a central subject, it will continue to look at the subject and turn automatically to stay aligned in the scene. With objects that usually cannot look at anything, it is a bit trickier. Again, Infini-D comes to the rescue with animation assistants that keep an object aligned along its path of motion. StrataStudio Pro enables you to easily align an object to its path of motion and make it bank like an airplane when it turns.

## StrataStudio bank turns

1. At time 0, the airplane is at rest (see figure 9.16).

2. After several seconds, a motion path has been defined with four key points (see figure 9.17).

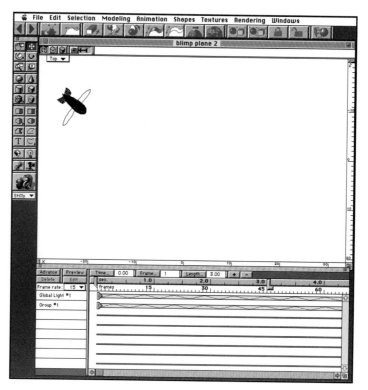

**Figure 9.16.** View of airplane at rest: time is 0 at frame 1.

3. For the first key frame an ease-in value is applied. Notice that the spline tension slider controls the smoothness of the rate of the acceleration. The End Lifespan checkbox in the lower-left corner is used to snuff a model out of existence at a key point without interrupting its motion—an airplane could disappear in mid-flight, for example (see figure 9.18).

4. The entire motion path is selected and the Align to Path Animator is opened. You can adjust the orientation of the model in the fast-shaded preview at the left by dragging it around with the mouse (see figure 9.19). This establishes the "normal" forward and upward direction. Clicking on the Bank on turns checkbox causes the plane to bank naturally, as well as to follow the path.

5. The resulting animation specifies a separate motion path for every part of the model (see figure 9.20).

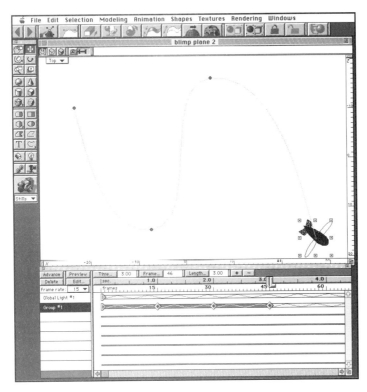

**Figure 9.17.** Defining key points for motion.

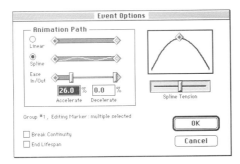

**Figure 9.18.** The Event Options dialog box where you can control acceleration, easing-in, and easing-out.

6. The camera is repositioned and the animation previewed. The plane now banks left-to-right as it flies out of the screen (see figure 9.21).

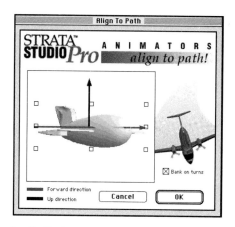

**Figure 9.19.** StrataStudio Pro's Align to Path dialog box where you can set the orientation of the model.

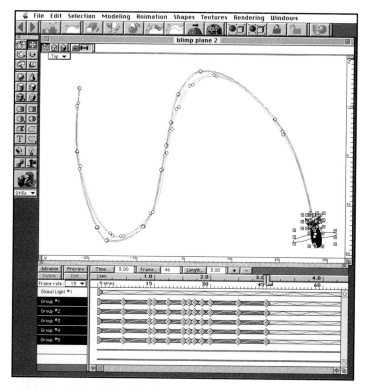

**Figure 9.20.** StrataStudio Pro displays separate motion paths for each part of the model.

# Manually smoothing motion

With programs that do not automate banked turns, you will find yourself creating subordinate key frames to make models rotate and align within the larger overall motion. For example, if a car is flying around a narrow oval track, it will rotate almost 180 degrees at each end of the oval, but rotation will be minimal along the long straight aways of the oval. In contrast, for an object flying around a circle, you can simply specify that it should rotate 360 degrees in the time it takes to go around the loop. An object flying around a square track or other corners takes careful handling. Here, you will want the object to rotate only as it comes to a corner. You will therefore need to create two key points for every corner. The object will begin to rotate just as it approaches the corner and finish a 90-degree rotation just after it rounds the corner. (For the effect of a fishtailing car, you can make it over-bank at the second key point, then add a third key point just beyond and have it rotate back to 90 degrees.) The important point is not to make the car turn constantly to complete a 360-degree rotation as it rounds the square, but to adjust the rotation so it matches the actions of a real car on a real square track.

# Infini-D's Animation Assistants

Infini-D's Animation Assistants are similar to StrataStudio Pro's without interactive controls (see figure 9.22). They provide a degree of natural behaviors, such as following a path and banking turns.

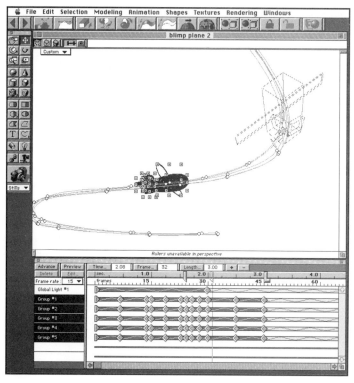

**Figure 9.21.** Your animation is previewed onscreen.

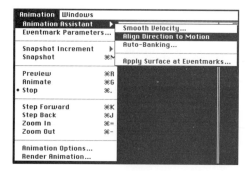

**Figure 9.22.** The menu where you can select your assistance from the Animation Assistant in Infini-D.

## Macromedia Three-D tweening

Macromedia Three-D offers a set of tools for creating realistic motions for animated objects. The first of these is the Graph Tracks. This is a graph showing the changes in parameters of an object over time. If you change the shape of the curve by dragging control points, you can modify parameters to your satisfaction.

A related dialog box called Tweening enables you to control the ease-in and ease-out values of an object in the selected key frames. You also can choose to make the motions Smooth (to create a natural-looking acceleration and deceleration); or you can choose Cyclic, which allows a series of frames to repeat continuously. This means the last frame in the cycle will flow smoothly into the first, so there is not a noticeable "jump" between cycles. One of the options enables you to use a formula (entered in Macromedia Three-D's Score) to control the motion of the object. This enables you to constrain motion relative to mathematical formulas, such as the acceleration due to gravity.

The capability to support mathematical formulae, or the results of calculations in motion cells, makes Macromedia Three-D an outstanding choice for use with a program like Working Model that generates motion based on real-world physical interactions. Working Model can export the results of its calculations right into Macromedia Three-D's animation Score.

In addition to standard motion tweening, Macromedia Three-D provides very good control over surface quality morphing. You can set surface values numerically and the program will automatically tween in-between values to create a smooth transition from one parameter to another. So, for example, an opaque object can disappear by turning transparent.

# Modeling for animation

Modeling for animation is no different than modeling for still images, with the exception that you may want to do more planning on the front end. For example, in still images, it does not matter if you model a character's mouth as one part or several parts. In animation, however, you will want to use several parts if you plan to make the character talk realistically. In many cases, animations will actually require less detail in models. For instance, you may want to simplify the background so that rendering is faster and the background does not distract from the foreground.

Animations are often created in several layers, enabling you to combine various animated backgrounds and foreground objects in interesting ways. More importantly, this enables you to perfect one part of an image at a time—requiring you to re-render only the parts that need corrections.

# Simplify background objects

Because speed is so much more of an issue when creating animation, it is important to optimize what you can do in a given amount of time. One of the most effective techniques is to substitute backgrounds and environments for background and environmental objects whenever possible, and to simplify the non-essential objects in your scene. If you are using multiple copies of a foreground model for background "extras," you can hide non-essential details on those models so that they do not eat up rendering time. This has an added benefit: The eye is naturally drawn to the most detailed, interesting objects in a scene. If you simplify everything but the foreground characters, they will automatically become the focal point of your animation.

# Bevels

As discussed earlier, bevels are extremely important for creating realistic objects. They are even more so in animation, because they catch and reflect light where flat surfaces tend to be rather, well… flat. If possible, use rounded bevels when animating because these are particularly effective at catching and reflecting highlights. Bevels also tend to provide an outline for extruded text that makes it much easier to read.

# Environment maps

To give a scene sparkle and the appearance of shininess, use environment maps and reflective surfaces liberally. Animated objects without the benefit of reflections tend to be dull looking, even when brightly lit. Often, you can use a very subtle environment map to give an object just the suggestion of light and shadow moving across its surface. At other times, you can use a dramatic environment map; for example, a flashing red-and-blue animated environment can create the effect of being at the scene of an emergency.

Static environment maps usually suffice when the main models in your scene are moving around; as a model moves it will catch and reflect the environment map on different surfaces, giving the object a rich sense of realism.

See Animation: Teapot Environment on the CD-ROM bound-in to the back of this book.

# Links and constraints

Links and constraints come into their own when animating. When creating still images, it is often adequate to simply move and tweak objects until they are properly aligned. When animating, however, it is crucial that objects and groups have defined relationships so that you need not move every part individually at every frame.

# Morphing

*Morph* is the accepted term for metamorphosis, or transformation, from one shape to another. (If you will bear the expression, this is a field that is rapidly changing shape.) Almost every 3-D company has a new and improved morphing tool in the works. A couple of Mac 3-D programs have special capabilities for animating unusual properties.

Infini-D enables you to morph any object created in a Workshop to morph into a different form of itself (see "Morphing a glass" later in this chapter).

Crystal TOPAS, like Macromedia Three-D, also enables you to morph between two spline objects with the same number of spline points. Even simple key-frame animators, such as Typestry, StrataVision 3d, and Presenter Professional, enables you to squash and stretch objects over time.

# Will Vinton's Playmation

This program enables you to animate an object's flesh. It uses the metaphor of skeleton and skin, enabling you to bend an entire model along a spine and have the skin fold on the inside of the bend and stretch on the outside like a real creature. You can even animate separate vertexes, or selected groups of vertexes, so that part of a model can move one way, while another part moves in a different direction. This results in incredibly organic motion.

# StrataStudio's particle morphs

StrataStudio Pro has made an art out of shape morphing. Extensions to the program enable you to blow things apart and fly back together in a new form, or simply morph smoothly between dissimilar objects without the visual blending that occurs in most 2-D morphing programs.

---

**Who morphs?**

- Infini-D
- Macromedia Three-D
- StrataStudio Pro
- Crystal TOPAS
- Playmation

---

# Prepare to morph

You may need to conform to some rules to accomplish smooth morphs in some programs. In Macromedia Three-D, for example, you must begin with two models created with the same number of control points. About the only practical way to do this is to build your end model by deforming your starting model (without adding points). MacroModel forms a good partnership with Macromedia Three-D in this respect, because it is fairly easy to use the Bezier spline-based modeler to derive vastly different shapes from the same starting block. Essentially, Macromedia Three-D tweens the positions of each point in the model at each frame in the sequence, using the beginning and ending states as the extremes.

Similarly, Sculpt 4D limits morphing to different forms of the same model. Inifni-D's morphing and modeling are part of the same process, so no preparation is necessary.

StrataStudio Pro enables you to morph smoothly between spline objects with different numbers of control points.

## Morphing a glass

Infini-D's morphing is very simple to use. You can morph between any objects that can be created in the same Workshop window (Lathe, Extrude, or Freeform). But with very complex surfaces (such as 3-D type), keep in mind that surfaces will look strange when they turn inside out to accomplish a morph.

1. Model a glass in the Lathe Workshop by drawing its outline with the Polygon tool (see figure 9.23). When it is complete, choose Exit Workshop.

2. Position the model, assign a texture and lights and select Snapshot (see figure 9.24). This freezes the model at that location in time.

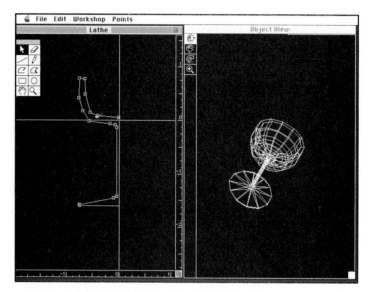

**Figure 9.23.** A glass model drawn with the Polygon tool.

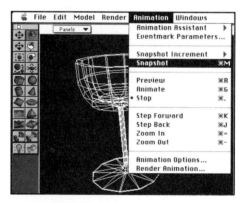

**Figure 9.24.** Choosing Snapshot from the Animation pull-down menu.

3. Move the timeline marker a few seconds, then move the model to a new location and rotate it. Double click on the model to open it in the Lathe Workshop once again. Select the Reshape Outline command, and drag the control points around to reshape the glass (see figure 9.25). Exit the Workshop and note that the model has been changed to reflect your edits. Choose Snapshot again to complete the morph.

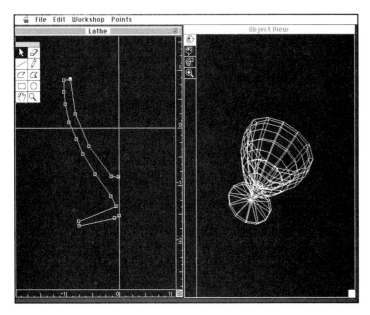

**Figure 9.25.** The glass has been reshaped and rotated.

4. To preview the morph, drag the time slider to intermediate points in your animation (see figure 9.26).

# Rotoscoping

Rotoscoping is the technique that allows you to map an animation or digitized video onto a background, or onto an object in your scene. Several 3-D programs enable you to use animated backgrounds and textures. These begin as animation files—although there is no accepted standard. Macromedia Three-D uses PICS, Infini-D uses QuickTime, and EIAS requires an EIAS Animation file. Otherwise, these programs use the animation file in the same way you normally use a still image as a texture or background. For every frame in the animation, these renderers step one frame through the animated texture, resulting in an animation within an animation—even an animation wrapped around a 3-D object.

315

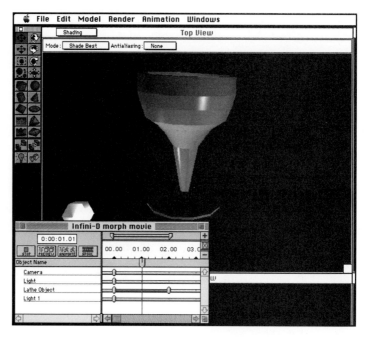

**Figure 9.26.** Moving the time slider previews the morph.

You may use an animated texture to put a movie on a cinema screen, to put video on a TV screen, or even to show clouds blowing past a window in an architectural rendering.

Animations and digitized video can be used for both backgrounds and textures in a number of 3-D programs. Some programs (such as Electric Image), require that you convert animations to specific formats. Infini-D and Strata's animators support QuickTime movies, while Macromedia Three-D uses PICS files.

**Several 3-D programs offer rotoscoping, including:**

- Macromedia Three-D
- StrataStudio Pro
- StrataVision 3D
- Infini-D
- EIAS

# Film loops

A seamless animation or *loop* is a clip that loops continuously so that the same series of frames plays over and over; it is impossible to determine where it begins and ends. Just as seamless textures are more convincing, loops can create the sense of ongoing activity in the background or on the surface of an object. To create animated loops, you can render them in 3-D of course, as well as turning to some digital trickery.

It is usually simple to create a 3-D animation that begins and ends in the same place—thus guaranteeing that the action in the animation continues smoothly without a break. For example, you can create an animation of machine gears grinding together and render it as an animation for use as a background. If you later composite this with an animation of a wrench dropping into the scene, you can create the effect of a wrench dropping into the machine.

For abstract moving animations, you can create an animation that moves in one direction—then reverse it and splice the two segments together. Using Adobe Premiere and Kai's Power Tools' Texture Explorer, for example, you can generate two background images with a smooth transition between them. You then can save this effect as a QuickTime movie; reverse the order of the images (but not the transition) using Premiere's Backwards filter; and generate a second QuickTime movie with the two segments spliced together. When you play the animation, the beginning frame is the same as the end and the entire movie loops seamlessly.

## Morphing a cloud video

It is possible to create very convincing seamless loops of natural video scenes by using one of the several new special effects programs that provide digital morphing.

Using a program like Gryphon Software's Morph, you can morph the end frame of a QuickTime video segment into the first frame. This creates the missing link between the first and last frames of a clip. With patience, this can be an effective technique, although it will probably take several attempts before the transition seems natural.

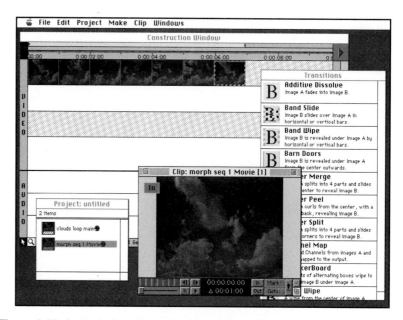

**Figure 9.27.** Adobe's Premiere is the best of the editing tools when working seriously with QuickTime. It can easily be used for creating endless film loops.

## Morphing tools

Several programs now provide digital morphing that can be used to create special effects film loops for rotoscoping. Elastic Reality from ASDG Software and VideoFusion from Video Fusion are both good candidates. *Elastic* reality enables you to morph parts of images at different rates (event-based morphing) for effects that go beyond simple transitions. VideoFusion, meanwhile, is a full-featured QuickTime effects tool that can be used for compositing and other QuickTime production effects.

# Physics-based animation

Physics-based or *physical modeling* and animation are widely used by high-end software (such as SoftImage), on UNIX platforms. But animation that obeys the laws of nature is gradually finding its way to the Macintosh.

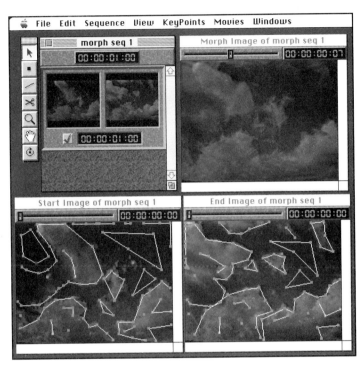

**Figure 9.28.** Morph uses control points to define important areas to transform.

It is important for a model to accelerate correctly when animating to make it resemble a real world motion; and if it is falling, it ought to fall at a normal rate. A physical-based animation program enables you to place a model in a scene (say 1000 feet off the ground), and apply "gravity" to the model. When you run the animation, the model accelerates (at 32 feet per second squared) and stops suddenly—or even bounces an appropriate distance depending on the material it is made of—when it hits the ground.

These animations are much easier to do if the computer automatically calculates the model's acceleration and animates accordingly. Physical animators can have built-in intelligence. A model may have parts labeled left leg, right leg, torso, and so on. A predefined motion for walking could be applied to this model, and the animation software can automatically apply the right kinds of motion to each part of the model. (The knees and ankles would bend appropriately and the model would walk at the right speed based on the length of its legs.)

By defining rules for different types of motion, you can automatically create movement to fit any situation. This kind of animation power is just around the corner for Macintosh users.

# Inverse kinematics

Inverse kinematics is a simple idea that is very difficult for the software developer to implement. For this reason, it is not widely available. In its simplest form, if you move a model's hand the arm will follow. This is the inverse of the normal modeler relationship, whereby a child has to follow its parent, but the parent is free to move where it likes. The rules of inverse kinematics mean that moving a hand to a certain position implies having moved the upper arm, forearm, and body in a certain way. In order to do this, you must establish rules of behavior for a child's link to its parent. For example, if you twist the hand, the forearm must twist an appropriate amount, as does the upper arm if you twist the hand too far. The first phase of this kind of relationship already exists in programs like EIAS and Infini-D that enable you to establish constraints on objects so that they can only move within certain limits of position and orientation relative to their parents. The capability to have the parent respond if the child tries to exceed these limits is probably not far away.

# OZ

VIDI's physical-based animation system, called OZ, should reach the anxious hands of animators early in 1994. Prototypes feature drag-and-drop animations that you can apply to models in a scene, as well as inverse kinematics. Demonstrations of OZ indicate that this will be an extremely powerful animation system when it finally ships.

# Working Model

Working Model, from Knowledge Revolution, is a physics-based motion simulation package that works in two dimensions, but has the capability to export its animations to 3-D software packages. For example, you can create an engine using joints, springs, and forces and Working Model will calculate the motion of the machine (see figure 9.29). If you export the key frame animation information to Macromedia Three-D and replace the 2-D models with their fully-detailed Three-D counterparts, you can render a fully realistic animation of the machine in action.

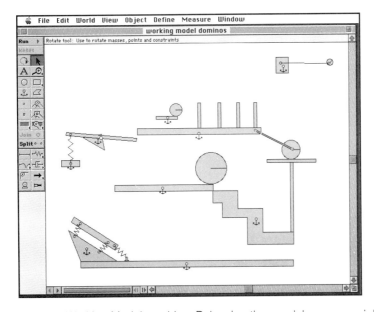

**Figure 9.29.** A Working Model machine. Releasing the pendulum, upper right, initiates a chain reaction of physical events.

The software provides a wide variety of physical constraints, such as springs, pulleys and joints. It can deal with collisions, wind resistance, gravity, and electrostatic charges. You can create a logo, for example, and generate an animation of 3-D letters crumbling and falling to the ground and bouncing chaotically (or rising into the air and blowing away). The program keeps track of the properties of components and the nature of constraints; it is automatically aware of kinematic relationships.

In addition to directly exporting animations to Macromedia Three-D, you can save a tab-delimited motion file for use in any program that supports this format (such as Electric Image Animation System). You also can export a DXF animation—a DXF file for every frame of an animation.

Because Working Model animations can rapidly fill a Macromedia Three-D score with data thereby slowing down processing to a crawl, it is best to export your Working Model data in several small chunks—rather than hundreds of frames at a time (see figure 9.30).

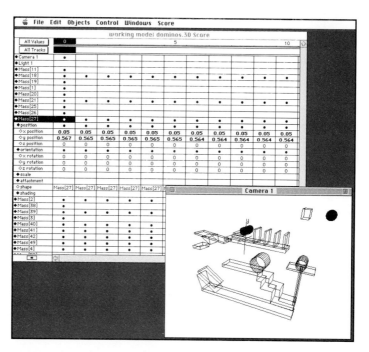

**Figure 9.30.** This model was imported into Macromedia Three-D from Working Model, complete with extruded models and motion descriptions for every cell.

# Formulas in animation

While they don't calculate the physics for you, EIAS and Macromedia Three-D both enable you to enter formulas to control the motion of objects. With some understanding of the formulas of physics, you can use these to create your own animations that obey physical laws.

By harnessing the power of Apple Events, it is likely that future versions of Macintosh 3-D software will communicate with programs like Working Model or Mathematica to generate 3-D animations from physical simulations—without any user intervention.

# Particle animation

*Particle animation* enables you to decompose a model into points: each with a characteristic shape (such as polygonal triangles or spheres). These particles can then be blown apart, crumpled by gravity, or blown away by wind. Very sophisticated particle animation, which is available on other platforms, enables you to create effects such as a snowstorm or exploding fireworks. Tornadoes and firestorms also can be generated by particle animators. While effects of this nature are in the future for Macintosh users, the first fragments of particle animation have begun to swirl onto the scene. When the PowerPC becomes a reality, many of these features will make a sudden appearance on the Macintosh.

Two Macintosh 3-D programs currently offer particle animation: Electric Image's Animation System and StrataStudio Pro.

StrataStudio Pro was the first commercially available Mac 3-D particle animator. It offers a variety of particle animation plug-ins that explode, shatter, and vaporize models. Particle morphing is an extension for StrataStudio Pro (due to ship around the same time as this book) that enables you to blow apart a model and have it reorganize the particles into a new model.

Electric Image's Animation System 2.0 will ship with an "explosion" extension called Mr. Nitro which is the direct result of an animation for the movie Terminator II.

# RenderMan

While several animation programs let you use RenderMan shaders directly, only Macromedia Three-D to date enables you to animate RenderMan shaders. For example, you could have a flaking paint shader where the flaking becomes progressively worse over time, or you could have a shader that uses green as the base color initially, but changes to red.

When animating, you can change the procedural parameters of surfaces over time, thus creating the effect of blushing, twisting, or peeling skin.

VIDI's Presenter Professional provides key-frame animation using RenderMan. Its level of animation control, however, is not as sophisticated as Macromedia Three-D. StrataStudio Pro, using Strata's Rend•X extension, will export RIB files and lights and will automatically convert texture maps into a RIB-compatilbe format. Texture morphing is not yet supported in this program.

# Animated lights

Animated lights are important to many kinds of night-time and darkened scenes. If you are depicting starships or other vehicles traveling by night, or if you simply want to create the effect of realistic lighting, you will want to experiment with putting lights in motion. Some of the methods you can use to do this include: putting lights on spaceships, causing street lamps to flicker, using visible lights (in Electric Image) as "explosions," sweeping "searchlights" across an object, or the sun slowly moving across a scene to show the passing of a day.

# Creating a flame

With StataStudio Pro or Infini-D, you can rotoscope a surface with animated glow and transparency maps to create the effect of flickering flames and other unusual lighted surfaces. Combining this technique with object morphing can create realistic flames.

# Summary

- Animation is based on key frames. Each *key frame* defines the state of a scene and the software automatically calculates all the action in between.

- *Key events* are similar to key frames, except that every object, including cameras and lights, has its own timeline and its key frames which are independent of every other. Even properties of an object can have their own timelines.

- Cameras can be animated like regular objects to provide a constantly changing point of view.

- Ease-in and ease-out provide smooth acceleration and deceleration to ensure that objects do not have sudden jerky motion changes.

- Modeling for animation does not need as much detail, particularly if they'll be moving fast; backgrounds can be simplified.

- Bevels are crucial in animation to give objects light-catching surfaces as they move. Environment maps are also important to make moving objects appear shiny.

# 10

# Rendering

R endering is where modeling, scene building, and animating payoff with the creation of realistic 3-D images. While *rendering* is concerned with the interaction of light and surfaces, the result of rendering is ultimately an image composed (in most cases) of colored pixels forming a bitmapped image. The rendering process diverges in one crucial respect from the way lighting and visualization of scenes occurs in the real world. In nature, light travels from a light source to an object that either transmits or reflects changed light to the viewer. What you see is reflected light, modified by interaction with objects and atmosphere.

The problem with this natural approach, as far as the 3-D user is concerned, is that most of the light that enters a scene is never reflected back to the viewer, but bounces out into space in some other direction. Three-D software, therefore, calculates the process in reverse: given the viewer's position and focus, the renderer determines what surface is visible and calculates the direction and source of all the light striking that surface point and determines how it reflects off the surface. Finally, the result of these calculations is that the renderer determines a color for the particular pixel in question.

A typical video-resolution image is 640-by-480 pixels (about 300,000 pixels) and the renderer steps through this process for each and every one of them! It is no wonder that rendering takes a long time.

Rendering remains the real bottleneck in Macintosh-based 3-D systems—but that limitation is fading rapidly. Programs like Strata's Virtual 3-D and Virtus' WalkThrough Pro are proving that real-time texture-mapped 3-D animation is a real possibility, while the impending release of speedy, RISC-based PowerPC Macs stands to turn the world on its three-dimensional ear.

While this chapter covers the basics of rendering, there are a number of advanced software and hardware options for greatly accelerating the speed and potential power of Macintosh 3-D rendering covered in chapter 13, "Advanced topics."

# Rendering methods

There are many types of rendering and each has its advantages. For the Mac 3-D user, these include:

- PostScript blending
- Wireframe
- Hidden line
- Flat shading
- Gouraud shading
- Phong shading
- Ray tracing
- Radiosity
- Ray Painting
- RenderMan

# PostScript blending

When you render with Adobe Dimensions or RayDream's addDepth, you are actually creating a rendering composed of many overlapping shapes that blend together visually. This is very similar to what you get when you create a blend in Adobe Illustrator or Aldus FreeHand. Each step in the gradation from black to white, and all the colors in between, is a solid block of color. The advantage of this is that a PostScript blend is infinitely scalable; the disadvantage is that as you increase the size of the image without increasing the resolution of the rendering, you get "banding" of colors. The other disadvantage of this method is that this is less realistic; it doesn't account for transparency, reflection, and other effects. Also, current versions limit you to white lights.

On the other hand, this is an extremely effective technique for producing artwork that needs to fit in to existing production methods. PostScript blends can be used to create surprisingly beautiful illustrations. Another advantage is that this art can be easily passed around and used in different types of documents at different sizes. Although they are difficult to compare to other rendering systems, addDepth renders a typical image in under a minute on a Macintosh Quadra, while Dimensions typically takes two to three times longer than that.

# Wireframe

Wireframe displays are the standard mode of displaying models during the modeling and scene building stages of 3-D (see figure 10.1). However, it is sometimes desirable to create a "wireframe rendering" of a scene or model. This is sometimes used when you want to create the effect of an unfinished project. It is particularly effective when composited artfully with a realistically rendered part of the same scene and gives the effect of a skeleton under a skin.

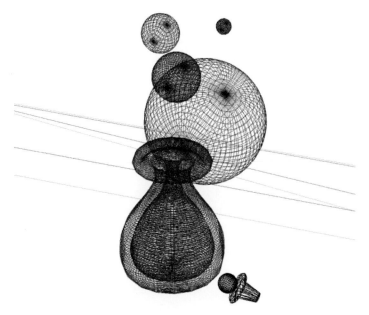

**Figure 10.1.** Wireframe rendering created in StrataStudio Pro.

A common use of wireframe renderings is Encapsulated PostScript (EPS), a format you can incorporate into most PostScript illustration and desktop publishing packages. Some 3-D programs will export an editable EPS wireframe that you can then modify in 2-D in a program such as Illustrator or FreeHand.

# Hidden-line rendering

Hidden-line rendering is a popular architectural, engineering, and technical illustration technique. *Hidden-line rendering* is essentially the same as wireframe rendering, except that foreground surfaces hide the lines of background surfaces (see figure 10.2) This creates the effect of outlined solid objects without shading. You'll usually use this rendering method when you want to create an image that looks as though it were hand-drawn in perspective. A hidden-line rendering can be touched up with "watercolors" in a program like Painter or Photoshop to create a very traditional-looking architectural rendering.

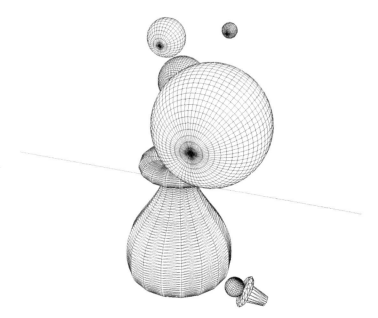

**Figure 10.2.** Hidden-line rendering created in StrataStudio Pro.

Hidden-line renderings are a standard in technical documentation, such as service manuals, because they print well in black and white and are easy to read—even at small sizes.

# Flat shading

*Flat shading* is the simplest and fastest method of shaded rendering. It derives its name from the faceted, polygonal appearance of the images it produces (see figure 10.3). This technique applies a single color to each of the polygons on the surface of a shape. This is the rendering technique favored by programs more concerned with display of information than photorealism. Mathematica is a good example of a special-purpose program that uses this technique. It enables you to graph the results of mathematical equations as shaded 3-D models.

**Figure 10.3.** Flat-shaded rendering created in StrataStudio Pro.

Because it is the fastest form of shaded rendering, it is commonly used by modelers to display geometry at the modeling stage. Some programs (such as VIDI's Presenter Pro), are fast enough at flat shading to provide rendering in near real-time while you work.

The drawbacks of flat shading are that it doesn't allow for realistic transparency, reflection, or texture mapping. It produces renderings that are unnaturally faceted and easily identifiable as being computer generated.

On the other hand, flat-shaded models are great for creating modernistic renderings with a high-tech video-game look.

# Gouraud shading

*Gouraud shading* (pronounced "juh-ro") goes one step further than flat shading by blending the edges of polygons toward their centers. This generates a very smooth rendering. But fine details, hard edges (such as an object's corner), and textures are "smeared" together resulting in rather blurry looking shapes (see figure 10.4).

**Figure 10.4.** Gouraud-shaded rendering created in StrataStudio Pro.

This is also a very fast rendering algorithm, so it is widely used for "smooth shaded" previews, and even for some finished renderings, such as those produced by Specular's LogoMotion. For animations where the shape of objects flying around in space is paramount, this can be a good solution.

Like other simple forms of shading, Gouraud is incapable of accurately depicting transparency, refraction, or reflection.

# Phong

*Phong* rendering (named for Bui Tuong Phong, an "illuminary" who determined how to smooth polygonal surfaces) calculates the shading of each pixel of an image based on the brightness, color, and direction of light sources striking that pixel; but it does not "trace" the light as it is reflected. While it is not as realistic as ray traced rendering, it is much faster in most cases. Phong shading, being the simplest form of realistic rendering, is the preferred method for most animations. EIAS, the most expensive general rendering system for the Macintosh, offers Phong shading as its "best" algorithm. With creative texture mapping and environment mapping, Phong rendering can produce images as realistic in appearance as ray tracings (see figure 10.5).

**Figure 10.5.** Phong rendering created in StrataStudio Pro.

Unlike ray tracing, which produces shadows as a matter of course, Phong shading goes through extra steps to produce shadows, usually reducing rendering speed. The two places where Phong shading completely breaks down are the mirror reflection of objects and refraction. While Phong shading does allow for environmental reflections and transparency (without refraction), mirror reflection and realistic transparency both require ray tracing for accurate depiction.

Although Phong shading generates very smooth surfaces, it does not smooth the faceted polygonal edges of coarse wireframes, so where smooth edges are important (particularly in high-contrast foreground and background relationships) you may want to increase the wireframe detail of your models (see figures 10.6 and 10.7).

**Figure 10.6.** Phong rendering of a coarse wireframe created in Sketch!.

**Figure 10.7.** The same model Phong shaded in Fine wireframe mode.

# Reflection maps

Color and brightness are calculated in reverse, from viewer to object to light source, in Phong rendering. However, only light striking a surface and bouncing towards the viewer is calculated, not light bouncing from one surface to another to the viewer; true reflections are not possible with Phong shading. This means you'll have to make creative use of environment maps to simulate reflections on surfaces.

For Phong renderings where you absolutely must have local reflections, it is possible to render the scene from the point of view of the object and use it as an environment map for that object. EIAS does this automatically, calling it "Automatic Environment," but the results can be slower than ray tracing.

# Ray tracing

*Ray tracing* is the most realistic rendering technique commonly available, and it is often referred to as "photorealistic" by 3-D programs. (However, Phong renderings can be just as convincing, depending on the scene.) Ray tracing follows the path of light rays from the light source to the surface of objects to the viewer. Unlike Phong rendering, ray tracing also accurately depicts the direction of light even after it is reflected, and the color and intensity of light as it bounces between and passes through objects.

Because ray tracing tracks the color and direction of light through a scene, it is capable of accurately depicting complex light effects. These effects include mirror reflection, shadows, transparency, and refraction: qualities that are only approximated by other rendering systems (see figure 10.8).

---

**Tip**
The only reason not to use ray tracing is time constraints. Typically a Phong rendering on a Quadra 950 may take ten minutes to an hour depending on the complexity of the scene. The same image that takes an hour in Phong

---

shading may take two days to ray trace if there are a lot of mirror reflections and transparent objects with refraction. Recursive reflections particularly wreak havoc.

**Figure 10.8.** Ray traced rendering with mirror reflections, transparency, and refraction. Created in StrataStudio Pro.

# Mirror reflection

In ray tracing, a ray of light bounces from one object to the next, carrying color and intensity as it goes. This means that an object's appearance will bounce around in a scene until it reaches the viewer. You see not only objects, but objects reflected off of each other as well. Mirror reflectance affects much more than glass mirrors. Some of the items that require ray traced reflections for a high degree of realism include: chrome or any other polished metal, shiny plastic, polished marble and tile, glass, lacquered wood, and ceramics.

# Recursion

Because objects in 3-D can have near or total reflectance, it is possible to create scenes where light rays bounce around infinitely from object to object, like a ball in a pinball machine with a bumper blocking every exit. This can result in a rendering taking forever when tracing a single infinitely bouncy light ray; and is particularly likely when there are a number of rounded reflectors in a scene (such as chrome pipes or spheres). Ray tracers, therefore, offer a setting to limit the number of "recursions" of a single reflection (see figure 10.9). Typically, this number is set at one or two, although for extremely reflective scenes (such as a hall of mirrors), you may want to bump the number up. Just be prepared to wait a very long time for your rendering to finish.

**Figure 10.9.** The expert settings dialog box in StrataVision 3d's textures control panel enables you to set limits on recursion.

# Transparency

Ray tracing is capable of accurately depicting the transmission of light through transparent objects. The most basic effect of this is that you can see other objects behind a transparent object. This also means that light can pass through a transparent or translucent surface, affecting surfaces on the other side. As light passes through green glass, for example, the light takes on the green color.

In the case of glass, for example, a material can have transparency combined with other surface qualities (such as reflection), so that some light will pass through the surface, while some will bounce off.

> **Tip**
> When using transparent objects, consider using a rendered background instead of post-compositing your image with an alpha channel. This is because transparency and particularly refraction are not carried through properly to alpha channel. If you want your background to show through naturally, you will need to render it into the scene.

# Refraction

At times, light may bend as it passes through a surface. This quality is known as *refraction* and is one of the major visual clues that distinguishes one "clear" material from another. The most common example of refraction is that of a glass lens.

Like mirror reflection, refraction is subject to recursion. It is possible to have a series of objects that bend light into a continuous loop.

# Radiosity

*Radiosity* is an advanced form of ray tracing that accurately depicts the interaction of light "under the surface" of surfaces. Since mirror-like surfaces are actually relatively simple in terms of how they reflect light (it merely bounces off), this algorithm is mostly used when you require extremely life-like matte finishes and shadows. Matte surfaces have a minute roughness that scatters light very subtly, giving the surface a soft-edge glow.

Examples of matte surfaces include: flat spray paint, asphalt, rough metal, sanded wood, and soft cotton fabric. Matte surfaces, although non-reflective, will often have a barely-perceptible glowing effect due to the interaction of light with the surface material.

**Radiosity:**
StrataVision 3d and Strata StudioPro are the only renderers that currently support it on Macintosh computers.

While radiosity combines the accuracy of ray tracing with the accurate depiction of surfaces, it is substantially slower than ray tracing. Thus it is suitable only for extremely critical renderings requiring extremely realistic results. It is seldom used for animations. Radiosity rendering practically requires some form of rendering acceleration (see figure 10.10).

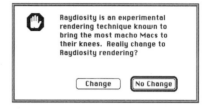

Raydiosity is an experimental rendering technique known to bring the most macho Macs to their knees. Really change to Raydiosity rendering?

Change    No Change

**Figure 10.10.** The warning box in StrataVision 3d, making it clear that radiosity is not for the faint-hearted.

# RayPainting

StrataStudio Pro has a new rendering method called "Ray Painting," that paints a surface with splotches of color as if it were being painted. This is much faster than normal ray tracing because the renderer need only sample a small fraction of the total pixels in the image. It uses the results of this to smear brush strokes in a logical fashion over an object's surface (see figure 10.11).

## Boolean rendering

Shade II and RenderMan both allow for Boolean operations during rendering. Just as you can subtract one volume from another in a solid modeler such as Zoom or form•Z, you can use RenderMan or Shade II to do this at the rendering stage. In Shade II, these effects have an additional option: If you subtract a sphere from the edge of a cube, for example, you can choose to have the texture of the sphere applied to the sphere-shaped void left in the cube—even while the rest of the cube maintains its original texture (see figure 10.12). This saves you from having to create multiple parts to get multiple texture maps on a single object .

**Figure 10.11.** Ray Painted ray tracing created in StrataStudio Pro.

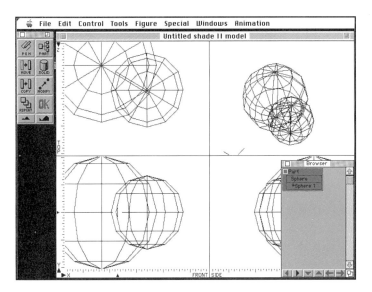

**Figure 10.12.** In Shade II, overlapping models can be set to render as boolean operators on one another.

# Rendering quality

Rendering quality is a subjective measure. Just what makes rendering high quality is up to the taste of the person using it. For our purposes, we'll define *high-quality rendering* as that which most resembles what we see with our own eyes in the everyday world. Of course, no computer program can ever hope to totally recreate a natural scene. But the capability to create the illusion of reality—hence the term *photorealism*—is the goal.

# Realism

A realistic image is one that accurately portrays real objects in everyday life in realistic settings. Many things contribute to the sense of realism:

- **Details.** These serve as clues to the authenticity of a subject. Shading and shadow, textures and reflections, modeled, and mapped details all lend to the illusion that you are seeing a real-world image.

- **Effects.** These may be as subtle as a minuscule grain on an object's otherwise smooth surface, or as dramatic as a bright red glow.

- **Control.** The careful placement and revelation of important parts of a scene. This may include one object serving only to carve into and reveal part of another object.

- **Organic appearance.** Nothing looks more computer generated than an image filled with perfectly smooth, perfectly symmetrical, perfectly geometric objects. Organic objects are lumpy, misshapen, and malformed.

# Detail

One of the distinguishing factors of high-end rendering systems (such as EIAS and Sculpt 3-D), is that they allow for a high degree of flexibility in texture mapping and rendering of details. At the low end of the spectrum, 3-D programs generally offer only simple texture mapping, but effects like multiple overlaid textures and animated textures are not supported.

It is important to keep in mind that detail can be created in many ways. Modeling creates the most realistic details at the expense of time and rendering speed. Many details can be created through the judicious use of texture maps, bump maps, and carefully placed backgrounds.

# Antialiasing

*Aliasing*, also called stair-stepping or jaggedness, is a problem of digital imaging that results from a computer's habit of working in terms of visible square pixels as the smallest unit of an image. It occurs at the edges of contrasting curved or diagonal lines, but its effect is devastating to the best-laid renderings. An easy way to picture aliasing is to try drawing a perfect circle on a sheet of graph paper by filling in squares. Even though you may generate an approximation of a circle, its edges are very jagged. ("You can't square a circle.")

Antialiasing combats the "jaggies" by blending the pixels at the edges of objects into the background (see figures 10.13 and 10.14). A black circle on a white background, for example, becomes a black circle with a thin ring of gray pixels on the outside edge blending in to the white background. When viewed from a distance, you can't tell exactly where the white background ends and the black ring starts—they appear to fit smoothly together. Even though antialiasing essentially works by smudging the edges of objects, the visual effect is that of creating a smooth sharp line.

**Figure 10.13.** Image rendered in Strata StudioPro, with no antialiasing.

**Figure 10.14.** The same model with a high degree of antialiasing.

# Supersampling

There are several different methods for creating antialiased edges. Most 3-D programs use the method of "supersampling." Essentially, *supersampling* renders a high-resolution image and uses the extra rendering information to determine the blending of the edges. The result is a normal-resolution rendering, with the high-resolution information being discarded after antialiasing.

The simpler and much less time consuming method of antialiasing is practiced by some 3-D programs as well as antialiasing utilities such as Jag II from RayDream. These programs can work on finished renderings (unlike supersampling, which is an integral part of the rendering process). This is sometimes called *interpolative* (or "averaging") antialiasing. It works by interpolating between pixels and their neighbors. When the program encounters an area of high contrast or color differential, it interprets between the contrasting pixels to blend the edges. In areas of gradual color or contrast variation, pixels are left alone in order to avoid unnecessary blurring of the entire image.

# Wireframe complexity

The wireframe complexity of an object in 3-D determines the level of actual geometric detail in a model. For example, a polygonal modeler may simulate a circle by creating a many-sided polygon; at a very low level of detail, this may be an octagon, while at a very high level of detail, it may use a 64-sided polygon that will much more closely resemble a circle.

Even in spline-based systems, wireframe complexity has a direct impact on the level of detail possible in a model. To create a bump on a surface between two splines, you will need to create several new splines to use as contours for the bump.

Wireframe complexity is often distinct from rendered smoothness. That is, it is possible to create a smoothly rendered image from a very coarse wireframe through the trickery of Phong rendering, and so forth. However, more complex wireframes will lead to more accurate, more detailed images. The trade off is that the increased volume of data required to increase wireframe complexity results in decreased speed (and increased storage requirements) throughout the 3-D process.

Most 3-D programs have options for increasing wireframe detail, usually while creating a model. Sketch!, on the other hand, benefits from its use of splines in that you can reset the wireframe complexity of models at any time. You even can work on a model in coarse wireframe mode, then switch to finely-detailed wireframes for final detail work. Sketch! also enables you to render in a different level of detail than the one in which you work. It also enables you to set different levels of detail for different models in a scene.

# Smoothness

The apparent smoothness of rendered objects is the result of a number of factors: the rendering algorithms in use, the detail of the wireframes being rendered, and the degree of abruptness in change over an object's surface.

Some rendering methods, particularly Gouraud, impose an automatic smoothing on surfaces (sometimes when it isn't desirable). This is because Gouraud shading determines the color values at the edges of polygons. It also blends the colors together toward the polygon's center: this is like buttering the edges of your toast and spreading the butter in towards the middle. When you use the Smooth shading option of many renderers (usually reserved for Phong and ray traced rendering), the program changes the surface "normals" (surface vectors) of facets to make a faceted model look smooth to the renderer.

# Speed

Rendering speed is an overwhelming concern of 3-D users. Fortunately, it is also a concern of hardware and software vendors. Even though 3-D modeling and rendering are becoming more and more complex and demanding more and more of rendering systems, rendering times are actually getting shorter—not longer. This is partly due to the speed of computers, but also due in part to the relentless optimization of rendering software. There are many user-controlled elements that affect the speed of rendering: the type of rendering, the complexity of the models being rendered, the detail or resolution of the rendering, the number of lights, special effects, texture maps, and many others.

Fortunately, the current availability of network rendering, workstation slave rendering, and even NuBus coprocessor rendering, is greatly assisting the quest for more speed (see chapter 13, "Advanced Topics"). In the near future, Macintosh PowerPC will be far faster than the current variety and rendering speed will start to take a back seat to creative control and software features.

# Speed factors

There are many factors that influence rendering speed, a few of which are subject to control by the 3-D user. While it is true that some 3-D rendering applications are much faster than others, it is more often the case that better 3-D applications provide for the creation of complex scenes in an efficient manner. For example, environment mapping is a much more time efficient technique than ray traced reflections. A program with good control over environment mapping techniques will often get the job done more efficiently than one that settles on ray tracing as the only way to create a reflection.

For users without a fully-loaded Macintosh, it is also important to keep in mind that the factors that affect speed are also generally the ones that affect memory requirements. Cutting down on any of them will lighten the load on system requirements.

## Rendering type

The type of rendering used contributes directly to the speed of rendering. Radiosity and ray tracing, respectively, are the slowest algorithms. Depending on what you are trying to achieve, RenderMan can also be extremely slow (and Pixar's 3-D scene building program lays itself bare to the Sunday punch "slo.place"). RenderMan, using one of the many acceleration options, is one of the fastest general-purpose rendering systems available to Macintosh. Phong shading is the fastest realistic rendering method available in most modelers, while Gouraud and flat shading are fast, but sacrifice rendering quality for speed.

## Scene complexity

When using Phong, or a simpler rendering system, the amount of time it takes to render a scene increases more or less linearly as you increase the number or complexity of any of these factors:

- Models

- Texture and environment maps

- Lights

- Reflections and refractions

- Shadows

On the other hand, ray tracing times increase exponentially. This is because every reflection of a surface is dependent on the reflections of nearby surfaces.

In general, the overuse of lights and shadows is the most common problem. Beginners are prone to rely heavily on ray-traced reflections because they make a scene realistic without bothering with environment maps.

# Image size

The size of the image you create also directly influences rendering times. Since a renderer calculates backward from each pixel in the image and the sum of all the lights and colors arriving at that point, doubling the number of pixels will typically double the total rendering time. Keep in mind that proportionally doubling the size of an image actually quadruples the number of pixels it contains (since you are multiplying both the horizontal and vertical dimensions). For example, a 640-by-480-pixel image will take four-times longer to render than the same image rendered at 320 by 240 pixels.

# Lights

Every light source adds a new element to the calculation of all affected surfaces. The addition of lights to a scene particularly can slow down ray-tracing because a single light can affect surfaces multiple times. This is why it is preferable in most cases to use a single light at full power, rather than two lights at half power. This makes it particularly bothersome when software vendors create programs that constrain the power of lights to a narrow range or even one or two settings; you will often need to use multiple lights where one would normally suffice.

# Mirror reflections

Ray traced reflections are among the most costly of rendering effects because—as far as the renderer is concerned—they require multiple renderings within a single scene. Recursive reflections can bring a renderer to its knees.

# Effects

Effects that affect rendering speed include the use of shadows, fog, and depth of field.

Shadows are particularly detrimental to rendering speed. For this reason, it is often possible to turn off shadow rendering for an entire rendering, or just for individual objects and lights. In many cases it is only the key shadow (cast by the key light) on the main subject that is of significant value in an image.

# Texture and environment maps

Environment and texture maps are costly in two ways. One is that the mere overhead of opening and manipulating a sizable bitmapped image file imposes its own time penalties. (This is an issue particularly when using a network distributed rendering system. In this case, each texture map must be copied over the network to every rendering node.) The other penalty imposed by the use of maps is that the renderer must go through the task of mapping the image onto the appropriate objects. Nevertheless, this is almost always faster than ray tracing reflections.

# Antialiasing

Antialiasing also significantly slows down the rendering process. Even interpolative antialiasing adds a final step at the end of rendering that slows rendering down. Many 3-D applications enable you to set a level of antialiasing; the higher the level, the longer rendering requires.

# Summary

- *Rendering* is the step that generates an image.

- There are many different types of rendering suited to different requirements.

- Rendering quality (aesthetically pleasing realistic rendering) depends on detail in the model, antialiasing, and lighting. Renderers vary widely in their depiction of these details.

- Rendering speed is influenced by the complexity of the scene being rendered and the type of rendering system being used.

# Working with images

T he uses of 3-D images are as varied as any other form of artwork. How you create them, of course, will have a lot to do with your intentions for the completed renderings.

There are many considerations, but none so important as final output. Will your still images be printed on a billboard, or used as slides in a presentation? Will your animation be used as a QuickTime movie on a CD-ROM, or will it be broadcast on network television? These considerations determine the type of 3-D output you'll need to create, and to some extent, the software you'll need to use.

This chapter makes no claims to be an all-inclusive guide to using 3-D images; rather, it should serve as a sampling of ideas and techniques.

- For print work, you'll need to get your images into a suitable desktop publishing or color separation program.

- For multimedia, you'll want to consider animation in a format such as QuickTime, and the programs which allow you to work in that format.

- For video or film, you'll either be bringing your animations to a post-production service bureau for output to video, or you'll be doing it yourself with the help of frame-accurate recording hardware and frame-by-frame controller software or hardware.

The considerations go beyond simple output, however. You may want to add detail work or special effects to your 3-D output. Or you may need to composite your images with other work so that your 3-D spacecraft flies over crowds of screaming earthlings or your architectural rendering is nestled into the landscape where it belongs.

# Compositing

The most common need for post processing after generating a rendering is compositing a rendered image with an imported 2-D background (see figure 11.1). Many 3-D programs enable you to import a background image before you render, but this tends to slow down rendering times significantly. The faster, more practical, and more flexible method uses the "alpha channel" to seamlessly composite a 3-D rendering with a 2-D background.

**Figure 11.1.** This scanned photo of a dog was composited in Photoshop. The bone was modeled and rendered in Strata StudioPro.

# The alpha channel

Standard photorealistic images on the Macintosh contain 24 bits of color information. This is enough to generate nearly 17 million colors. But the Mac operating system actually allows an image file to contain 32 bits of information. In most 3-D programs, and most 2-D image

353

processing programs, the 8-bits of extra are saved as what's commonly known as the *alpha channel*. This is a grayscale image that is usually used to provide transparency information. The advent of the alpha channel greatly changed the way users can work with images on the Mac.

Imagine viewing a clear wine bottle you've created in a 3-D program against a polka-dot background. Because the bottle is clear, you will see the patterned background through the glass. Where the wine label and the cork are, you will not see the pattern. Where the wine itself is, you will see the background, but it will be greatly obscured by the colored wine. Even on the glass of the bottle itself, you will see varying amounts of the background, depending on the transparency of the glass and glare off the surface. Now suppose you decide that you hate polka dots. You really wish the model was placed in front of blue tiles. In programs that don't support the alpha channel, you would be forced to return to the scene builder, open the model, replace the background and—horrors!—re-render the image. For a difficult ray tracing this might take a couple of days. On the other hand, if you created the image in a program that has alpha channel support, you would simply open the image in Photoshop (or another alpha channel-aware image processor) choose Load Selection, copy the selection, and paste it over an image of blue tiles. The transparency of the glass and the wine will be maintained and the tiles will show through just like the polka dots did, and in the same places. In fact, you won't be able to tell the image wasn't rendered in front of the blue tiles in the first place!

Alpha channel support can be even more crucial for video effects. Say, for example, that you have created a flying 3-D logo with an alpha channel. You could easily composite the logo with digitized video previews of this week's football highlights, or you can composite multiple layers of graphics, so that the word ITALY flies in over a moving 3-D map of that country. Programs such as Adobe Premiere, CoSA's After Effects, and VideoFusion's VideoFusion, enable you to composite animations using alpha channels for transparency. Some sophisticated video switching hardware enable you to "key" graphics directly over video using the alpha channel.

For programs such as Sketch! that don't support alpha channel masking, you'll have to settle for other methods. Just as not all 3-D programs currently support alpha channels (although eventually they will), not all file formats retain alpha channel information. The following section explains common file formats, and which ones do maintain transparency information.

# File formats

Three-D stills and animations come in many formats destined for many kinds of output. Fortunately, the Mac specializes in moving these image formats around from one program to another, so the techniques that apply to the standard formats can usually be applied to the non-standards as well.

For still images, the main standard is PICT (technically PICT2), a format that handles photorealistic images as well as the transparency information in an image. Animations aren't quite so simple. There are compression formats designed to be played back at full size and speed on the Mac, such as QuickTime and Electric Image's FAST. There are formats that retain 100 percent of the quality in every frame of an animation, the most conspicuous examples being PICS and numbered sequences of PICT files.

Each of these formats has its own uses and its own adherents. Which formats you'll use depends largely on what you plan to use the resulting images for.

# Color depth

Each pixel in a bitmapped image contains a certain amount of data—1 bit, 8 bits, 16 bits, or 24 bits. While it's not necessary to know it to get your work done, 2 raised to the power of the number of bits (for example, $2^8$ for 8-bit) is the number of different colors available to an image. One-bit graphics are black and white; 4-bit graphics support 16 levels of gray or 16 different colors; 8-bit graphics support 256 colors (or levels of gray); 16-bit gets you into the thousands of colors; and 24-bit supports over 16 million colors. It's important to note that most image formats can support images in any of these color depths. Image color depth goes hand in hand with the color depth of the display system for which the images are intended. If you're using an 8-bit display, 24-bit images will look just like 8-bit graphics—that is, you won't be able to see a lot of the details. Keep in mind, however, that 3-D renderers are based on Apple's 32-bit QuickDraw, and even images destined for 8-bit output are initially rendered in 24 bits of color. (As explained earlier, the "extra" 8 bits is sometimes used for an alpha channel). Each file format has its own niche, depending on the ultimate use of the image.

# 1-bit

Black and white graphics are usually used for wireframe and hidden-line renderings. These files are very compact, even at large sizes. A screen-size 640-by-480 pixel image requires about 64K on disk.

# 8-bit

Eight-bit color provides for a complete range of tones in grayscale (and is a popular format for desktop publishing), but produces "banding" when used for full-color continuous-tone images, such as those produced by 3-D rendering. It is possible to create realistic 3-D images in 8-bit with a technique called *dithering,* which blends dots of a few different colors together to create the appearance of many different shades of color. Since this requires a "screen" of colors, dithering reduces an image's resolving power for showing fine details, and sometimes results in strange and unnatural colors when an image has many areas that fall outside of the palette's gamut. (*Gamut* is the range of colors supported.)

Eight-bit images are popular in multimedia because they are very compact, compared to 24-bit graphics, and they load and display quickly when used in animated presentations. In addition, most Macintosh systems are not equipped with expensive 24-bit-color hardware, while 8-bit is now the Apple standard. A very effective and common technique for using 8-bit images is to dither using a custom palette of colors, rather than the standard Mac palette. Simply put, an image that contains many blues and greens can be dithered much more smoothly and invisibly with a palette that contains primarily green and blue colors. Some programs, such as Macromedia's Director, can do this automatically, while others, such as Equilibrium's DeBabelizer, have refined custom palettes and dithering to an art.

An 8-bit 640-by-480 image requires about 256K on disk—four times the space of a 1-bit image.

# 16-bit

This color level is offered on some of the newest Macs as a compromise between expensive 24-bit color and underpowered 8-bit. While not photorealistic, it does offer a very broad range of color tones. Sixteen-bit color closely approximates the range of color supported by NTSC video, so it's a good compromise solution for video producers who need to preview Mac-generated graphics before laying them down on tape. Sixteen-bit graphics dithered to a custom palette are almost indistinguishable from 24-bit graphics, unless the image contains a very broad range of colors and tones. Sixteen-bit is also adequate for QuickTime movies used for CD-ROM and other multimedia applications. A 640-by-480 pixel image at 16-bit is about 460K.

# 24-bit

Twenty-four-bit video is photorealistic to all but the most discerning eye and it's the best you can get from the Macintosh, although 64-bit graphics are rumored to be around the corner. In fact, Macs with 24-bit graphics are used by many people as color correction and retouching stations. Twenty-four-bit color is practically required if you want to see all of the subtle shading and details generated by 3-D rendering.

While 24-bit graphics are of sufficient quality for any application, they have one very significant drawback: the files are very large. A screen-resolution 640-by-480 pixel, 24-bit image takes about 900K of disk space. A high-resolution image suitable for printing at 150 lines per inch on an 8.5-inch-by-11-inch page requires about 24M of disk space!

# Still formats

Color depth is only the first decision in creating and saving 3-D graphics. File formats are the next hurdle to overcome. These, too, are subject to the requirements of your ultimate use of the images. In general, Macintosh software will specify which formats are best to use.

- **PICT. PICT2** (usually referred to as just "PICT") is the standard format for exchanging 2-D image files on the Macintosh. While it supports vector graphics, its primary use for 3-D users is in storing and transporting 2-D bitmaps. The format supports 32-bit images (24 bits of RGB color and 8 bits of alpha). This is the most widely supported image format on the Mac, and is the standard for use in multimedia programs, as well as many image editing programs.

- **EPS (AI).** EPS (which stands for Encapsulated PostScript) is the Adobe Illustrator format, primarily used for storing PostScript line art for use in Adobe Illustrator or Aldus FreeHand. It is sometimes known as "editable PostScript." Adobe Dimensions and RayDream's addDepth both can save files in this format. It has the advantage that files are scalable and resolution independent. You can open an EPS (AI) file in Illustrator and ungroup and edit parts of the image without any resulting degradation of image quality. You can also save one of the lines in an illustration as a "clipping path" which allows you to automatically wrap text around it in a desktop publishing program.

- **Scalable EPS.** This is the format normally saved by addDepth and Dimensions. Like EPS (AI) files, this format can be squashed and stretched and printed at any size without "pixelizing." However, it's not editable in Illustrator or FreeHand.

- **EPS bitmap.** Like a PICT, this stores photorealistic images in bitmapped format and can include a screen-resolution preview "header" image used for placing and cropping the image in desktop publishing and illustration programs. It will print correctly on a PostScript printer. Like any bitmap, enlarging the image results in pixelization or loss of image quality.

- **TIFF.** The TIFF format (which stands for Tagged Image File Format) is also a bitmap image format, often used instead of PICT. It has the advantage that it is more cross-platform compatible and allows for a high degree of compression. It is also a popular format with desktop publishing software, as it prints quickly due to the compression which can be moved quickly over the network and decompressed by the printer. TIFF can also store an alpha channel.

- **Image.** Image files are the standard still image format created by Electric Image Animation System.

- **JPEG.** This is an image file format that denotes that the image has been compressed using a standard JPEG compression system. (JPEG stands for Joint Photographic Experts Group, the organization that defined the JPEG compression standard.) JPEG images are very compact, although the compression is "lossy" at high levels of compression, meaning that a certain amount of image data is thrown away during compression. This is an excellent format for storing large numbers of images. QuickTime ships with a JPEG component so it can open and save this format (see "Animation Formats," below, for more about QuickTime). Hardware accelerators make JPEG compression lightning fast.

- **Photoshop.** Adobe Photoshop saves a file format that retains an unlimited number of channels in addition to the alpha channel. Photoshop calls the alpha channel "Selection" or "Channel #4," but the program enables you to save and name as many channels as you need. These extra channels work as place holders which can be used to quickly and accurately select different parts of an image. When saving a Photoshop document in another image format, such as PICT or TIFF, only the primary alpha channel ("#4") is retained.

As with animations, there are many other types of image files on other platforms. Your best bet on the Mac is to stick with the file types listed here, and resort to a powerful image translator, such as DeBabelizer (described in this chapter), for converting files to formats for other platforms.

# Animation formats

In terms of file size, if still images have a slight weight problem, then animation files register on the Richter scale. While a screen-size 24-bit still image weighs in at about 1M, an uncompressed NTSC-resolution animation tips the scales at around 30M *per second*. Fortunately, efficient techniques exist for storing, compressing, and ultimately transporting these behemoths to their destinations.

## Numbered PICT

This format is no different than standard PICT, except that some programs can generate every frame of an animation as a PICT file, with each frame numbered sequentially. This is a good choice where absolute fidelity and maintaining the alpha channel is required. It is also the least efficient storage method in terms of compression and playback. It's popular with video producers, who record their images to video tape and backup the image files to DAT tape or other high-capacity backup media. If a frame is "dropped" when recording on a professional tape deck, it's a simple matter to open the single missing PICT file and insert the image into the blank space on the tape. With numbered PICTs, it's also easy to renumber images to rearrange their order of appearance on a tape. A final consideration is that numbered PICTs can easily be opened by image editing programs for retouching or rotoscoping with a painting tool, for example.

## QuickTime

QuickTime is actually an architecture that supports a range of file compression formats for 3-D animation, sounds, and still images. QuickTime uses different compressors (see figure 11.2), which are essentially different file formats that work within the QuickTime architecture. Every format allows you trade image quality for compression and speed, and to set the frame rate. You must have the QuickTime extension in the Extensions folder in your System folder in order to use its features. Most Mac 3-D animators now have an option to save movies in QuickTime format. If yours doesn't, you can use a variety of software to convert other types of animation files to QuickTime. For 3-D users, the most important compressors include:

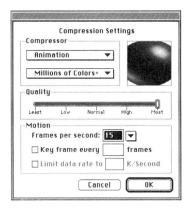

**Figure 11.2.** The QuickTime Compression settings dialog box.

- Animation—Millions of Colors +

  This compressor is the most commonly used for storing 3-D animations. It saves the first image, and then saves only subsequent changes from one frame to the next, resulting in a complete, compact file with the alpha channel intact. Because animation backgrounds tend to remain fairly static, with only foreground objects in motion, this is an effective technique enabling rapid compositing of files.

  The "Animation—Millions of Colors" compressor (without the "+" leaves out the alpha channel, resulting in increased speed and smaller files. (It's the format used for the QuickTime animations included on the CD-ROM.)

- Video

  This is the best format to use when you need high-quality clips that play in real time on faster Macs. The only setting option is "Color." This setting and the Compact Video compressor are appropriate when using rotoscoped (moving) backgrounds, since the whole image changes from frame to frame. Animations will play back faster at this setting, but with a noticeable loss in image quality compared to the Animation compressor.

- Compact Video is as much as ten times slower to compress than Video, but it plays back about twice as fast. It's a very lossy format, but appropriate when you need animations to play back from CD-ROM at high frame rates or in large sizes or from slower Macs. ("Lossy" compression is a type of compression that throws away some data in order to achieve greater compression efficiency. The result is more or less loss of image quality.)

- None

  A non-compression compressor analogous to saving a series of sequential PICT files. It results in the least degradation of image quality, as well as the least benefit in terms of storage and playback.

- Photo-JPEG

  This compressor is used primarily for compressing still images. It simply saves the image in JPEG format. JPEG accelerator boards typically come with their own QuickTime compressor that supplements this one.

# PICS

PICS is a format originally introduced by VIDI, specifically designed for storing animations. Macromedia's Director has probably done the most to popularize the format, and it is now an ubiquitous standard only recently usurped by QuickTime as the method of choice. Most 3-D animation programs can save a PICS file, and most multimedia and video production programs can open one.

Like numbered PICT, PICS maintains all of the quality in an image and retains the alpha channel. (In fact, the PICS format essentially saves PICT files of each frame into one file.) It has the advantage of keeping every frame in a single file, although it is much more difficult to repair or replace if a frame or two is corrupted. PICS doesn't require

QuickTime to work, a significant consideration for users of older system software or those low on RAM. A recent version of PICS works like the Animation compressor in QuickTime, storing the differences between subsequent frames.

# EIAS Animation

This is Electric Speed Image's format for animations created by its Animation System. The format has little practical use unless you're going directly to tape from Electric Speed Image's Projector application. Other programs don't support it, so you can't use the format as a medium of exchange. You will need to store files in this format if you plan to use animated textures or backgrounds in EIAS Animation because the program won't accept other formats. Transporter translates to and from Image format to other more standard formats.

# Adobe Photoshop

Adobe Systems Inc.'s Photoshop is by far the most important image processing tool available on the Macintosh. It is often compared to a Swiss Army Knife—many different tools in one—and it is as good at image compositing and color separation as it is at painting and special effects. There are other programs that perform individual functions better, but if you work with 3-D images on the Macintosh, it's pretty hard to get by without Photoshop. The following are a few examples where the 3-D user is likely to need Photoshop:

- **Compositing images.** Because of Photoshop's robust support for alpha channels (you can have unlimited channels in a single document) it is the ideal platform for merging 3-D graphics with other images.

- **Textures and backgrounds.** Photoshop gives you an unlimited source of material to use as textures and backgrounds. You can use it to create glow maps, smoke swirls, bump maps, seamless tarantula fur textures, and thousands of other surfaces and effects, both real and imagined. It's also the interface supplied with many color scanners, the cornerstone of a 3-D creator's texture supply.

- **Details.** Touch up images to add subtle highlights and shadows, paint bits of grime on walls, or "strip in" an all-important fly on the nose of a statue.

- **Generate special effects.** Photoshop plug-in tools such as Paint Alchemy and Kai's Power Tools enable you to add unique special effects to renderings. You can filter a photorealistic image to look as though it were painted with watercolor or sketched with charcoal, for example.

- **Image retouching and color processing.** Balance the colors in an image and paint out unwanted glitches.

A "Try Me" version of Photoshop 2.5 is included on the CD-ROM.

# Compositing images

Photoshop enables you to use the alpha channel in a variety of ways. The most common is compositing a 3-D rendering with a photograph or other 2-D image. This is generally a very easy process, primarily consisting of copying and pasting.

1. Begin by generating a 3-D rendering in a program that supports an alpha channel, in this case Strata StudioPro (see Figure 11.3). Render a fairly complex scene, being sure to check "Render alpha channel as background" in the **Environment effects** dialog box. Also be sure to leave antialiasing turned on when rendering.

2. Launch Photoshop and open the background image. This should be at least as large as the 3-D image. Next, open the 3-D image, so they're open at the same time.

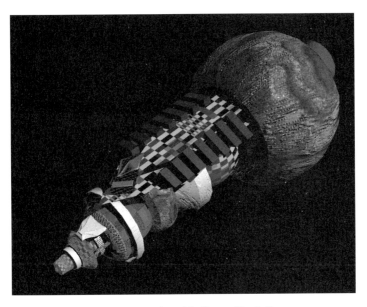

**Figure 11.3.** A complex image, rendered in Strata StudioPro.

3. With the 3-D image active, choose **Load Selection,** which uses the alpha channel to select image with the background masked out (see figure 11.4).

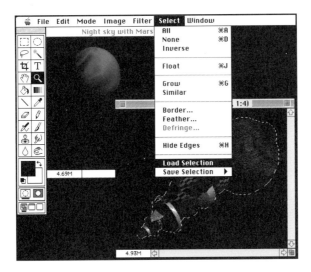

**Figure 11.4.** Choose **Load Selection** to mask out the background in the image.

If the background is selected instead of the foreground—the selection marquee runs around the outside of the image box—it means that the alpha channel is reversed. This is a common problem, because some programs, particularly those used for video production, require it. Choosing **Inverse** from the **Select** menu switches the selection without altering the alpha channel itself.

If the **Load Selection** menu option is grayed out in the **Select** menu, the image doesn't contain an alpha channel. Consult your 3-D application's documentation to see how to render with an alpha channel.

4. Once the objects are selected by a marquee, choose **Copy** from the **Edit** Menu (see figure 11.5).

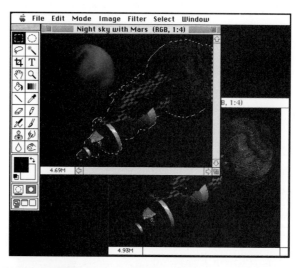

**Figure 11.5.** Choose **Copy** from the **Edit** menu.

5. Click on the background image to select it and choose **Paste** from the **Edit** menu. While the selection is still active, you can drag the objects around with the mouse. Click on the background to paste the 3-D objects in place (see figure 11.6).

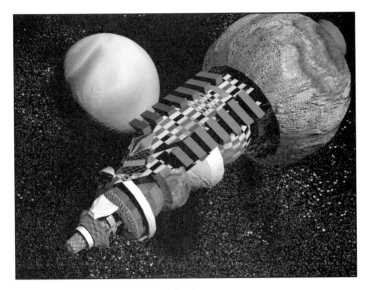

**Figure 11.6.** Pasting the background in place.

Note that the foreground objects maintain the antialiasing generated in Strata StudioPro so that there is no jaggedness between foreground and background (see figure 11.7).

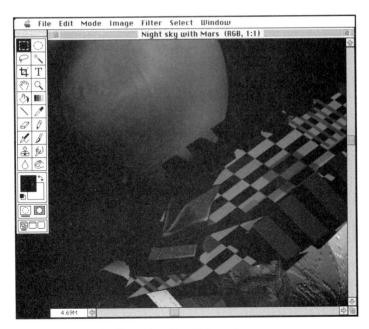

**Figure 11.7.** Note that the figure is still antialiased.

# Faking a shadow

The following technique is an example of how you can use the alpha channel and Photoshop in combination to create unusual effects.

1.  Begin by opening a 3-D rendering with an alpha channel in Photoshop (see figure 11.8).

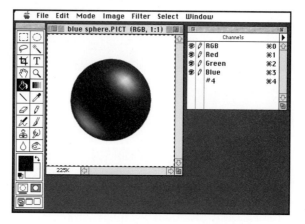

**Figure 11.8.** A rendering of a sphere, opened in Photoshop.

2.  Open the **Channels** palette (under the **Window** menu) and click on #4. This will reveal the alpha channel (see figure 11.9). Choose **Select All** from the **Edit** menu and choose **Copy.**

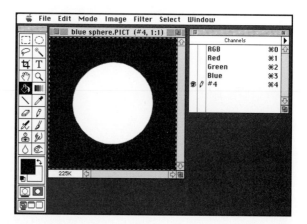

**Figure 11.9.** The alpha channel.

3. Use the **Channels** pop-up menu to create a new channel, #5, and paste in the copied channel. With the channel still selected, click on the foreground/background color switcher near the bottom of the tools palette to make the background color black (this causes edge pixels to fill in black during the Distort operation.) Choose **Distort** from the **Effects** submenu under the **Image** menu. Drag the corner points of the marquee until the channel is squashed to a shadow-like shape (see figure 11.10).

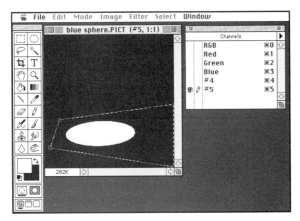

**Figure 11.10.** Changing the shape of the new channel.

4. **Select All** to highlight the whole channel and choose **Gaussian Blur** from the **Blur** submenu under the **Filter** menu. Set the level to 5 pixels (see figure 11.11).

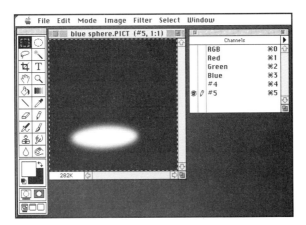

**Figure 11.11.** The blurred channel.

5. Click on **RGB** in the **Channels** palette to return to the color image. Choose **Load Selection #4** from the **Select** menu to select the 3-D object (see figure 11.12), then choose **Copy** from the **Edit** menu to copy the object to the clipboard.

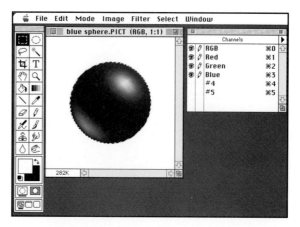

**Figure 11.12.** The selected RGB sphere.

6. Choose **Load Selection #5** to load the distorted alpha channel. Make sure that black is selected as the foreground color. In the **Edit** menu, choose **Fill.** Set the fill values to **Foreground**, **80 percent opacity**, **Apply normally**. This will paste a "shadow" over your object—do not be alarmed (see figure 11.13).

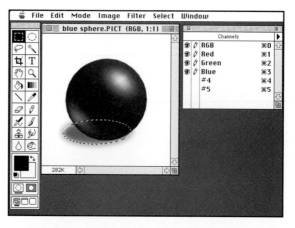

**Figure 11.13.** The sphere, with the shadow pasted over it.

7. Choose **Load Selection #4** once again. Select **Paste Into,** which pastes the color sphere into the selected area (see figure 11.14). This covers the portion of the shadow that lies behind the sphere, and completes the image.

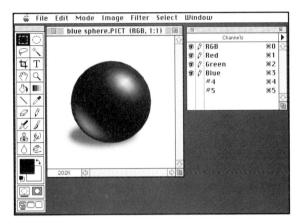

**Figure 11.14.** Pasting the sphere over the shadow completes the image.

# Motion blur

Animations and still images gain a great deal of realism from the addition of motion blur. With the **Motion Blur** filter (under the **Blur** submenu in the **Filters** menu) you can easily create this effect in Photoshop. While the Motion Blur filter is effective by itself, you can create really interesting images by pasting a sharp version of the object at the end of the blur trail, then blurring this slightly. This creates the effect of a photograph flashed at the end of the exposure.

1. Begin by opening a rendering with an alpha channel.

2. **Load selection #4** (the alpha channel) and **Copy** the image.

3. **Select all** and apply the motion blur. Set a direction by dragging the line in the wheel, and set the amount to 40 pixels (see figure 11.15). The results are shown in figure 11.16.

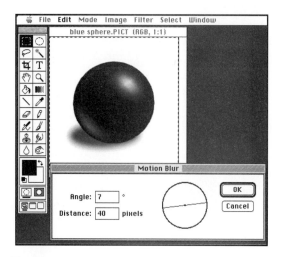

**Figure 11.15.** The Motion Blur dialog box. The result of this blur is shown below.

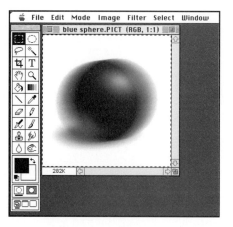

**Figure 11.16.** The results of the motion blur.

4. Choose **Paste** and drag the pasted object to one end of the blur trail (see figure 11.17). Click on the background to lock the selection into place.

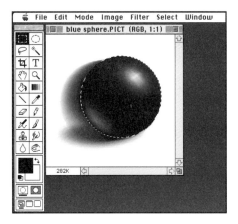

**Figure 11.17.** Drag the object to the end of the blur.

5. **Select All** and choose **Motion Blur** again. This time set the amount to 10 pixels (see figure 11.18).

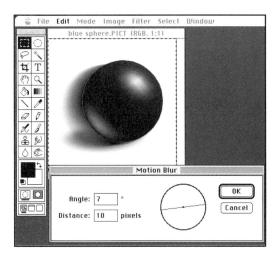

**Figure 11.18.** Applying the motion blur again.

6. The result is shown in figure 11.19. Note that the first blur creates a streaking tail; the second blur gives the foreground object's surface a subtle movement.

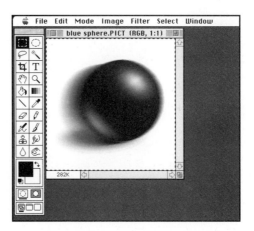

**Figure 11.19.** The completed motion blur.

# Fractal Design's Painter

Fractal Design's Painter is every bit as unique as Photoshop in its own ways. It does support alpha channels, so you can easily make simple compositions in the program, and it supports third-party plug-ins, like Kai's Power Tools, so it's an outstanding program for creating textures and backgrounds. What really sets Painter apart, however, is its "natural media" painting (see figure 11.20). Painter offers a wealth of painting tools that closely mimic real-world art supplies. You can paint with oils, watercolors and acrylics and you can draw with charcoals, pastels, crayons, felt pens, ink pens and pencils, to name a few. The other unique capability of Painter is its Cloning feature. This enables you to paint over an existing image, pulling colors from the original, but creating strokes with the brushes in hand. You can also get colors from a regular palette. You can even automatically adopt the painting style of masters. This makes it deliciously easy to turn a rendered 3-D haystack into an "automatic Monet."

**Figure 11.20.** Image rendered in Sketch! and "cloned" in Painter with pastel brushes.

While it's possible to create some really strange fakes—what if Van Gogh had painted spaceships?—the possibilities for elegant architectural renderings and presentation illustrations, for example, are almost endless.

# DeBabelizer

If Photoshop is a Swiss Army Knife for still images, then Equilibrium's DeBabelizer is something like a Cuisinart for images and animations (see figure 11.21). While it lacks painting tools, and many of Photoshop's pre-press tools, DeBabelizer has a wealth of indispensable power for the 3-D user. Among other things, it supports third-party Photoshop plug-ins, so filters and special-effects tools designed to enhance Photoshop also work in DeBabelizer's powerful, complex batch-processing environment.

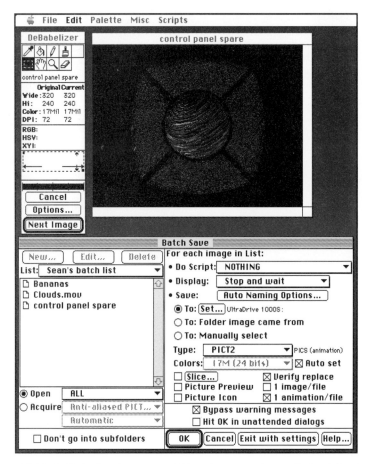

**Figure 11.21.** DeBabelizer has powerful batch processing tools for doing just about anything to a bunch of images or animations.

DeBabelizer is a batch image processor. It allows you to convert most image file formats to most other formats. It allows you to adjust the color palettes of images, or to composite one group of images with another. DeBabelizer also has full support for alpha channels (as well as for other kinds of masking).

But, it's very difficult to summarize precisely what makes DeBabelizer good. The following is a sample of how a resourceful 3-D user might put it to work:

- Composite a series of images against a single background or composite one animation over another.

- Convert a folder full of 640-by-480-pixel 24-bit PICS files into a single 320-by-240-pixel QuickTime movie using the Animation compressor.

- Generate a single color "Super palette" based on the dominant colors in all of the images of a 24-bit animation. Dither the animation using this palette to play as well as possible on an 8-bit Mac.

- Legalize the palette of an animation so colors will display correctly on NTSC video.

- Convert a QuickTime movie to an Electric Image Animation format for use as an animated texture map.

- Convert a flying logo to Vidco f/x format for overlaying onto video.

- Use a procedural blend to merge a Kai's Power Tools texture over everything a specific shade of green or purple in a series of numbered PICTs.

- Reduce a disk full of differently-sized PICTs, TIFFs, and EPS bitmaps to the same size and resolution and store them in one folder on another disk.

- Generate a series of 3-D terrain models in DXF format, by applying Knoll Software's CyberSave filter to extract height values from gray values in every frame of a QuickTime movie.

- Replace the white highlights in every frame in a PICS animation with yellow, so Macromedia Director won't turn them transparent during playback.

- Prepare a batch of images as textures and corresponding bump maps for use in a 3-D program.

Anything you can do in DeBabelizer can be saved as a script, and scripts can call other scripts, so it's possible to create very complex image processing procedures that are totally automatic. You can also perform actions on "batches" of files, so that the same script can be repeated automatically for every image in a folder or animation, for example (see figure 11.22). A new version of DeBabelizer is AppleScript compatible, so you can even use QuickKeys or another Apple Script-compatible program to control it.

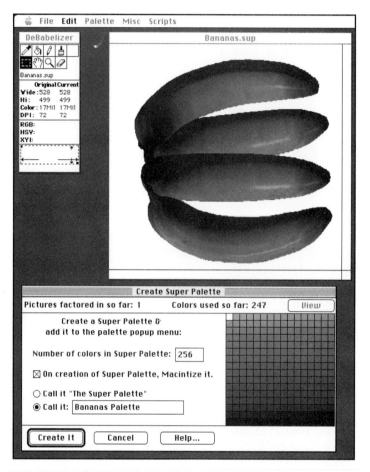

**Figure 11.22.** One of DeBabelizer's strongest features is the fast and beautifully-handled batch reduction of color palettes to single palettes. This is a coup for multimedia developers.

# Desktop publishing

Desktop publishing itself is beyond the scope of this book; however, there are some issues which will make your life easier when generating images for use in programs like QuarkXPress and Aldus PageMaker. The first consideration is which rendering format to use. Dimensions and addDepth are naturals because they automatically save in EPS format. This makes it easy to incorporate images into desktop pages.

When rendering bitmap images, however, you'll need to determine what file type is best suited to the work you're doing. EPS bitmap and TIFF are standards.

# Making and using a clipping path

A clipping path is a feature of EPS images which allows you to save a mask along with an image. This is analogous to the alpha channel, and is used by desktop publishing programs to automatically flow text around graphics. You can use the alpha channel in Photoshop to create a clipping path for a 3-D image.

1. Open a 3-D rendering created with an alpha channel background. The rendering in figure 11.23 was created in StrataVision 3d. Choose **Load Selection** to select the 3-D object (see examples earlier in this chapter for details).

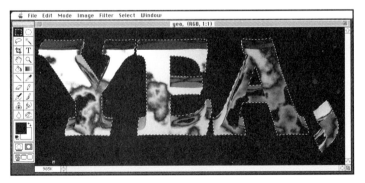

**Figure 11.23.** A rendering created with an alpha channel background.

3. In the **Channels** palette, choose **Make Path** (see figure 11.24). A tolerance of 2 or 3 pixels is usually sufficient. Drag around the

whole image with the path selection tool to select the whole path, choose **Save Path** from the Channels pop-up menu, and save the path as Path 1.

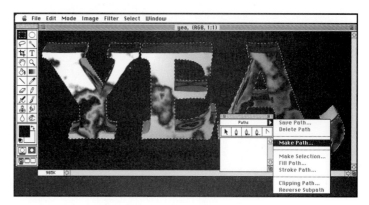

**Figure 11.24.** Choose **Make Path** in the **Channels** palette.

4. Again, in the Path pop-up menu, choose **Clipping Path** (see figure 11.25). In this dialog box, choose the pull-down menu of paths, choose **Path 1**, and set the flatness to 1. Since the paths should not overlap, choose the **Non-Zero Winding** option and click on the **OK** button.

**Figure 11.25.** Choosing **Clipping Path** from the **Path** pop-up menu.

5. Save the image as EPS with an 8-bit preview; leave the other options unchecked.

6. In QuarkXPress, drag a new picture box over an existing block of type and import the EPS image through the **File** menu. The text is automatically displaced to wrap around the image box (see figure 11.26).

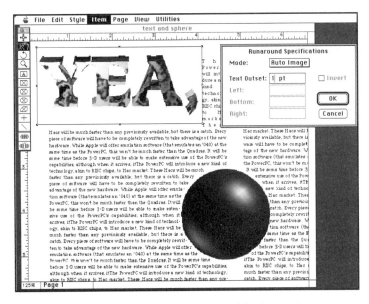

**Figure 11.26.** The text automatically wraps around the image box.

7. With the image box still selected, choose **Runaround** from the **Item** menu. In the pop-up menu choose **Auto Image** and set the amount to 1 point. The results are shown in figure 11.27.

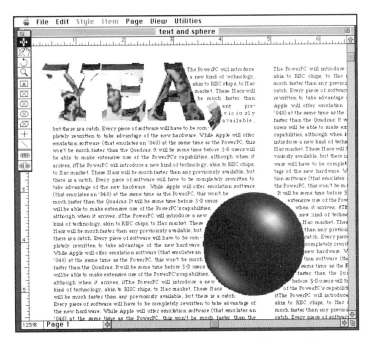

**Figure 11.27.** Notice how the text neatly wraps around the graphic.

# Color management

If you're producing color separations, consider using the EFIColor System from Electronics For Imaging Inc. It uses sophisticated color profiles for different printers and types of printing, in order to produce the best possible separations. There is a standalone version called Cachet, a set of Photoshop calibration tables, or a version included with QuarkXPress.

# Animations

The uses of 3-D animation are endless. Once you have determined the size, resolution, frame rate, and file format, and have actually rendered an animation, there are many applications that can help you put it to use.

# QuickTime

There are now several capable editing programs designed for creating complete movies from QuickTime clips. In addition to the Apple Movie Player, which can serve as a rudimentary editor for QuickTime, there are a host of more creatively flexible applications. All of the commercial applications for QuickTime editing and effects support alpha channel compositing with still or moving images. VideoFusion and After Effects also support field rendering for extra-smooth video graphics (described later in this chapter).

- **Adobe Premiere.** This is the most flexible of the QuickTime editing applications currently available. It offers many styles of transitions and filter effects, as well as titling and animation of video windows. With the proper hardware compression, such as SuperMac's Digital Film or Radius' VideoVision Studio, it supports real-time full-screen, full motion play back of video.

- **Diva's VideoShop** is another high-power QuickTime editing application. There are also some low-end movie editors designed for editing and adding special effects to QuickTime

382

productions, including Avid's Sparrow and VideoFusion's QuickFlix, but these don't include the features needed for professional video output and special effects.

- **VideoFusion** is a special effects program aimed at compositing and adding effects to QuickTime animations and video. Its most interesting features are the pan zoom rotate tools, which can spin video around any or all axes simultaneously.

- **CoSA's After Effects** is very much aimed at the video graphics professional. It provides high-quality sub-pixel animation of video clips and unlimited layering using alpha channels.

# Video

Video editing is a very specialized discipline requiring lots of expensive hardware. There are, however, easy and inexpensive ways to output video in a manner that can be easily transferred to video by a service bureau.

# Frame-by-frame recording

Frame-by-frame recording is a multi-step process requiring a frame-accurate video deck that can be controlled via a serial link or a custom connection, a video encoder (which may or may not include Genlock) and software and sometimes hardware, used to control the display and recording of graphics. Essentially, the process works by opening one frame of animation at a time, displaying it (through the encoder) on the video system, and recording subsequent frames on the video tape.

Since the video hardware alone is extremely costly, this work is often done by service bureaus. However, some advancements have come along to bring this type of video animation into the realm of reasonable for small businesses.

# Software animation controllers

There are several software-only animation controllers that work in conjunction with a variety of video hardware systems. Popular software programs include:

- Auto-PICT QT

- DQ-MAC232

- MacAnimator Plus

- MacVAC

## DQ-MAC232 and EVO-9650

One example of a highly effective, relatively low-cost solution for putting animations on hi-8 tape is Diaquest Inc's DQ-MAC232 software (see figure 11.28), paired with a Sony EVO-9650 video deck. The video deck is controlled via the Mac's serial port, so no NuBus hardware is required. There are many different video encoders available on the market, ranging in price from a few hundred to a few thousand dollars. Examples include the TruVision NuVista+ and the Radius VideoVision. All of this can be had for about the price of a fully-loaded graphics Mac.

Using this setup, you load a "play list" in the DQ-Mac software, specifying the frames to record and the starting points and stopping points of both the animations and the video tape. When you click on the Record button, the software takes over, running the tape deck forward and back, loading and displaying the subsequent frames of video, and hitting the tape deck's "record" button at the appropriate moments. The software also will automatically composite images with alpha channels, so you combine a foreground and background animation, for example.

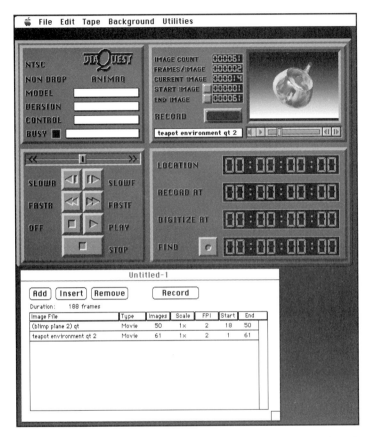

**Figure 11.28.** The DQ-MAC232 interface, showing a QuickTime movie to be recorded. The cue for animations on video is the window at lower left.

## DQ-Animaq

By far the most popular hardware-based animation controller is the DQ-Animaq from Diaquest. This board controls two decks at a time, frame-grabbing from one, compositing those images with an existing animation, and outputting the result to the other. The board and associated software are about the price of a high-end Mac, making this an economical solution for sites willing to spring for the video decks. Optional software provides a capability called QuickPass. This allows the board to grab and record frames of video at full quality and very high speed. (It does this by grabbing every seventh frame starting and frame one with, for example, the deck playing at full speed. When it reaches the end, it rewinds and grabs or records every seventh frame starting at frame two, and so-on. This eliminates the delays caused by the deck's having to "pre-roll" before every frame.)

The software for outputting video to tape is indistinguishable from the DQ-MAC232 software.

## Electric Image Animation System

Electric Image Animation System (EIAS) has long been able to control video devices through the Diaquest board. But it also offers another option: Saving animations on Exabyte Corp.'s 8-mm backup drives in Abekas backup format.

The Abekas video system is very high quality digital video, providing high fidelity without the intricacies or pitfalls of recording to video tape (such as tape stretch). It uses specialized recording and play-back hardware and costs about the same as a nice home. Most cities have at least one service bureau with an Abekas system, and most of these are equipped with Exabyte backup drives. Once you've saved your animation in this format, you simply carry the Exabyte tape to the service bureau, and for a very reasonable fee, transfer the animation directly into the Abekas system. It's a completely digital solution, and the result is top quality.

## Exabyte drivers

Just as EIAS can record its animations to Exabyte tape in Abekas backup format, two new general animation packages are available to provide the same functionality to users of other Mac animation software.

- ASDG, a company known for special effects on SGI workstations and other platforms, offers Abekas drivers for the Macintosh and other platforms.

- Knoll Software (founded by John Knoll, one of the authors of Photoshop and the creator of the CyberSave Photoshop plug-in) offers a driver package called Missing Link that can save images and their alpha channels in a variety of configurations.

Both write Abekas backup format files to Exabyte tape, but they offer a variety of features for compositing graphics, as well.

Top-of-the-line Exabyte drives retail for about $2,000, and the tapes (identical to 8 mm Hi-8 camcorder cassettes) cost about as much as a premium VHS tape. Exabyte drives are much faster than DAT, so your time is spent rendering, not recording. This is a vastly more economical solution than investing in video hardware, unless you own a service bureau or are outputting animations full time. And, it probably makes a lot more sense to pay the small fee every time you lay an animation on tape than it does to go out and buy a professional animation deck.

# Field rendering

So what is field rendering, anyway? NTSC video is made up of two fields (never mind the confusion caused by makers of video digitizers hyping "60-fields per second" vs. "30-fields-per second" performance). Each of the two fields are made up of alternating horizontal lines a single pixel thick. If you hold your open hands in front of your face, fingers interlocked, you'll get a good idea of what fields look like— one hand is the odd field, the other hand is even. Video actually displays these fields in sequence, first the even one, then the odd. The result—Oh, foolish eye!—is that we see smoothly flowing motion at a rate of 30 frames per second. We never notice that every other line on the screen goes blank every 30th of a second. We do, however, notice that single-pixel horizontal lines in graphics flicker perceptibly, and that the top and bottom edges of shapes seem to jump up and down minutely. This is due to this alternating display or *interlacing* of fields.

Since a frame of video is actually comprised of two fields (for convenience, you can think of these as frame "1a" and frame "1b"), many animation systems are cheating when they record a single image to a frame of video—1a and 1b both get the same image. The visual impact of this is very subtle: graphics are slightly jerky as they move across the screen. This is because we're used to half the frame changing every 60th of a second. Instead, the animation systems are changing the image every 30th of a second.

When field rendering, on the other hand, every field receives a new image that has changed subtly since the last. For practical purposes, this almost increases the frame rate from 30 frames per second to 60. Field rendering has two immediate effects: the first is that you'll have to render twice as many frames, which means rendering will take twice as long. The second is that you'll need hardware that supports recording to fields. This means an encoder and video deck with synchronized timing mechanism suited to field recording.

# Multimedia

Interactive media, non-linear media, multimedia—call it what you will—the concept is really fairly simple: enabling people to exercise personal control over what they see and hear. The questions that arise from this idea are hardly so simple. For the multimedia author, the question is often: What do people *want* to see and hear?

An obvious answer is that they want to see things they haven't seen before—and that's where 3-D comes in. It's one thing to see a tea kettle whistling frantically on top of the stove. It's quite another to see it explode, blowing away the walls and windows but leaving the kitchen otherwise unscathed.

Such scenes are possible using the Mac and 3-D software. The software also makes it possible to create new and unusual interfaces and strange vehicles to transport passengers of your media through unfamiliar worlds.

There are as many ways to incorporate 3-D into media as there are kinds of media. Some of the most common uses today include:

- Interface elements

- Scenery and props

- Animations

# Authoring tools

Macromedia Director, despite a programming interface that is hard to love—and even harder to work with—is still the standard tool of choice for creating interactive media on the Mac (see figure 11.29). Fortunately, there are several very good products giving Director competition.

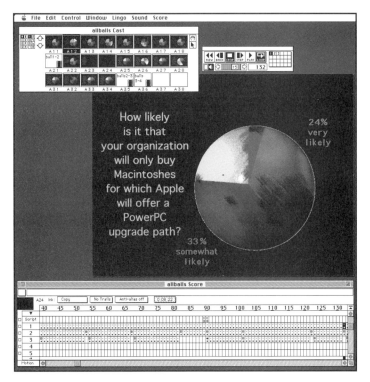

**Figure 11.29.** Interactive presentation created in Macromedia Director. Courtesy of the Alpha Channel, San Francisco, California.

For those looking to try something different, there are two really outstanding authoring tools available on the Mac: Passport Producer Professional from Passport Designs Inc., and Authorware Professional from the same company that brings you Director.

These programs occupy different ends of the spectrum for creating interactive media. Producer Pro offers buttons with a modest amount of interactive functionality, as well as a wonderful time-based approach to producing animation. It costs about as much as a mid-level

3-D package. Producer Pro is specifically created for delivering synchronized media from the Mac. It uses QuickTime and SMPTE time code, so you can, for example, set a QuickTime movie and a MIDI music file to play on the same beat.

Authorware is the high end of the price spectrum. What you get for the money, however, is an authoring package that goes far beyond Director in terms of user interactivity and tracking of user responses. The other thing you get is a programming system that even a 3-D artist can understand. Authorware costs more than the most expensive Mac, but if interactive development is what you do, this program is worth the money. It's a great bargain if you can get it through Macromedia's educational discount program.

# Color palettes

While 3-D software is capable of producing photorealistic animations and graphics, most Macs aren't capable of displaying them. The standard display system is now 8-bit color—paltry compared to the 17 million colors 3-D software can generate. There is, however, a way to display images and animations on these Macs without most of the color posterization and banding you'll get if you simply open a 24-bit image on an 8-bit system. The trick is to "dither" the image with a custom color palette. Essentially, what you want to do is limit the palette you're using to the 256 colors that form the majority of the image. In general, even continuous-tone images of natural scenes are limited to certain ranges of color. A park scene might be mostly greens and browns, for example.

Photoshop enables you to do this through its Index Color command. When you save an image with an Adaptive palette, Photoshop adjusts the palette to reflect the colors in the image.

DeBabelizer actually has the best approach currently available. It surveys every image in a batch (all of the images you plan to use in a Director presentation, for example), and creates a single palette which it uses to dither every image. This means an entire presentation, animation or whatever, can use the same 256-color palette. This results in great performance gains during playback and eliminates alarming flashes of bizarre color on the screen as the Mac readjusts its system palette to the current image. (See "DeBabelizer," this chapter).

# Creating a console

Three-D software makes it very easy to generate buttons and control panels for use in multimedia applications. Buttons are generally very simple shapes, so it's easy to create any button you need with just about any 3-D software. The following example uses Alias Sketch! to create a 3-D track ball.

1. In the Top view, create a sphere at the center of the working plane in Sketch! (see figure 11.30). In the **Materials** dialog box, give the sphere a texture and bump map.

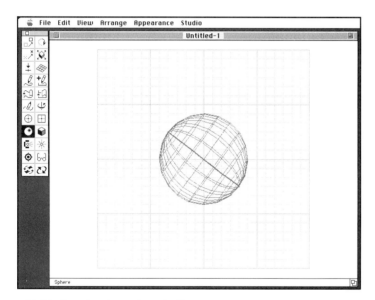

**Figure 11.30.** Creating the sphere in Sketch!

2. Draw a 2-D shape that takes up one quarter of the space around the sphere (see figure 11.31).

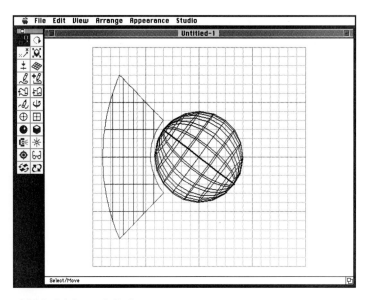

**Figure 11.31.** Adding a 2-D shape.

3. Use the Extrude tool to give this shape depth (see figure 11.32).

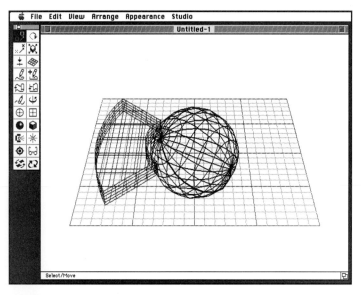

**Figure 11.32.** Adding depth to the 2-D shape.

4. With the Resize tool, shrink the top face of the extruded object to bevel the top edge (see figure 11.33).

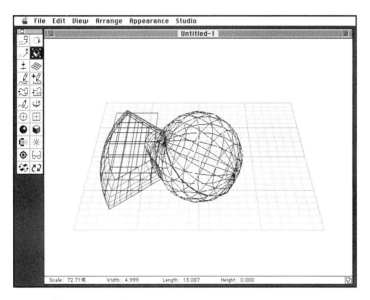

**Figure 11.33.** Shrink the top face to bevel the top edge.

5. In the **Materials** dialog box, apply a texture and a bump map (see figure 11.34). This bump map uses an arrow. Use the **Position Materials** command to rotate the bump map into position. Do a test render of just the button to make sure it's positioned properly.

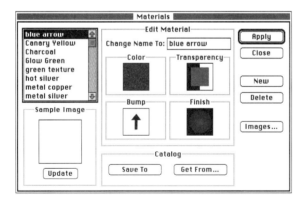

**Figure 11.34.** Apply a texture and bump map through the **Materials** dialog box.

6. Select the button, choose **Duplicate** from the **Edit** menu, and choose the Rotate tool from the Tool palette. (Duplicating the button in this order preserves the orientation of the bump map relative to the bottom.) Move the rotation point to the center of

the sphere and move the duplicate button around until it's opposite the first. Repeat this step for the third and fourth buttons (see figure 11.35).

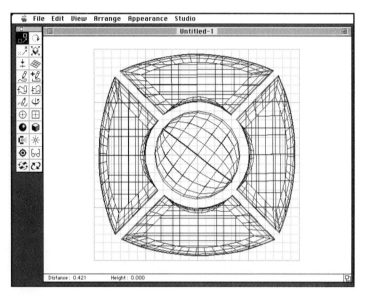

**Figure 11.35.** Duplicate the first button to create the other four buttons.

7. Set two lights on opposite sides of the model, far away, with one light slightly weaker than the other. Set the background to black and render the image (see figure 11.36).

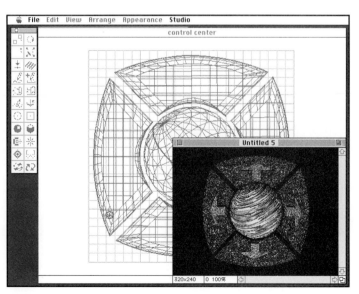

**Figure 11.36.** The final rendered image.

# Animating still images

CoSA's After Effects is a remarkable package designed specifically for producing broadcast-quality video animation. You can use it to make the most out of your 3-D renderings. For example, you may want to animate and render a model that takes four hours to render, but you need 60 frames of animation in 24 hours. After Effects enables you to perform varieties of pans, zooms, squashes, and more esoteric effects (even 3-D rotation) to any image or QuickTime file.

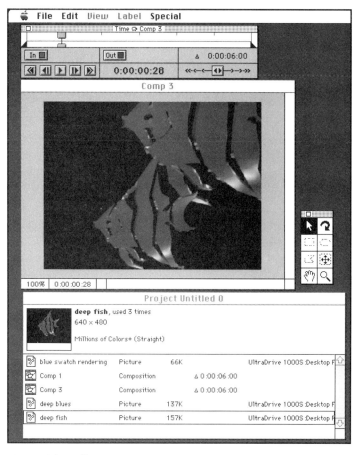

**Figure 11.37.** After Effects can be used to composite multiple layers of graphics and animation almost effortlessly.

After Effects provides stunning automatic compositing of images with alpha channels (see figure 11.37). The program does "sub-pixel" animation and can be used for field rendering. *Sub-pixel animation* means that the program works at higher resolution than your screen, so images animate very smoothly, and field rendering means you can double your frames-per-second setting in your 3-D program when rendering and export it to tape via After Effects to get the best-possible animations.

# Summary

- Working with 3-D images often begins with compositing—the overlay of 3-D graphics onto other images.

- Still images and animations can be saved at different bit depths with trade-offs in storage and image quality.

- QuickTime has become the accepted Mac animation format, but videographers and multimedia developers still rely on PICS and other formats.

- Adobe Photoshop is by far the most popular Mac image editing and compositing application. It has endless uses in 3-D.

- Painter and DeBabelizer are programs at the opposite ends of the spectrum that both offer powerful image processing capabilities.

- Three-D can be incorporated easily into desktop publishing projects.

- Putting animations on video requires frame-by-frame recording methods.

- Field rendering is a method of doubling the frame rate of an NTSC animation.

- Three-D is a compelling part of modern multimedia design.

- Many programs are available that can animate still 3-D images.

# RenderMan

R enderMan is unquestionably the most ambitious of all 3-D rendering systems. Not only is it extremely powerful on the Macintosh, but it is available to many other kinds of computer systems, becoming a kind of universal 3-D language. While many products take advantage of it, RenderMan is not a Macintosh product in and of itself, though a number of Macintosh products are built around it.

RenderMan is a system from Pixar (a company created in the alchemy of Lucasfilm) for the depiction and rendering of realistic 3-D images. RenderMan takes input in the form of geometry, lights, and "shaders," and generates rendered images. Unlike other 3-D systems, RenderMan is application-independent. In other words, it acts very much like a PostScript printer—you send it a RIB (RenderMan Interface Bytestream) file, and it processes a picture. The beauty of the system is that any machine that runs RenderMan can render a RIB file created on another machine. The other unique aspect of RenderMan is that Shaders—the algorithms that define surfaces and how they are rendered—are separate from RenderMan itself. As long as a shader obeys the very flexible rules set down by RenderMan, the renderer should be able to use it. This means that RenderMan has almost open-ended power: it can create images with the realism of ray tracing or radiosity, but is not limited to using one method for an entire scene. Essentially, each object in a scene can have its own rendering system attached in the form of a Shader.

# The 3-D "printer"

Just as PostScript is a language for defining 2-D images, RenderMan is a language that defines 3-D objects and surfaces.

It's very common for 3-D users to model and build scenes on a Macintosh or other personal computer and to send these scenes to a powerful workstation for rendering. Macintosh users can even use add-on acceleration hardware, such as YARC Systems Inc.'s NuSprint or MacRageous boards, which are essentially high-speed RISC computers on a NuBus board (see chapter 13, "Advanced Topics"). A special version of RenderMan, in this case YARC RenderMan, accepts RIB files created on the Mac and generates renderings at very high speed. Alternatively, you can network the Mac to one or more UNIX machines from Silicon Graphics Inc. or Sun Microsystems (running their own versions of RenderMan) for high-speed rendering.

The reason companies like Industrial Light and Magic and others that make extensive use of 3-D are able to put RenderMan to such good use is that it's possible to create an infinite variety of very realistic surfaces by writing custom RenderMan shaders. In addition, RenderMan's device independence means the images can be rendered at extremely high speeds using networks of high-powered computers.

# Choosing RenderMan

The version of RenderMan that runs on the Macintosh is called MacRenderMan. Anyone with a Mac and software that can generate RIB files can theoretically generate the same type of images that Industrial Light and Magic creates for blockbuster movies. Be aware, however, that the computing power at the disposal of ILM's RenderMan makes the fastest Mac look like a gnat on the knee of a brachiosaurus.

MacRenderMan is supplied with Pixar's ShowPlace, but is also available as a separate product. RenderMan appears on the Mac as a Chooser device. This means you select RenderMan in the Chooser, then select from among the various flavors of RenderMan available. These include "VectorRMan," which renders a wireframe view of the scene, and "PhotoRMan," the renderer of choice for photorealistic rendering. Just like printers, copies of RenderMan running on the network are automatically available for your rendering jobs (see chapter 13, "Advanced Topics").

When you select one of these RenderMan versions, it becomes the default rendering "printer." The system also comes with a program called RenderApp, which works very much like the Print Monitor application supplied with every Mac. Anything you send out for rendering is processed by the RenderMan "device" and returned to RenderApp, or a substitute, as a finished image.

MacRenderMan is a distributed processing system. This means that it can divvy up a single rendering job among several different copies of RenderMan located on the network. Each of these rendering slaves renders its portion of the image and sends it back to the rendering Mac for assembly into a single image. This is a classic case of division of labor, and it works great. (Distributed rendering systems are also available for RayDream's Designer, Strata's products, and Infini-D; see chapter 13, "Advanced Topics," for further explanation.)

# RenderMan Shaders

Shaders are procedures used to compute details of a surface used in a rendering. For the purposes of most Mac users, some types of shaders are used behind the scenes, such as light source shaders (which are supplied with MacRenderMan and modified by your scene building application). The shaders of most interest to end users are typically surface shaders and, sometimes, volume shaders.

Technically speaking, shaders are text files which specify some of the parameters for a whole range of possible variables that make up a surface quality. Really skilled RenderMan users can open a shader, modify it using a word processor, and wield magic on a 3-D scene. George Lucas' special effects studio, Industrial Light and Magic, was the cradle of RenderMan technology and the company remains the greatest master of this sorcery. The company uses the technology to create liquid-metal cyborgs, rippling submarine monsters, and Tyrannosaurus dinosaurs, among other fantasia. Fortunately, most users are insulated from the details of shaders by the fact that most programs which support RenderMan offer shaders in a format that makes it easy to apply "textures" without understanding the underlying technology.

## Surface shaders

Surface shaders (see figure 12.1) are the most common shaders you'll have to deal with because they define the color and texture of a surface, much the way procedural shaders (often used for wood and marble) do in other rendering systems. Commercially available shaders from the Valis Group are sometimes as simple as "paint" or as complex as "metal bubbles."

**Figure 12.1.** RenderMan rendering generated in Macromedia 3-D using a variety of surface shaders.

# Displacement shaders

Surface shaders can include displacement, which handles the deformation of an object's surface and the creation of irregularities. When applied to a surface, you can create realistic pits, ridges, threads, or other displacements of a surface's volume.

Displacement shaders can include materials such as glass, wood, or metal. Displacement shaders define changes in the volume of an object. For example, a brick displacement might actually modify the surface of an object to rise at the brick's surface and fall inward at the mortar between bricks. Unlike a bump map, which creates the illusion of a bump by changing the shading on an otherwise smooth surface, a displacement shader actually modifies the volume of the object.

# Looks

Shaders are an extremely powerful format, and a skilled programmer can create all kinds of unusual surfaces. However, RenderMan shaders have traditionally been extremely mysterious. Their power lies in the ability to configure the many parameters that determine an object's surface appearance, but most 3-D users lack the sophistication, time, or patience to program shaders. Some programs allow you to set these parameters without manually typing in program code, but programs such as Presenter Professional and MacroMedia Three-D still require you to set values for characteristics such as "X(float)," "UpVector" and "AtVector" to get the most out of RenderMan shaders. Needless to say, most designers don't immediately perceive the value of floats or the ups and downs of AtVectors.

Fortunately for novice users, Pixar has introduced an easy-to-use shader format called Looks that comes with both Typestry and ShowPlace. In addition, the Valis Group is updating all of their commercial shaders to offer this format.

Looks makes it much easier for a 3-D user to use textures. Unlike other forms of RenderMan shaders, Looks includes a visual preview of each texture. This means that, for once, you can see a sample of the material you're applying to an object before you render the scene. This is not as helpful as a real-time preview of an object with the texture applied, but it's better than pure guesswork. Hopefully, all programs that support RenderMan output will eventually offer support for the Looks format. This means that you'll be able to preview surfaces and other RenderMan effects, at least to some extent, from within your scene-building application.

Currently, however, the non-Pixar applications that support RenderMan (such as Presenter Professional, Macromedia Three-D, Sketch!) do not have any support for the Looks format, so you'll have to take the well-traveled, but more confusing, slow road.

## Glimpse

Looks are actually divided into two parts in the current version— Looks Masters and Looks Instances. A master contains all of the default settings for a particular Look. Since you'd probably be unhappy if you edited a Look, didn't like what you got, and couldn't figure out how to edit it back again, Pixar has made the Looks Masters uneditable. However, the Glimpse utility, which comes with Showplace and Typestry, enables you to knock off as many different variations of the Master as you like. For example, you might want to change the grain colors in a wood shader or modify the degree of refraction in a glass texture. Glimpse enables you to do this, as well as to make many other modifications to looks, all starting with a Master.

The interface essentially allows you to modify individual parameters of a shader through a graphical interface. This format protects the user from having to program shaders or truly understand the workings of all of a shader's parameters. You are free to experiment to see how changes will affect your designs. Glimpse also allows a designer to simply make selections such as choosing a color from a color picker or specifying an amount of lumpiness with a slider bar (rather than specifying a color number or typing in a displacement value). Once you have defined an Instance, it is saved and applied to an object from your 3-D application. Wisely, Glimpse doesn't let you change the Looks Master itself.

# Programming shaders

For those who want to go beyond what's available in commercial and on-line libraries of RenderMan Shaders and Looks, it's possible to write your own shaders. This technical and complex undertaking requires detailed knowledge of the RenderMan interface, an understanding of surface qualities, and a practical grasp of computer programming in a language such as C. In short, it's beyond the scope of this book, except to say that with some effort, shader programming can yield wonderful results. It's possible to create shaders that will generate almost anything you can see. What is possible and what is practical don't always coincide, however. The single-purpose renderers that come with most 3-D applications (at least on the Mac) have the advantage that they are complete and are easy to work with. At the commercial level, so are the programs that use RenderMan. RenderMan, being a rendering language rather than a specific application, is relatively unlimited, but mastering the language is not for the casual practitioner.

> **Tip**
> The author encourages anyone interested in programming
> Shaders—or just learning a lot more about RenderMan—to
> read the *RenderMan Companion* (Steve Upstill, Addison
> Wesley, 1990). No author could hope to come close to
> documenting this system better than this authoritative
> textbook. And, for those who can handle the frequent
> intrusion of mathematical formulae and program code, it's
> a very interesting read.

# The Valis Group

A specialized division of Pixar, The Valis Group, is particularly
devoted to creating new shader packages and clip models for use
with RenderMan. Many of the most original and creative RenderMan
shaders available to RenderMan users have the VG initials on them.

# Summary

- RenderMan is Pixar's rendering system that runs on many
  different platforms. It works like a printer for creating 3-D
  images.

- MacRenderMan works is the standard Mac version of
  RenderMan. Other Mac versions include YARCRenderMan and
  NetRenderMan.

- Shaders are RenderMan's equivalent of textures. They are
  available in a variety of file formats for different gnerations of
  RenderMan-compatible software.

- The Looks format, unlike the format is more or less What-You-
  See-Is-What-You-Get. You can modify Looks with a utility called
  Glimpse.

# 13

# Advanced topics

W hile some people may consider the very act of creating a 3-D image an "advanced topic," compared to traditional 2-D techniques, it is nevertheless sometimes necessary to go beyond the day-to-day basic requirements of modeling and rendering. This chapter attempts to shed light on some of the most important techniques used to take 3-D to a higher level: translating and transporting models between applications; smoothing the facets of polygonal models; coping with the many file formats endemic to 3D; and accelerating rendering through special hardware and software and distributed processing.

# Transporting models

Because no 3-D tool is perfect, many users take advantage of multiple applications. Architects, for example, often work in a full-featured CAD application when designing structures, but export their models to a program such as StrataVision 3d for photorealistic ray tracing. Animators, who rely on programs like Electric Image Animation System and Macromedia Three-D, must use a separate application to build their models. Moving models between applications is by no means as simple as it is in the 2-D world, where file formats like EPSF, QuickTime, and PICT guarantee that graphics files are compatible from one application to the next. The list of available file formats for 3-D is almost as long as the list of applications themselves. And some programs greatly complicate matters by supporting some—but not all—of a file format's features.

With recent releases of 3-D software, some measure of help has arrived. MiniCAD+, for example, exports native StrataVision 3d-format files, so rendering a MiniCAD+ plus model is as simple as saving in one program and opening in the other. Modeler Professional, from VIDI, exports Electric Image's FACT format; it can also render directly to RenderMan as does Macromedia's MacroModel. Alias' Sketch! outputs RIB files, but you will need Pixar's ShowPlace to apply lights and shaders. Working Model, a 2-D physics simulation package, exports its animations directly to Macromedia Three-D.

# 3-D file formats

Things, however, are not nearly so rosy with most applications. In general, they rely on a few key file formats, including DXF, RIB, and IGES, to name a few. (Electric Image Animation System's Transporter lists about 20 file formats in its import menu.) Usually, the support for these standards is somewhat less than "standard." Often a subset of the possible formats is supported. Conversely, a program may import a particular file format, but not all of the included objects will make it in translation. It is common, for example, to import a complex object from another program, only to find that it renders as "inside-out." Other problems include holes in surfaces that disappear when moved to another application or groups of objects that are combined into single inseparable objects when imported. There are many tricks for dealing with these problems, but there are no standard techniques. In cases where a file does not convert accurately, you may need to modify it in the original application to make it work when exported. Many programs offer a variety of export settings that affect your ability to export a model.

Fortunately, Apple is reportedly working on a 3-D "meta-file" format. This would be analogous to the 2-D PICT format. Any program that supports the meta-file could read models, lights, and other 3-D features from another program that also supports it. The time frame for the release of this format has not been established. Vendor support will hopefully follow when it does.

# DXF

The Drawing eXchange Format (DXF) is the AutoCAD standard file format developed by Autodesk Inc. Originally a 2-D format (2D DXF), it has been upgraded to include the 3D DXF specification (which is the only one that really matters for 3-D applications). Often, the 3D DXF format is referred to as simply "DXF." This is the most widely supported file format by far. Its strengths are in defining and exchanging polygonal (faceted) geometry. This makes it a natural for exchanging architectural drawings and other polygonal primitives, but it is weak at defining spline-based surfaces and other curves (except for circles and arcs).

DXF has become a de-facto standard for exchanging geometry from one program to another—but the way programs support the format is erratic, to say the least. DXF is not particularly adept at communicating curves, so DXF files tend to be much larger than equivalent spline-based models. DXF is a more-or-less reliable format, however, so it is widely supported and used. DXF can carry color and layer information which you can use to transport object groupings intact.

# IGES

The Initial Graphic Exchange Specifications (IGES) standard defines far more types of objects than most programs support. That makes it a good format for importing documents (if you can read all of the possible features in an IGES file you can read just about anything). But exporting a file to IGES is by no means a guarantee that another 3-D application can read it.

Unlike DXF, which is widely supported in both directions, IGES is widely supported as an export format, but few programs on the Mac offer the option of importing an IGES file.

# RIB

RenderMan Interface Bytestream (RIB) files are the standard medium of exchange for RenderMan geometry lights and shader information. The advantage of this format is that it has integral support for splines. Because RenderMan is available on most platforms, it is a natural for distributed rendering and general file exchange for users of RenderMan-compatible products. On the other hand, because the file format includes the specifications for shaders, it is difficult and therefore unpopular to implement in applications that are not aimed at using RenderMan.

# 3DGF

The 3-D Geometry File format (3DGF) is Macromedia's attempt to create a 3-D file format standard. It is positioned as a substitute for RIB because both file types support the same types of geometries (except for NuRBS, which RIB supports, but 3DGF does not). It is also a spline-based architecture. It does not, however, carry shader information like RIB.

# Kandu's Cadmover

Cadmover, from Kandu Software Corp., is a commercial software application specifically created to translate one 3-D file to another format. Because this is its specialty, Cadmover tends to be very good at what it does. For users of CAD software—particularly less widely-supported applications—who want to convert their models to a particular format, this program is a great time saver.

# Smoothing

A common complaint is that objects that appear smooth in one application import with obvious facets on curved faces. Most 3-D programs that do ray-tracing or Phong shading have a way to smooth faceted surfaces. Some programs enable you to adjust this setting so that intersections beyond a certain angular threshold (such as the inside or outside corners of a cube) will not be smoothed, while the relatively gradual angles on faces and the surfaces of spheres and cylinders are smoothed over. Smoothing is achieved by adjusting the normals on faces so that they blend into adjacent faces. Like bump mapping, this is a rendering trick; it doesn't affect the actual geometry of a model.

# Acceleration

There is no getting around the fact that 3-D rendering is slow. The publishers of 3-D applications have made a science of optimizing their algorithms, but things can still proceed at a snail's pace even on lightning-fast Macs. There is hope, however, for people determined to do 3-D on a deadline. The choices are fairly simple: faster hardware or faster software. There are a number of options on both fronts, but the user will have to balance speed, cost and convenience to come up with an equation that works.

# Faster hardware

You can soup up your Mac only so much. Even the fastest 68040 accelerators will bring only a few orders of speed to slower Macs. Quadras are fast, but not that much faster than Mac IIs. To really accelerate the hardware end of rendering, you will need to look to some of the more advanced technology on the market.

## RISC

Reduced Instruction Set Computing (RISC) chips are the same ones used in high-end graphics workstations by Silicon Graphics. These chips are currently about ten times the speed of the fastest MAC.

By putting one or more separate RISC chips in your Mac, in the form of NuBUS boards, you can achieve 3-D rendering power comparable to the RISC-based workstations. This approach brings workstation performance to the Mac, while maintaining the friendly productive front end for which Apple is so adored. The down side to this approach is that RISC processors can be used only for rendering (or other applications for which custom software has been written). Because the Apple operating system still runs on 68030 or 68040 chips on the Mac's motherboard, modeling and other functions are not accelerated. However, rendering is by far the slowest part of any 3-D project, so the boards from Integrated Device Technology and YARC are exceptionally good values for the serious 3-D user.

# YARC boards

One of the great advantages of the YARC board is that software publishers have written distributed processing software for it, so that you can have more than one YARC board in your system and get a proportional benefit.

YARC's boards (the fast NuSprint and faster MacRageous), are available bundled with YARCRenderMan (the YARC version of RenderMan). RenderMan users see the YARC board as just another RenderMan Chooser extension. When you go to render, your job is shipped across the NuBus to the YARC board and the rendering is displayed on your screen as it is completed in unbelievably fast time.

VIDI's Presenter Professional uses the YARC board when ray tracing if you have the YARC version. (Presenter Pro also can use YARCRenderMan directly.)

Byte by Byte's Sculpt 3D RISC and Sculpt 4D RISC also enable you to take advantage of one or more YARC boards for high-speed ray tracing.

Specular Inc.'s BackBurner rendering engine includes a YARC component, so in addition to distributed rendering, users can directly address the YARC board for acceleration without the trouble of network maintenance. Users can render Infini-D images and animations at many times normal speed using this software.

In all cases, the YARC boards accelerate rendering anywhere from five to 20 times the speed of a Mac.

# IDT CZAR

Integrated Device Technologies' CZAR board is another RISC chip on a NuBUS board. This one, however, emulates a Silicon Graphics workstation, and supports the TorqueWare/VideoBits rendering solution for StrataVision 3d and StrataStudio Pro.

VideoBits' Flash Tracer rendering software is available bundled with TorqueWare. The two programs together allow you to achieve SGI-class rendering speeds inside your Mac.

# PowerPC

The PowerPC will introduce a new breed of RISC technology to the Mac market. These Macs will be much faster than any previously available, but there is a catch. Every piece of software must be completely rewritten to take advantage of the new hardware. While Apple will offer emulation software (software that emulates a 68040 chip) at the same time as the PowerPC, this will not be much faster than the Quadras. It will be some time before 3-D users will be able to make extensive use of the PowerPC's capabilities (although when it arrives, it will open up many doors of opportunity for powerful 3-D applications on "Macs").

Many 3-D vendors have plans to ship native PowerPC versions of their software the same day Apple ships the first PowerPCs.

# Distributed processing

As with hardware acceleration, software vendors are struggling to make the heavy demands of their renderers reasonable in a production environment, without requiring users to make huge additional hardware investments. One of the ways they can do this is with distributed processing. Also called *distributed rendering*, this technique harnesses the power of several computers to perform the work of one in much less time. Users of UNIX workstations have long had this capability, so it is with belated enthusiasm that Mac users are approaching this technique.

# How distributed rendering works

Distributed rendering is simple in concept, but generally not so easy to implement. Essentially, it operates on the division of labor principle (see figure 13.1).

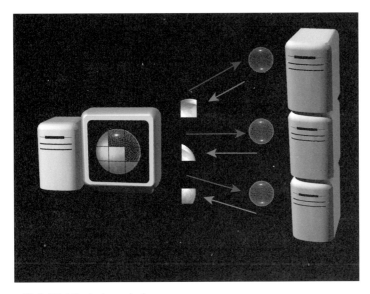

**Figure 13.1.** Distributed rendering.

1. A *master* computer (usually the computer used for modeling and scene building) is connected to one or more *slaves* via a network. This reverses the traditional client-server relationship, in which many clients command the resources of one server.

2. The master sends the entire model and scene description, complete with texture maps, over the network to every slave machine. Each of these slaves then has everything it needs to render the entire scene, if necessary.

3. The master makes rendering assignments, instructing each slave to work on a different slice of the total scene. The slaves render their slices as quickly as possible and send the results to the master.

4. The master machine receives each slice of the final rendering and assembles it like a jigsaw puzzle. As each slave finishes a slice, the master assigns it a new missing piece of the rendering to complete the puzzle.

Distributed rendering can be implemented in a variety of schemes. There are currently four software-only distributed rendering systems available on the Mac: Strata's RenderPro, Specular's BackBurner, RayDream's DreamNet, and Pixar's NetRenderMan.

Essentially, each of these packages works the same way: You install a slave application on each machine on the network and you configure it to allow access to unused processor time. (RenderPro's slaves include a calendar to schedule when the Mac will be available, so rendering does not interfere with the owner's regular work.) Specular's AutoBurner works like a screen saver, only allowing access to a Mac when the keyboard has been idle a specified amount of time.

When a rendering job is requested by the user at the master Macintosh, the master checks the network for available slaves and if it finds them, initiates a network rendering.

The advantage of distributed rendering is that you can take advantage of existing networked Macs and have them all collaborate on a single project. The disadvantage is that rendering pretty much must take over the slave Mac to do any good. If the owners of the slave Macs are working on their machines, CPU cycles are withheld from the distributed rendering process and it does not do much good. Essentially, this means you will need to reserve distributed rendering for after hours—a common practice, anyway, since rendering usually puts an end to modeling and other tasks for quite a while.

The other significant limitation of distributed rendering is the speed of the network. For users with a slow LocalTalk network, the time it takes to send models, textures, and environments over the wire tends to negate the advantage of having multiple machines working on the same image or animation. Because there is a certain loss of efficiency for every machine added, the performance curve tends to level off after you add a dozen machines or so. With Ethernet, distributed rendering is much more viable, since the files are piped over the network much more quickly and network performance doesn't interfere with the process.

The final problem with this type of software is that, like any renderer, the slaves are memory-and CPU-hungry. Even if you manage to network a roomful of Mac Classics and install distributed rendering software on each one, you are not likely to see much of a performance gain over rendering on your master Quadra 950. The performance gained is almost directly proportional to the speed and availability of the Macs used as slaves.

One of the requirements of a distributed rendering system is that the master must be able to keep track of slaves as they are turned on or off, or crash during a rendering or for some other reason. All of these systems manage the ins and outs of distributed rendering without much trouble.

# NetRenderMan

NetRenderMan is unique among distributed rendering software because it allows the master Mac to access any version of RenderMan available on the network. Thus, you may have a Mac calling on the services of a Quadra, a Mac II with a YARC board, and a Sun or SGI workstation, all at the same time. NetRenderMan is also unique in that it's now bundled with MacRenderMan. You get three rendering slave nodes for free.

# Render Pro

Strata's distributed rendering software is extremely efficient at accessing network resources, so it closely approximates a linear performance gain as you add Macs to the chain. As mentioned, it includes a calendar to restrict access, so owners of slave machines can lock out the rendering access, except at specified times.

# BackBurner

Specular's distributed rendering software, BackBurner, includes a screen saver that automatically allows access to the slave when its owner has been idle for a specified amount of time. A YARC rendering engine is available for BackBurner which means anyone rendering with BackBurner can access a YARC board on the network.

# DreamNet

Like the other distributed rendering systems, DreamNet offers access control by the owner of the slave Mac. RayDream expects big things for the DreamNet system software in the form of products from other vendors.

# RocketShare

Radius Inc. offers a hardware device that is particularly well suited to distributed rendering. The Radius Rocket (with optional RocketShare software) is a NuBus board that acts like a separate Macintosh on the network. You can install one or more of these boards in a Macintosh and each can be running a copy of the distributed rendering software. The main Macintosh CPU, acting as the master, distributes the rendering jobs to the slaves running on each of the Rockets. Since the network is the NuBus, the network bottleneck is completely eliminated, resulting in very fast renderings on a "single" Mac.

# UNIX workstations

Power 3-D users may not be content to use only the Macintosh. Studios such as Disney and Industrial Light and Magic, and business sites that rely on intensive 3-D output (such as Boeing), are likely to rely on high-power UNIX computers such as those from Sun and Silicon Graphics. These have the processor speed and computational power to be many times faster than the fastest Macintosh. It is possible to network Macs with these powerful machines to get the best of both worlds. For example, you could do your modeling on the Macintosh, send the results over the network to a Silicon Graphics Indigo for rendering (at 10 times Macintosh Quadra speeds), then incorporate the final image into your documents using desktop publishing software on the Mac. TorqueWare also allows access to SGI processing power and opens it up to access from software like VideoBits' rendering engine for StrataVision 3d.

The most powerful modeling and animation software in existence is available for the SGI platform (and the SGI machines go on up to models that provide real-time rendering for virtual reality). Wavefront, Power Animator, and others are used extensively for creating Hollywood special effects. Expect to pay close to $50,000 just to get your foot in the door with these systems.

Currently, Macintosh users can render on the SGI using the aforementioned FlashTracer from Torque/VideoBits; Electric Image Animation System users can render to SGI as well; and users with the SGI version of RenderMan also can take advantage of the workstation's rendering speed. UNIX versions of RenderMan are also available for other high-end workstations.

# Summary

- Transporting models involves finding file formats in common between two programs. Sometimes, you can go through an intermediate program to translate files.

- Currently, programs that support one file format do not necessarily support all of the same features; so files may need a lot of fine tuning before they can be exported and before they can be imported into another program.

- Several 3-D file formats are de-facto standards, including: DXF, IGES, and RIB.

- Acceleration is primarily applicable to rendering speed, although a faster computer will make everything proportionately faster.

- Hardware acceleration in the form of RISC coprocessors can make rendering five to 20 times faster than a single Macintosh alone.

- The NuBUS boards from YARC are the most widely supported acceleration hardware for 3-D rendering on the Mac.

- Distributed processing enables you to harness multiple Macs to do a single rendering.

- Those craving the utmost in rendering power can send renderings over a network for processing on a UNIX workstation.

# Macintosh 3-D applications

W hile the following is undoubtedly an incomplete listing, these products are the core of Macintosh 3D applications (and indispensable related products) currently and soon-to-be available. Corporations are listed alphabetically.

# Adobe Systems Inc.

1585 Charleston Road
Mountain View, CA 94039

Phone: (415) 961-4400
Fax: (415) 961-3769

## Dimensions

- 3-D PostScript

A demo version of Dimensions is included on the CD-ROM.

System requirements: System 6.05 or greater, 2M RAM, hard disk.

Dimensions can extrude or lathe Illustrator-format outlines. Can map an Illustrator illustration as a label. Supports white Sun-type lights and requires that fonts be saved as outlines in another program to be able to extrude them. Rendered images are editable PostScript objects.

## Photoshop

- Image processing
- Painting

A demo version of Photoshop is included on the CD-ROM.

Used for painting textures and compositing images using alpha channels and other types of mattes. Also used for touching up and adding details to 3-D renderings.

Almost mandatory for working with bitmap graphics on the Macintosh.

# Premiere

- QuickTime editing

A demo version of Premiere is included on the CD-ROM.

Premiere is the, well, premiere QuickTime editing application on the Macintosh. It includes all kinds of features for compositing and adding special effects to QuickTime movies and animations created in 3D. It's also great if you want to create animated backgrounds and textures for rotoscoping.

# Aldus Corporation

9770 Carroll Center Road, Suite J
San Diego, CA 92126

Phone: (619) 695-6956 or (800) 888-6293
Fax: (619) 695-7902

# Super 3D

- Modeling

- Scenes

The first Macintosh 3-D application. Supports Hidden-line and wireframe rendering.

# Alias Research Inc.

110 Richmond St. East
Toronto, Ontario M5C1P1

Phone: (416) 362-9181 or (800) 267-8697
Fax: (416) 362-0630

## Sketch!

- Modeling

- Scenes

- Rendering

A gallery of Sketch! samples is included on the CD-ROM.

System requirements: Macintosh IIci minimum, System 6.05 or newer, 8M RAM (12 recommended), 9M disk space, 32-bit QuickDraw, 24-bit color recommended.

Sketch! is a free-form 3-D modeler that uses unique navigational tools and a powerful spline-based modeling system offering "putty" surfaces.

Features include: unlimited cameras; one texture per object; bump and transparency mapping; lights include Spot, Point, Sun and Ambient; export formats include, DXF, EPS, PICT, RIB, TIFF, Alias PIX, and StyleGuide; rendering formats include: Ray tracing, Phong, Gouraud, flat shading, hidden line, wireframe, and EPS wireframe; export RIB geometry.

## UpFront

- Modeling

- Scenes

- Rendering

System requirements: Color Classic or better Macintosh, 4M RAM, System 6.05 or later. Recommended: 8M of RAM, math coprocessor, color monitor.

UpFront is designed as a basic 3-D package for visualization and illustration. It's particularly suited to architectural design. Sun can be positioned and automatically animated for time of day.

UpFront is a polygonal modeler with simple solid modeling features for doors and windows. You can save unlimited views, and animate the camera using basic key frames. Only distant lights are supported. Export formats include: DXF, PICT, EPS, RIB, Alias PIX, TIFF, Draw, PICT, Architrion, Swivel CMD, Comma Text, and Tab Text. Rendering types include: flat shading, hidden line rendering, Editable PostScript, and RIB export.

# The Alpha Channel

72 Delmar Street
San Francisco, CA 94117

Phone: (415) 626-4744
Fax: (415) 626-4744

# Expert Set 3D

- Textures

A set of sample textures is included on the CD-ROM.

The Expert Sets are CD-ROM volumes of complimentary backgrounds, textures, bump maps, and surface effects maps that are ready for use in 3-D applications. The Alpha Channel also creates Expert Sets for use in multimedia presentations and standard slide show presentations.

# Anjon & Associates

714 E. Angeleno, Unit C
Burbank, CA 91501

Phone: (818) 998-7925

# Playmation

- Integrated

System requirements: 68030 Macintosh, Math coprocessor, 4M hard
disk space, 5M RAM.

Playmation produces very life-like character animations; however,
the 1.0 Macintosh version suffered from its direct port from the DOS
platform. It's a non-Mac-like program, and all windows are modal
(you can't switch between programs while you work in Playmation).
In addition, the modeling and animating modules are separate
programs; textures are based on a small set of procedural shaders;
and although it creates very realistic "feeling" living creatures, it
doesn't offer tools for creating very complex objects.

Features include: a unique patch-and-spline-based modeler uses
"spines" and "skins"; uses two windows per view; animation is event-
based, with multiple time lines; tools for animation include complex
spline motion paths and character animation controls (such as being
able to assign a spine to an object and have surfaces bend along this
spine); one texture is allowed per object; supports bump maps and
transparency maps; light types include spot, point, sun, and ambient;
export formats include DXF; rendering format is Ray tracing.

# Artifice Inc.

PO Box 1588
Eugene, OR 97440

Phone: (503) 345-7421
Fax: (503) 346-3626

# Design Workshop

- CAD

- Visualization

Designed as a basic 3-D visualization, concept and design program, particularly for architecture design. Calculates and renders architectural models for the path of the sun on a given day of the year. The program supports unlimited layering and polygonal surface modeling with Boolean effects for windows and doors.

You can save unlimited views. Includes sun lights only. Saves in PICT, EPS, DXF, Claris CAD, and Architrion formats. Rendering types include: radiance, flat shading, wireframe, and hidden line.

# Ashlar Inc.

1290 Oakmead Parkway, Suite 218
Sunnyvale, CA 94086

Phone: (408) 746-1800 or (800) 877-2745
Fax: (408) 746-0749

# Vellum 3D

- Computer-aided design and drafting

System requirements: SE/30 or faster Macintosh, 4M RAM, 5M hard disk space, System 6.05 or later.

A powerful drafting and modeling environment for creating complex precision shapes. For scene, building, animation and rendering, you'll have to export to another application.

Modeling tools include precision spline and polygonal CAD tools for drafting and design. Export formats include: DXF, IGES, EPS, PICT, Vellum, and DXB.

# Autodesk Inc.

2320 Marinship Way
Sausalito, CA 94965

Phone: (415) 332-2344 or (800) 964-6432
Fax: (415) 331-8093

## AutoCAD Release 12

- CAD modeler

- Renderer

AutoCAD is an industry-standard high-end CAD program, with a limitless range and depth of powerful, customizable modeling tools and a programmable work environment. The optional extension to AutoCAD, AME, provides solid modeling functionality. Add-on modules from other companies provide capabilities such as RenderMan support and ray tracing.

An advanced CAD application customizable to any 3-D task. Light types include: spot, point, sun, and ambient. File export formats include: DXF, IGES, EPS, and PICT. Formats supported by AutoCAD can be supplemented with add-on export tools. Render type is Gouraud.

# Autodessys

2011 Riverside Drive
Columbus, OH 43221

Phone: (614) 488-9777
Fax: (614) 488-0848

# form•Z

- CAD

- Design

System requirements: Macintosh II or better, 5M RAM, math
coprocessor, 5M hard disk space, System 6.04 or later.

Powerful, fairly easy-to-use solid modeler. Combines NuRBS and
polygonal geometry. form•Z has extensive Boolean support, enabling
you to easily carve objects with one another. The program has a high
degree of integration with its 2-D tools for exporting models as plans
and importing plans and turning them into models.

form•Z's capabilities include: can save multiple views; light type is
limited to sun; extrudes fonts with bevels; saves in PICT, DXF FACT
(Electric Image Animation System), STL, 3DGF, RIB, EPS, and IGES
formats; renders with flat shading, hidden line, wireframe, Phong, and
Gouraud.

# Byte by Byte Corp.

9442-A Capitol of Texas Hwy. North, Suite 650
Austin, TX 78759

Phone: (512) 795-0150
Fax: (512) 795-0021

# Sculpt 3D/Sculpt 3D RISC
# Sculpt 4D/Sculpt 4D RISC

- Integrated

RISC adds support for YARC's NuSprint and MacRageous accelerator
boards. The 4D versions add basic animation tools. Sculpt is due for a
major upgrade around the end of 1993 which will add splines and an

overhauled interface. Currently, it's one of the most powerful 3-D applications on the Macintosh for high-end users, supporting very detailed modeling and rendering. The trade-off is in a Byzantine, non-standard interface.

Sculpt is a Polygonal modeler that use a three-plane view. Animation in the 4D versions is basic key frame. Multiple textures per object, as well as surface quality maps, are supported. Light types include: spot, point, sun, and ambient. Export types include: DXF, PICT, and EPS, but many formats are available through "file machine" translators. Rendering styles include ray tracing, Phong, Gouraud, flat shading, hidden line, and wireframe.

# CrystalGraphics Inc.

3110 Patrick Henry Drive
Santa Clara, CA 95054

Phone: (408) 496-6175
Fax: (408) 496-6998

# Crystal TOPAS for Mac

- Integrated

Ported from the powerful PC version, Crystal TOPAS Macintosh has been in a state of limbo. A new-and-improved version is due in 1994. The PC version features powerful spline-based control of animation parameters and shape morphing. The modeler is polygonal and animation is based on key frames with one time line. Texture options include environmental reflection mapping, bump maps, glow maps, and transparency maps. Light types include spot, sun, point, and ambient. Export options include DXF, IGES, and RIB. Rendering options are Phong, flat shading, and wireframe.

# Diaquest Inc.

1440 San Pablo Ave.
Berkeley, CA 94702

Phone: (510) 526-7167
Fax: (510) 526-7073

## DQ-Animaq

- Animation control hardware

Diaquest's Animaq boards are the industry standard hardware for controlling frame-accurate video decks and managing the laying out of animations onto video. The QuickPass option for capturing QuickTime makes them a virtual necessity for serious rotoscoping of video-resolution images.

## Mac-232

- Animation software

This software enables you to put animations directly onto videotape if you have a frame-accurate animation video deck. The software works just like Diaquest's hardware boards, except that some of the high-speed features of the boards are not supported.

# Dynaware USA Inc.

950 Tower Lane, Suite 1150
Foster City, CA 94404

Phone: (415) 349-5700 or (800) 445-3962
Fax: (415) 349-5879

# DynaPerspective

- CAD

- 3-D visualization

System requirements: Macintosh II or later, 2M RAM, 8-bit color or better, hard disk.

DynaPerspective is a 3-D design and visualization package with lots of tools specifically for architectural design. It offers a polygonal modeler with architecture-specific tools. Simple animation using key frames. Export formats include: DXF, PICT, Wireframe, Hidden line.

# Electric Image Inc.

117 E. Colorado Blvd., Suite 300
Pasadena, CA 91105

Phone: (818) 577-1627
Fax: (818) 577-2426

# Electric Image Animation System

- Scenes

- Animation

- Rendering

Electric Image features the most complete set of animation tools available on the Macintosh. Features include spline-based parameter curves and detailed control of individual motion parameters. EIAS is the industry-standard animation program on the Macintosh. It's very expensive, but for the professional video and multimedia animator, it justifies its price with power. EIAS includes complete animation

device control so you can render directly to video. The program also
directly controls various animation hardware and can record directly
to Abekas video recorders or to Exabyte tape drives in Abekas
format. Version 2.0 was due to ship around the same time as this
book. This version includes sound synchronization, particle animation and SGI rendering support.

EIAS's file import formats include: Architrion II, Cad-3d (Atari),
Cubicomp, Cyberware, DXF (Macintosh and PC), FACT (EIAS),
Filmroll, Generic (text), Lightwave (Video Toaster), MacConcept,
Macintosh 3D (text), Movie.BYU, MPS Demo, OFF (.geom, Digital
Equipment Corp.), OSU (.DETail, Ohio State, Phoenix 3D, Sculpt 3D
(Macintosh and Amiga), Super 3D (text), Swivel 3D, TWGES
(VersaCAD/PC), Videoscape (Amiga), Wavefront .OBJ, Zing (Pro 3D),
Zoom, 3D Turbo, 3DGF Binary (Macromedia 3D).

A font extrusion module, Mr. Font, generates high-precision beveled
models from outline fonts. Bevels can be treated as separate objects
for separate texture mapping.

Unlimited animated cameras are allowed and animation is event-
based with individual time lines for even minute parameter changes.
You can apply a single texture as well as a label to any object. Surface
quality maps can be used to modify most parameters, including glow,
transparency, and specular reflectance. Electric Image is the only
Macintosh 3-D program with visible lights. These include: spot, point,
sun, and tube lights. Output formats include: DXF, EPS, PICT,
QuickTime, Numbered PICT, and PICS. Rendering formats include
Phong, Gouraud, flat shading, and wireframe. Distributed rendering is
supported to one other licensed Macintosh; SGI rendering is also
optional.

# Equilibrium Technologies

475 Gate Five Road, Suite 225
Sausalito, CA 94965

Phone: (415) 332-4343
Fax: (415) 332-4433

# DeBabelizer

- Image processing

System requirements: Macintosh with System 6.07 or later, 700K RAM.

DeBabelizer is almost a must-have for the professional Macintosh animator and multimedia developer. It's an image processing program that can perform a wide range of standard operations on large batches of files. You can write scripts to perform often-repeated functions, such as image resizing or palette reduction, then set the program running and walk away. DeBabelizer will convert almost any image format on the Macintosh to almost any other format.

# Fractal Designs Inc.

335 Spreckels Drive, Suite F
Aptos, CA 95003

Phone: (408) 688-8800

# Painter

- Painting

- Image processing

Painter is a "natural media" paint program that supports pressure-sensitive drawing tablets (such as those from Wacom). Its paint brushes and paints look and act like natural artist's tools.

You can use Painter to create textures and backgrounds. It's also a good choice for compositing images. In addition, you can "clone" 3-D renderings using Painter's brushes to get realistic-looking painted images.

# HSC Software Inc.

1661 Lincoln Blvd., Suite 101
Santa Monica, CA 90404

Phone: (310) 392-8441
Fax: (310) 392-6015

## Kai's Power Tools

- Image processing

Requires Photoshop or other program that supports Photoshop
plug-ins.

Kai's Power Tools is an indispensable Photoshop plug-in that provides an endless variety of seamless textures and other special
effects for the 3-D user. It can be used by any program that supports
Photoshop plug-ins, including RayDream Designer, or PICT files
created with KPT can be saved and imported into 3-D programs.

# HumanOs

11956 Bernardo Plaza Drive, Suite 510
San Diego, CA 92128

Phone: (619) 451-7892

## Presto 3D

- Modeling
- Rendering

This is a simple 3-D application for creating bitmapped 3-D images. It includes a polygonal modeler and flat-shaded renderer. It has the distinction of being the lowest cost modeling and rendering program available on the Macintosh.

# Integrated Device Technologies

2975 Stender Way
Santa Clara, CA 95054

Phone: (800) 345-7015
Fax: (408) 499-4048

# CZAR

- Acceleration

Requires a Macintosh II, Torque Systems TorqueWare software.

This is a RISC-technology NuBUS board that supports VideoBits' FlashTracer rendering software for StrataVision 3d and StrataStudio Pro. Essentially, it's like having an SGI workstation on a board available for acceleration of rendering.

# Intergraph Corp.

289 Dunlop Blvd.
Huntsville, AL 35894

Phone: (205) 730-2700 or (800) 345-4856
Fax: (205) 730-9491

# MicroStation Mac

- General CAD

High-end extensible, programmable CAD system. Direct competitor to AutoCAD.

# Kandu Software

2305 N. Kentucky Street
Arlignton, VA 22205

Phone: (703) 532-0213
Fax: (703) 533-0291

## CADMover

- Translation utility

Three-D file translation software. CADMover currently supports the following formats: IGES, MiniCAD, MacDraw, PICT, DXF, MSC/PAL, Super 3D, Sculpt 3D/4D, ZOOM, FOCUS text, 3DGF, Dimensions, CGM, PostScript, HPGL, MacDraft, and Dreams. The standard translation package can be supplemented with add-on translators. CADMover is a godsend for users needing translation between incompatible formats. However, the software has one pitfall: a brain-dead copy protection scheme and the need to have add-ons "factory installed."

# Knoll Software

PO Box 6887
San Rafael, CA 94903-0887

Phone: (415) 453-2471
Fax: (415) 453-2471

# CyberSave 2.0

- 3-D modeling utility

Requires Photoshop or Photoshop plug-in-compatible application. CyberSave is a plug-in for Adobe Photoshop that converts grayscale images to rectangular or polar 3-D objects. It saves in CyberWare and DXF formats.

# Knowledge Revolution

15 Brush Place
San Francisco, CA 94103

Phone: (415) 553-8153 or (800) 766-6615
Fax: (415) 553-8012

# Working Model

- Simulation and animation

A demo version of Working Model is included on the CD-ROM.

Working Model is a mathematically-accurate physics simulation system that enables you to build 2-D models and set them in motion using physical laws. Forces and mechanical influences can be used to create machines and other simulations that respond to inverse kinematics. Animations created in Working Model can be exported directly, as key frames, to Macromedia 3D, or motion values can be exported in tab-delimited format, and translated into position, rotation, and time values in programs such as Electric Image Animation System; 3-D models can then be substituted for their 2-D place holders.

# Macromedia Inc.

600 Townsend St.
San Francisco, CA 94103

Phone: (415) 252-2000 or (800) 945-4601
Fax: (415) 442-0190

## Swivel 3D Professional/ SwivelMan

- Integrated

A demo version of Swivel 3D Professional is included on the CD-ROM.

Requires System 6.07 or better, 5M RAM, 5M disk, 8-bit or better color.

Profile-based polygonal modeler with outstanding object linking. Uses single-window world view. Animation uses basic key frames.

Assign and configure RenderMan shaders and apply sun and ambient lights. Animate shaders and render

Available as SwivelMan bundle with MacRenderMan.

## LifeForms

- Animation

A demo version of LifeForms is included on the CD-ROM.

Also available from:
Kinetic Effects Inc., Suite 310

1319 Dexter Ave.
Seattle, WA 98109

Phone: (206) 283-6961

Uses key frames to animate human figures. You can export animations directly to Macromedia 3D or Swivel 3D or save them as wireframe QuickTime movies.

# Macromedia Three-D

- Scenes

- Animation

Animate 3-D objects in a single world view window, set cameras for new points of view. Animation is event-based with multiple time line score, similar to Macromedia Director score. Control event parameters at a minute level of detail and set spline motion paths for objects. Supports ease-in and ease-out, but no object tracking or banking. Small library of primitives. Bump maps are supported as are rotoscoped backgrounds. Shape morphing is also supported. Light types include point and sun. The program extrudes outline fonts. Rendering types include Phong and flat shading. RenderMan support is very good; can animate shaders and render directly.

# MacroModel

- Scenes

- Animation

- Rendering

A demo version of MacroModel is included on the CD-ROM.

Requires System 6.07 or better, 8M RAM, 8-bit or better graphics, 6M hard disk space.

MacroModel is a spline based free-form modeler. It uses a single active drawing window of a fixed size and offers extremely quick real-time shading. You can push, pull, twist, nudge, and bend surfaces easily.

Texture formats are limited to solid colors and internal procedural shaders and surface qualities. Lighting options include point, sun, and ambient. Rendering is limited to Gouraud. MacroModel exports geometry, lights, and textures in RIB format for RenderMan rendering. The program automatically extrudes outline type, with bevels, and it exports DXF, Macromedia 3D, and Swivel 3D formats.

# ModelShop II

- Modeling

- Visualization

A demo version of ModelShop II is included on the CD-ROM.

Simple polygonal modeler for architectural design and visualization.

# Mira Imaging Inc.

2257 South 1100 East, Suite 1A
Salt Lake City, UT 84106

Phone: (801) 466-4641
Fax: (801) 466-4699

# HyperSpace

- 3-D digitizing and modeling

Mira Imaging's HyperSpace systems come in about a dozen configurations. They enable you to digtize real-world models (such as clay sculptures or other physical models) in 3-D. These files can be saved in standard 3-D formats, such as DXF, for use in scene building, animation, and rendering applications.

# Pixar

1001 West Cutting
Richmond, CA 94804

Phone: (510) 236-4000
Fax: (510) 236-0388

## MacRenderMan

- Renderer

RenderMan is available as a stand-alone product that includes
shaders, the MacRenderMan application, and NetRenderMan, which
enables you to render on multiple Macs, or other RenderMan servers,
over a network. It is also bundled with ShowPlace, and an internal
version is included with Typestry. It's also available as an add-on
product for other programs that support it. Optional modules are
available for distributed processing on YARC boards, SGI and SUN
workstations, and other platforms.

## Showplace

- Modeling

- Scenes

- Rendering

A Showplace demo is included on the CD-ROM.

Showplace requires a Macintosh with a math coprocessor, System
6.07 or later, 8M of RAM, 13-21M hard disk, 8-bit color or better.

Showplace is Pixar's direct interface to RenderMan. It enables you to
build simple models, construct scenes, apply Looks-format shaders,
and render final images. It is also an important intermediary between
modelers that can export RIB files and RenderMan itself. Showplace
can be used to open a RIB file, apply lights and shaders, and send the
rendering job to RenderMan. Simple modeling is provided via plug-in

extensions. The program ships with lathe, terrain, and window shade modelers. Showplace allows you to save multiple cameras. You can apply one texture per object. The program offers spot, point, sun, and ambient lights. A type tool enables you to extrude fonts.

# Typestry

- Modeling

- Scenes

- Animation

Requires a Macintosh II or better, System 6.07 or higher (Multifinder under 6.07), 8M RAM, 5M hard disk, 8-bit color or better.

Typestry is a simple-to-use tool for creating 3-D artwork out of fonts. It allows you to extrude and bevel font characters, arrange fonts for a logo in 3-D space, add lights and Looks textures and render the scene using the internal version of RenderMan or MacRenderMan. Typestry supports simple-to-use key frame. Lights are limited to front-and-back suns. Can apply separate textures to bevels. Export formats include DXF, EPS, PICT, and RIB.

# The Valis Group

2270 Paradise Drive
Tiburon, CA 94920

Phone: (415) 435-5404
Fax: (415) 435-9862

# Pixel Putty

- Showplace modeling extension

A spline mesh surface modeler, Pixel Putty is available as an option for Showplace.

# Looks and Shader collections

Valis offers a wide variety of textures in Looks and Shader format for use in programs that support RenderMan.

# RayDream Inc.

1804 N. Shoreline Blvd.
Mountain View, CA 94043

Phone: (415) 960-0766
Fax: (415) 960-1198

## addDepth

- 3-D PostScript

Imports Illustrator or FreeHand line art, extrudes with bevels. Enables you to apply different textures to faces, sides and bevels. Renders a shaded PostScript image which can be exported to Illustrator or FreeHand or used directly in a desktop publishing package. Enables you to draw Bezier curves or import PostScript line art and extrude. No lathing tool. You can apply multiple textures per object (one each to sides, bevels and faces). Lighting is limited to white suns. Export formats include PICT, FreeHand, editable PostScript, and EPS.

## DreamNet

- Distributed rendering

Requires System 7 program linking.

Distributed rendering software for use with RayDream Designer. Sold in multi-user packs.

# RayDream Designer

- Modeling

- Scenes

- Rendering

A gallery of Designer samples is included on the CD-ROM.

Low-cost modeler and renderer with high-end features. Designed for illustrators. Spline modeler enables you to build complex free-form shapes. Supports texture and surface quality mapping, as well as direct drawing on model surfaces. Open architecture allows for effects plug-ins as well as additional features in the future. Modeler is based on Bézier (illustrator-style) splines and works in a single world view. You can use cameras to create multiple views. Apply multiple textures per object. Surface effects include bumps mapping, glow mapping, transparency mapping and others. Lighting options include spot, sun, point, and ambient. Can extrude fonts with bevels automatically. Can save in DXF, EPS, and PICT formats.

# Asym Technology

924 Carl Road
Lafayette, CA 94549

Phone: (510) 943-6157
Fax: (510) 943-3213

# ZOOM

- CAD

- Solid modeling

Complex CAD-accurate solid modeler.

# Silicon Graphics Inc.

2011 N. Shoreline Blvd.
Mountain View, CA 94039-7311

Phone: (415) 960-1980
Fax: (415) 549-0595

High-end graphics workstations.

# Specular International

479 West Street
Amherst, MA 01002

Phone: (413) 253-3100 or (800) 433-7732
Fax: (413) 253-0540

## Backburner/YARCBurner

- Distributed rendering for Infini-D

Accelerates Infini-D rendering by distributing tasks over multiple Macs. A YARC module is optional for those with access to a YARC board on the network. YARC board optional.

## Infini-D

- Integrated

A demo version of Infini-D is included on the CD-ROM.

Requires: Macintosh II or better, 4M RAM, System 6.07 or later, 8-bit graphics or better, hard disk.

Infini-D is a full-featured application that covers all the bases for the multimedia animator and graphic artist. Includes a polygonal, profile-based modeler that uses "workshops." Four window working worlds with unlimited cameras. Event-based animation offers multiple time lines but not control over minute parameters. Animation Assistants provide control over parameters such as ease-in and ease-out, banking, and aligning to motion. Multiple textures per object, as well as bump, glow, transparency, and other effects maps. Shape and surface morphing. Light types include spot, point, sun, and ambient. Lights are limited to 1x and 5x power. Infini-D automatically extrudes fonts with bevels. Export types include DXF, PICT, PICS, QuickTime, and EPS. Rendering styles include ray tracing, Phong, Gouraud, flat shading, hidden line removal, and wireframe.

# LogoMotion

- Logo modeling

- Animation

- Rendering

LogoMotion was not shipping in time for a summary in this edition of the *Macintosh 3-D Workshop*. Based on previews, the program extrudes fonts and EPS line art and enables you to easily create animations. Rendering is limited to Gouraud shading.

# Strata Inc.

2 West St. George Blvd.
Ancestor Square, Suite 2100
St. George, UT 84770

Phone: (801) 628-5218
Fax: (801) 628-9756

# Rend•X

- RenderMan Rendering

Requires StrataVision 3d or StrataStudio Pro, MacRenderMan.

RenderMan output to RIB format from StrataVision 3d or StudioPro. Automatically exports geometry, lights and textures in RIB format.

# Render Pro

- Distributed rendering

Requires System 7, AppleTalk network, program linking StrataVision 3d or StrataStudio Pro.

RenderPro is Strata's highly-efficient distributed rendering system that operates on multiple Macs on the network, and provides rendering plug-in as interface to StrataVision 3d or StrataStudio Pro. You can get near-linear rendering speedups by hooking up several fast Macs on a fast Ethernet network.

# StrataType

- Modeling

- Rendering

Simple application for quickly generating realistic extruded type with bevels. Ideal for desktop publishing. One texture per object. Sun and ambient lights. Exports DXF, EPS, PICT, and StrataVision 3d files. Uses Phong rendering.

# StrataVision 3d

- Integrated

A StrataVision 3d Player demo is included on the CD-ROM.

Requires a Macintosh II or later with math coprocessor, 3M of RAM, 40M hard disk, System 6.07 or later , 8-bit color or better.

StrataVision 3d is a polygonal modeler that uses one or more simultaneous views of a scene. It provides rudimentary animation with key frames and a single time line.

StrataVision 3d has outstanding texture mapping. Only one texture per object is supported, but multiple effects maps can be used to significantly alter a surface's appearance. These include: bump maps, glow maps, transparency maps, and others. Light types include spot, point, ambient, and suns. The program automatically extrudes fonts with bevels. It will also extrude bitmapped images based on the bitmap's gray values.

It supports the following file formats: DXF, IGES, EPS, PICT, MiniCAD, PICS, QuickTime, Super 3d, Swivel 3D, and TIFF. StrataVision's rendering options include RenderMan (with the optional Rend•X plug-in), radiosity, ray tracing, Phong, Gouraud, flat shading, hidden line removal, and wireframe. In addition to RenderPro, acceleration is available from Torque and Video Bits in the form of the TorqueWare/Flash Tracer tandem.

# Studio Pro

- Integrated

A Studio Pro Player demo is included on the CD-ROM.

System requirements: Macintosh II or later with math coprocessor, 5M of RAM, 40M hard disk, System 6.07 or later (System 7 recommended), 8-bit color or better.

StrataStudio Pro is one of the newest integrated 3-D modeling, animation, and rendering packages on the Macintosh. In many ways, it resembles the older StrataVision 3d. However, a number of important features set it apart: a Bézier-based 3-D modeling mode and extensive high-level animation features such as event-based key framing and particle animation.

This is the best all-around integrated package on the Macintosh for beginning and intermediate users of 3-D software interested in animation. It gets particularly high marks for its ease of use.

The animation tools include an event-based time score, spline motion paths, animation plug-ins that provide auto ease-in and ease-out, banking and particle animation features. Parameter-level animation is not possible in the current version, however. One texture is allowed per object, but the surface quality mapping options are as good as StrataVision's. Shape morphing is supported. Lights include point, sun, spot, and ambient.

Type can be easily imported and extruded. File formats supported include: DXF, IGES, EPS, PICT, and RIB (with optional Rend•X plug-in). Rendering options include: radiosity, ray tracing, Phong, Gouraud, flat shading, hidden line removal, and wireframe rendering. Acceleration is optional with Render Pro or TorqueWare.

# System Soft America

## Shade II

- Integrated

This program was developed, and continues to be upgraded in the United States; however, at the time of this book's publishing, Shade II was only available in Japan.

The program has a mix of very powerful high-end spline-based modeling features, with many awkward animation tools, and an attractive but non-standard interface.

It uses Spline (NuRBS) based modeling with automatic edge alignment and other powerful features. Modeling and scene building are done in a four-window setup.

The program automatically uses a YARC board if present in the system.

# Torque Systems Inc.

835 Emerson St.
Palo Alto, CA 94301

Phone: (415) 321-1200
Fax: (415) 321-1298

## TorqueWare

• Acceleration

Requires Flash Tracer rendering software (sold in bundle), SGI workstation or IDT RISC hardware, Macintosh II or later.

Currently used to accelerate StrataVision 3d and StrataStudio Pro rendering on an SGI workstation or IDT NuBUS RISC board. TorqueWare is the interface software between the Macintosh and the RISC system; FlashTracer (from Video Bits) is a rendering module that accelerates rendering.

# Video Bits

612 Fremont Ave., Suite 3
South Pasadena, CA 91030

Phone: (818) 403-0151
Fax: (818) 403-0148

# Flash Tracer

• Accelerated rendering

Requires TorqueWare software (sold in bundle), SGI workstation or IDT RISC hardware, a Macintosh II or later.

Currently used to accelerate StrataVision 3d and StrataStudio Pro rendering on an SGI workstation or IDT NuBUS RISC board. TorqueWare is the interface software between the Macintosh and the RISC system; FlashTracer is a rendering module that accelerates rendering. Supports Ray tracing rendering.

# View by View

1203 Union St.
San Francisco, CA 94109

Phone: (415) 775-6926
Fax: (415) 923-1205

# Turbo 3D

• CAD

• Visualization

Requires Macintosh with math coprocessor, 5M RAM and System 6.05 or later. Eight-bit or better color monitor recommended.

Turbo 3D is a CAD-accurate, highly-complex solid-modeling system for design and visualization of large architectural projects. It is for serious users of 3-D and demands a very dedicated student. Capable of building highly-complex solid polygonal models. Animation is for basic visualization and includes key frames and time of day lighting. Rendering used is flat shading, wireframe, and hidden line removal.

# Virtus Inc.

117 Edinburgh S., Suite 204
Cary, NC 27511

Phone: (919) 460-4530 or (800) 847-8887
Fax: (919) 460-4530

## Virtus Voyager

- Visualization

Run-time player for Virtus WalkThrough presentations (see below).

## Virtus WalkThrough

- Modeling

- Visualization

Requires a Macintosh II, with 2M RAM, a hard disk, 8-bit color or better.

WalkThrough is a simple polygonal modeler combined with a sophisticated, real-time navigational interface that enables users to "walk through" a model and look at it from many perspectives. The program can import a variety of models, so you can walk through designs created in other applications. The whole package is particularly well suited to architectural designs, though it works well with other types of models.

Animation is user-controllable in real time: it's the closest thing to "virtual reality" available on the Macintosh to date. The program can export a PICS or QuickTime movie, as well as export models in the following formats: DXF (2D/3D), Claris CAD, and MacDraw II. Rendering types include flat shading and wireframe.

# Virtus WalkThrough Pro

- Modeling

- Visualization

This program was not shipping in time for inclusion in this book. It's scheduled to include real-time texture mapping and transparency and realistic shading and lighting during walk-throughs.

# Visual Information Development Inc.

16309 Doublegrove St.
La Puente, CA 91744

Phone: (818) 918-8834
Fax: (818) 918-9935

# Presenter Pro

- Integrated

A Presenter Pro Player demo is included on the CD-ROM.

Requires a Macintosh II or better, 5M RAM, 20M of hard disk space, System 6.07 or later.

Presenter Pro is really two applications: Modeler Pro, where models are built and grouped, and Presenter, a scene builder and animator. Modeler Pro is a powerful modeler based on 3-D splines. It has good modeling controls all around. It is available as a separate product, Modeler Pro.

The Presenter portion of the package enables you to place and aim cameras and lights, assign textures and set up renderings. Unfortunately, it hasn't received the same attention devoted to the modeler. For example, you can't move objects by dragging in the scene builder. Texture mapping allows for a texture and a label. Bump maps are also supported. Presenter Pro has excellent support for the standard RenderMan Shader format, but this has been threatened by Pixar's introduction of the proprietary Looks format.

Light types include point, sun, spot, and ambient. Output formats include: VersaCAD, WaveFront, Dimensions, EPS, IGES, DXF, PICT, RIB, and FACT (Electric Image).

# OZ

- Animation

- Rendering

VIDI has announced a new animation system due to ship late in 1993, to compliment the Modeler portion of Presenter Pro, called OZ. This program is scheduled to include physical modeling and animation and inverse kinematics.

# YARC Systems Corp.

975 Business Center Circle
Newbury Park, CA 91320

Phone: (805) 499-9444
Fax: (805) 499-4048

# MacRageous II/NuSprint

- Accelerators

Require a Macintosh II and specially adapted rendering software.

YARC boars are extremely high-speed RISC NuBUS boards that provide super-fast rendering acceleration for the following 3-D products: Sculpt RISC and Sculpt 4D RISC; VIDI Presenter Pro YARC version (ray tracing and RenderMan); Infini-D (using YARCBurner extension); all programs that render with MacRenderMan (using YARCRenderMan); Shade II.

Using a YARC board is as simple as plugging it in, installing a YARC application, and rendering.

# Macintosh 3-D Workshop CD-ROM

**T**he CD-ROM included with this book has everything you need
to get started with 3-D. Working try-out versions of software
enable you to see how it looks and feels to work in 3-D. An
interactive tutorial, developed with Mac 3-D tools, guides users
through many of the essential techniques of 3-D. Images from the
book are reproduced in color with explanations of how they were
created.

Image galleries from a number of vendors provide a look at some of
the amazing images created with Macintosh 3-D software. A library of
sample models (in several standard formats) is a toy box full of
surprises. A huge library of textures, backgrounds, bump maps and
effects maps supplies lots of material to work with.

### Requirements
To use the CD, you'll need a CD-ROM drive that works with
your Mac. Most of the applications require that you copy
them to your hard disk before launching. While requirements vary for each application, a Mac LC II or better, 13-
inch color monitor and 5M of free RAM are recommended.

# Macintosh 3-D Workshop Interactive

A full-color interactive guide to lighting, surface qualities, texture and
environment mapping, rendering, and animation. Images and examples from the book are reproduced in color, along with many not-
found-anywhere-else 3-D illustrations and interactive lessons about
key 3-D concepts. See how multimedia and 3-D really work together.
This software is available only on this disc! The interactive guide
requires a 13-inch color monitor and 4M free RAM. You'll also need to
install the HyperCard player and QuickTime (also on the disc).

# 3-D Software

Not one, not two, not three, but—count 'em—eight working 3-D programs from different vendors. These are try-before-you buy versions that let you do everything but save your work. The try-out version of Infini-D even lets you save small renderings and QuickTime movies.

The try-out programs on the CD-ROM have specific system requirements. In all cases, you'll get much better performance if you copy the folder containing the software to your hard disk before launching the application.

## VIDI's Modeler Professional

This is the "digital clay" portion of the Presenter Professional package. Push, pull, and distort splines on any part of a model's surface. This version allows you to save your models up to a 100K limit.

The program will run on any Macintosh SE/30, Macintosh II, Quadra, Performa, or Centris which has a math co-processor, operating system version 6.0.3 or higher (including 7.1), and 32-bit QuickDraw. Though Presenter Professional will run on a system with 2M of free RAM, 4M or more are recommended. A 20M or larger hard disk with 4M of free space is required to install and use this online introduction to Presenter Professional's modeling module.

## Infini-D

One of the premiere integrated modeling, rendering, and animation systems on the Mac. The program enables you to do morphing and multiple-layer texture mapping among other neat tricks. This demo version allows you to save your work in small sizes. Requires 4M or more of free RAM.

457

# Adobe Dimensions

Extrudes and renders Illustrator and FreeHand line art as 3-D PostScript. Some sample line art is included, but for best results, you'll want to try creating your own outlines with Adobe Illustrator or Aldus FreeHand. Two versions of Dimensions are supplied—for those with and without an FPU (math coprocessor). A minimum of 2M free RAM is; 4M is recommended.

# form•Z

A powerful solid modeler that lets you carve objects with other objects. Copy the entire folder to your hard disk before launching (about 5M). To use the demo version of form•Z, drag the entire form•Z folder to your hard disk. The demo version of form•Z won't work if any of the files are moved out of this folder. The program requires 3M free RAM; more is recommended.

# Macromedia Selections

The following Macromedia 3D applications demonstrate a wide range of 3-D technologies. They are all System 7-compatible and 32-bit clean. A math coprocessor is needed, so the applications won't work on Macintosh models II, IIx, LC, and IIsi without a separate math coprocessor card. System requirements are: a Macintosh II or better, System v.7.0 or later, 8M RAM or more, 8-bit graphics or better, and 5M of hard disk space.

# Life Forms

Enables you to choreograph realistic human motion with accurate 3-D models.

# Macromodel

A powerful free-form modeler that enables you to work with 3-D surfaces the way you work clay with your hands.

# ModelShop II

Build polygonal models and visualize architectural objects.

# Swivel 3D Professional

One of the best tools for linking and constraining models to move in particular relationships to one another.

# Other Try-out Software

Because no 3-D program is an island, this disk includes important software that supplements and enhances the capabilities of any 3-D application.

# Adobe Photoshop

Photoshop is the most important image processing tool on the Macintosh. No serious 3-D user can live without it. This version enables you to open 3-D images and experiment with many of the techniques used in the book. Photoshop requires a minimum of 3M free RAM; 5M or more is recommended.

# Adobe Premiere

Premiere is like Photoshop for QuickTime. Import and edit your
animations, composit them with other video for "rotoscoping" and
add titles and special effects. Premiere requires a minimum of 4M free
RAM.

# Working Model

This is a unique physics simulator that enables you to build a model
and set it in motion. It's a 2-D program, but you can easily export
your animations to 3-D programs like Macromedia 3D to instantly
generate physics-based 3-D animations. To install Working Model,
you will need a Macintosh computer (68000-based computers, such
as the Mac Plus, SE, Portable, Classic, and PowerBook 100, are not
supported) running System 7 or later, approximately 4M of free disk
space and 3M of free RAM. A floating-point math co-processor (FPU)
is recommended but not required. To start the installation, double-
click on the file "Double-Click Me to Install."

# Image galleries

Sample images and animations created by many different users in
many Mac 3-D applications.

- **Alias Sketch! TV.** Interactive tour of images created in Sketch!.

- **Byte by Byte.** Gallery of images created in Sculpt.

- **Pixar.** Selection of RenderMan images.

- **Strata Gallery.** Interactive overview of Strata's 3-D products.

- **VIDI.** Slide show of unique images created in Presenter
  Professional.

# Sample models

Models used to create many of the illustrations in the book are included, as are samples of digitized 3-D objects from a couple of impressive third parties.

## Macintosh 3-D Workshop examples

Includes many models used in the book, including a scale-model steam locomotive, a smoothly-swept chambered nautilus, and a space station, to name a few. Models are supplied in native, DXF, and RIB formats. You can open these models in most 3-D applications.

## Mira Imaging

Sample models in DXF format and a gallery of models in an unusual 3-D player. There's also a guide to Mira's HyperSpace 3-D digitizing systems.

## Illustrative Impressions

Several unique models in DXF format and a gallery of 3-D models with an interactive 3-D player.

## More sample models

Many sample models come with the try-out applications listed under "3-D Software," and "Other Try-out Applications."

461

# Backgrounds and Textures

Every 3-D user needs more seamless textures, bump maps, and effects maps. Powerful 3-D images also call for environment maps and high-quality backgrounds. These textures and effects maps can be used with any 3-D application that supports bitmapped textures. The disk contains two collections:

## Wagstaff's Favorites

Folders full of the author's favorite home-brewed textures. These include lots of variations on several themes, with matching bump maps and effects maps for creating highly-realistic and unusual surfaces. There's also a collection of interesting and fanciful backgrounds and environment maps.

## The Alpha Channel

The disk contains two complete sets from the Expert Collection 3D. Visually and thematically matching backgrounds, textures, and bump maps make it easy to create attractive, color-coordinated 3-D graphics for multimedia and video.

# QuickTime

Apple's QuickTime (version 1.6) is included, so you can play the latest QuickTime movies and open images saved in QuickTime format. The QuickTime extension must be installed in the Extensions folder, in the System folder.

# HyperCard Player

The latest version of the HyperCard Player enables you to use the Interactive Macintosh 3-D Workshop. You can also use it to run other HyperCard-based applications.

# MACINTOSH 3-D WORKSHOP

---

**B**

---

## M

---

**T**

---

---

## U-V

---

# About the CD-ROM

The CD-ROM included with this book is in HFS (Macintosh) format, and includes interactive tutorials, an original texture library, and working versions of 3-D software. The try-out version of Infini-D even lets you save small renderings and QuickTime movies. For more information about the disc contents, see the "What's on the disc" appendix.

Different applications and files on the disk have different requirements; we recommend a **color Macintosh** with **System 7** and **5M of RAM** (and a **CD-ROM drive!**) as a minimum. Some of the applications require more memory, and some must be copied to your hard disk to work.

## The disc includes:

### Macintosh 3-D Workshop Interactive

A full-color interactive guide to lighting, surface qualities, texture and environment mapping, rendering and animation. Images and examples from the book are reproduced in color, along with many not-found-anywhere-else illustrations and interactive lessons about key 3-D concepts. See how multimedia and 3-D really work together. This software is available only on this disc!

### Image Galleries

Sample images and animations created by many different users in many Mac 3-D applications.

### Sample models

Models used to created many of the illustrations in the book are included, as are samples of digitized 3-D objects from Mira Imaging and more.

### 3-D Software

Not one, not two, not three, but—count 'em—*eight* working 3-D programs from different vendors. **Infini-D try-out** is one of the premiere integrated modeling, rendering, and animation systems on the Mac. This demo version allows you to save your work! Use it to open and render sample DXF models, also on the CD. **Adobe Dimensions TryOut** extrudes and renders Illustrator and FreeHand line art as 3-D PostScript. **form•Z try-out version** is a powerful solid modeler that enables you to carve objects with other objects. **Life Forms try-out version** enables you to choreograph realistic human motion with accurate 3-D models. **Macromodel try-out version** is a powerful, free-form modeler that enables you to work with 3-D surfaces the way you work clay with your hands. **ModelShop II try-out version** enables you to build polygonal models and visualize architectural objects. **Swivel 3D Professional try-out version** is one of the best tools for linking and constraining models to move in particular relationships to one another.

### Other Try-out Software

Because no 3-D program is an island, this disk includes important software that supplements and enhances the capabilities of any 3-D application. **Adobe Photoshop** is the most important image processing tool on the Mac. This tryout version lets you open 3-D images and experiment with many of the techniques used in the book. **Adobe Premiere** is like Photoshop for QuickTime. Import and edit your animations, composit them with other video for "rotoscoping," and add titles and special effects with this tryout version. The **Working Model try-out version** is a unique physics simulator that lets you build a model and set it in motion.

### Backgrounds and Textures

Every 3-D user needs more seamless texturess, bump maps, effects maps, environment maps and high-quality backgrounds. The disk contains two collections—**Wagstaff's Favorites**, folders full of the author's favorite home-brewed textures, and **Alpha Channel Expert Collection 3D,** two complete sets from the 3-D collection #1.

### QuickTime 1.6
### HyperCard Player